Truth is a
Strange Fruit

By the same author
Ten Men Dead (1986)

Truth is a
Strange Fruit

A personal journey through
the Apartheid War

David Beresford

First published by Jacana Media (Pty) Ltd in 2010

10 Orange Street
Sunnyside
Auckland Park 2092
South Africa
+2711 628 3200
www.jacana.co.za

ISBN 978-1-77009-902-9

Cover design by publicide
Front cover photo of David Beresford © Ellen Elmendorp
Set in Ehrhardt 12/16pt
Job No. 001293
Printed and bound by Ultra Litho (Pty) Limited, Johannesburg

See a complete list of Jacana titles at www.jacana.co.za

To Ellen

Butterfly moments, she said.
So they are.
We try to pin them down with words,
like the gorgeous creatures in still ranks
on the pages of lepidopterists' trays.
There is a desperation about it,
as if by chloroforming the moments
with memory
we can keep what has been
and hold back the march
to mortality.

David Beresford

Strange Fruit

Southern trees bear strange fruit,
Blood on the leaves and blood at the root,
Black bodies swinging in the southern breeze,
Strange fruit hanging from the poplar trees.

Pastoral scene of the gallant south,
The bulging eyes and the twisted mouth,
Scent of magnolias, sweet and fresh,
Then the sudden smell of burning flesh.

Here is fruit for the crows to pluck,
For the rain to gather, for the wind to suck,
For the sun to rot, for the trees to drop,
Here is a strange and bitter crop.

Lyrics: Abel Meeropol (aka Lewis Allan) / Vocals: Billie Holiday

This book contains verbatim extracts from evidence to the Truth and Reconciliation Commission. These extracts are identified by volume and page numbers of the Final Report (Volumes 1–7, Juta Law, 1998) and, in a few instances, references to hearings of the TRC.

Introduction

The story is told of a photographer in Vietnam who was blown up by a landmine. The American soldiers he was accompanying, thinking he was dead, tossed his body on to the back of a truck. He recovered consciousness to find himself lying on a pile of corpses. Managing to grab the camera hanging around his neck, he raised himself on one elbow and began photographing them.

In 1991, as correspondent for *The Guardian* in Johannesburg, I had a comparable if less grotesque experience. My newspaper sent me to cover the first Gulf War. Writing a feature article in the back seat of a Land Cruiser, I developed symptoms that were diagnosed a year later as early evidence of 'the shaking palsy', Parkinson's disease.

Like that photographer in Vietnam, I decided it was 'business as usual'. I continued to work as the Johannesburg correspondent of *The Guardian* and its sister newspaper, *The Observer*, trying to convince myself that Parkinson's disease was merely another assignment. I told myself I was like a foreign correspondent who had unexpectedly been given a visa to a strange and foreign land.

As I rushed about, hurriedly jotting down notes, I told myself I could hear the distant sound of the ship's siren summoning me home. Parkinson's disease was that land of foreign experience. Home was the cure that never came.

It was from that land that I covered the creation and proceedings of the Truth and Reconciliation Commission. The TRC was a body designed as a national confessional intended to give South Africa a new beginning through transparency and the articulation of the truth about the past.

By the time I had started writing this book, the statutory mandate of the Commission to investigate crimes of the apartheid era had long expired. The material from which the seven-volume report had been culled was transferred to the National Archives in Pretoria and authority over it was claimed by South Africa's Department of Justice.

The material is made up of documentation – including statements by victims and perpetrators of political violence during the apartheid era – which I am told take up half a kilometre of shelf space in the Archives. I use the term, 'I am told', deliberately. I have literally been forbidden sight of the collection on 'security' grounds.

The National Archives, with bullet-proof windows, and access-controlled by an 'air-lock' door under the watchful eye of security guards, resemble from the outside the headquarters of a ministry of defence, or those of a secret service, rather than a centre for scholarly research.

Bureaucrats at the National Archives and the Justice Department – including members of South Africa's National Intelligence Service who became inexplicably involved – seemingly decided that 'the truth' was something with which the public could not be entrusted. Accordingly, they placed the documentation under 'high security' and refused to give access to librarians, researchers and journalists.

I was warned by archivists of the obstacles that would be put in my way by the Ministry of Justice. So I sent in formal requests for material on a handful of incidents to 'test the water'. I am still waiting for a reply.

It is difficult to understand why the TRC has done nothing to remedy this. I am told that at their last meeting before shutting themselves down the commissioners formally resolved to place all of their documents in the public domain. But the laptop computer that contained the only record of the minutes of the meeting was stolen. The commissioners should be able to reconstruct the missing minutes without much difficulty, but that has not been done.

It is not the only peculiar action – or lack of it – by the TRC. I used to characterise this project, in conversation with friends, as a 'popular version' of the seven-volume Final Report. It was my intention to produce a single volume that would give the South African public access to the work of the Commission.

Then I discovered to my surprise that there was a specific requirement in the enabling legislation for the TRC that a 'popular version' of the report be published. I wrote to the Ministry of Justice, offering to write it for them. They never replied.

To complicate matters further, it turned out that a 'popular version' had not only been written, but published. After much effort, I managed to obtain a copy. Unfortunately, it was written entirely in German.

The TRC's claimed knowledge of 'the truth', or even its aspiration to know it, suggests a certain hubris on its part. What is the truth anyway? Can anyone claim to 'know' it?

The commissioners tried to deal with the question preemptively by announcing, in the first of the seven-volume Final Report, that there were different kinds of truths. There was 'factual', or 'forensic' truth; 'personal' and 'narrative' truth; 'social ... truth'; and 'healing and restorative truth'.

In terms of those definitions, this book is what the TRC would no doubt characterise as a 'personal' truth. Explaining what is meant by this term the Final Report quotes its chairman, Archbishop Desmond Tutu, as commenting that it is 'important that everyone should be given a chance to say his, or her truth as he or she sees it ...' The comment was obviously aimed at 'perpetrators' and 'victims' and not the media. But if 'everyone' should be given a chance to say his or her truth; if the 'personal' truths of perpetrators and victims demand recognition, so do the 'truths' of the media, which also have a personal element that is too often ignored.

After all, the importance of the Press has been long acknowledged. As Oscar Wilde put it: *'Somebody – was it Burke? – called journalism the fourth estate. That was true at the time no doubt. But at the present moment it is the only estate. It has eaten up the other three. The Lords Temporal say nothing, the Lords Spiritual have nothing to say, and the House of Commons has nothing to say and says it. We are dominated by Journalism.'*

It is with that justification, of truth being a many splendoured thing, that this book stands as 'my truth': a collage, or montage of what might be described as curiosities, ruminations, observations, anecdotes, snatches of remembered dialogue, letters, and stories centring around the momentous years that form the mandate of the TRC, 1960–94 – the years of what I have chosen to call 'the Apartheid War'.

It is about incidents and memories, going back to childhood rites of passage, which, one way or another, have affected my perceptions of South Africa, of apartheid and of myself. I have allowed it to range widely, from stories like that of the Cosas boys and Maki Skosana – the girl horribly murdered by members of the students' organisation as a result of what appears to have been mistaken identity – to the Bisho massacre, which I covered in the company of a puddle of brains and which may have determined the course of South African history. From Shucks, the execution monitor, to the butcher's shop known as death row. From the ghastly aftermath of the Rwanda genocide to the attempts by French surgeons to fix my Parkinson's with electrodes buried deep in my brain, and the death of my beloved brother. Interlaced throughout is a series of extracts from the Commission's Final Report that, for me, sum up the pain and brutality of those years.

I have left acknowledgements to the end of the book and it

does not detract from them to make one exception: the family of the so-called 'station bomber', John Harris. His widow, Ann Wolfe, generously gave me access to the love letters she and John exchanged as he awaited the hangman for eight months in 1964/5. I came across them quite by accident and they drew me deeper into the extraordinary and, at times, perplexing story of the first and only white person to be executed for a political offence.

My frustrations had been growing about getting access to TRC documents, and I wondered if I had taken on too much with the false assumption that all doors would be open to me. On a trip from Johannesburg to Cape Town, I stayed overnight at a sheep farm in the Karoo owned by two friends, Maeder and Leslie Osler (rugby fans may recognise the surname as that of two brothers, Bennie and Stanley, who were 'greats' of Springbok history).

If you are going to cry on someone's shoulder there is no better place to do it than on those of Maeder and Leslie over a bottle of red wine and a plate of hot soup on a Karoo farm after a long winter's drive from Johannesburg. In the course of this happy conversation, Maeder said in passing: 'Of course Jonty's got the letters.' Now, as anyone who knows Maeder knows Jonty is his best friend. Jonty Driver – the former headmaster of Wellington School in the UK and, like Maeder and Leslie, an anti-apartheid 'struggalista' from student days. But I hadn't a clue what he meant by Jonty 'having the letters'. So he explained and suddenly life took on luminosity again.

It so happens that I had previously written on the 1981 IRA hunger strikers, based on a remarkable cache of prison letters, but it seemed too much to stumble across another one, particularly as intimate as this. When I reached Cape Town I contacted Jonty who put me on to Ann, and soon scanners and fax machines were running and I was reading, with astonishment, the handwritten correspondence from death row more than 40 years ago.

They provided me with something of an emotional narrative

and set me on a quest to discover the truth behind that fateful July afternoon at Johannesburg's main railway station. It is that exploration on which I finally concentrate and which I hope will contribute to John Harris's place in the pantheon of South African patriots. Equally I hope it will contribute to the recognition of capital punishment as the abomination it is. In its Final Report the TRC recorded that between 1960 and 1994 over 2 500 people were hanged by the State.

While this book is less about the Commission than I originally intended, I would like to pay tribute to the TRC. To me the seven-volume report and its further documentation is a national treasure, a latter-day equivalent to England's Domesday Book. In it are recorded, not the goods and chattels of a kingdom, but more importantly the stories of a people who make up a nation.

Push me further as to why I have written this book, and what it is all about, and I am likely to turn to a story about a photographer in Vietnam who was blown up by a landmine ... And that of a little boy who, one afternoon a long time ago, was refused the means to escape reality.

The keeper of the books

The small boy looked dumbly up at the municipal librarian as she repeated herself: 'You can't have read three books in a morning. You only took them out today!' she said, indignantly, once again inspecting the smudged library card. 'Anyway, you're only allowed to take three books a day,' she added uncertainly, reassuring herself in her mind that the principle was well entrenched in natural law, even if there was no foundation for it in library regulations. 'You should get outdoors and do something healthy,' she added, marching decisively off.

'What am I going to do now?' the boy asked himself in terror at the thought of reality with cavernous jaws and bloodied teeth waiting to leap on him at the bottom of the library stairs. 'I'll write them,' he reassured himself and immediately felt calmer. 'I'll write books,' he murmured as he nervously looked around from the top of the stairs. 'Maybe I'll start by writing newspapers,' he thought, gaining courage as he made his way down. 'Or maybe I'll just read a bit slower,' he reflected as he ran for his bicycle leaning against the jacaranda tree in the rain of a monkey's wedding.

Promontorium prassum

An American writer, William Manchester, described apartheid South Africa as 'a very strange society'. It was something of an understatement. After all, this was the society that insisted a black concert pianist played from behind a screen so as not to contaminate the white orchestra with which he was playing; contaminated with what has never been explained.

The society where a stocking packet featuring a pair of naked legs was banned by the censors ... until the manufacturers agreed, for the sake of modesty, to clothe the legs in (transparent) plastic bags. The country where a Pretoria bus driver was sacked for failing to pick up a Japanese passenger, only to be reinstated when he protested he thought it was a 'Chinaman'.

But apartheid South Africa can rarely have been seen in its full panoply of strangeness as when three white actors in a rowing boat landed on a 'whites-only' beach in the little coastal town of Mossel Bay. To be met by seven more white men wearing curly wigs and painted black. The occasion was the 500th anniversary of the 'discovery' of South Africa by Europe, with the landing at Mossel Bay of Bartolomeu Dias. But if the original landing was memorable, its commemoration was at least notable for the bizarre, if unintended commentary on the state of the country after the centuries of Christian rule heralded by the arrival of the Portuguese explorer.

The ceremonies were marked by one of the most complete snubs to the South African authorities by a subordinate racial group – the 'coloureds', who form a majority of the local population, but can fairly be said to have stayed away from the proceedings in their thousands.

Only a few handfuls of coloured people – most seemingly passers-by – were to be seen among the crowd of about 2 000 whites who gathered on a hillside. They were there to witness the arrival of a replica of Dias's caravel and the theatrical re-enactment of the first meeting between Europeans and the indigenous population at the time, the Hottentots, or 'Khoikhoi'.

Little is reliably known about Bartolomeu Dias's momentous voyage in search of what Ptolemy called the *'Promontorium Prassum'* – the legendary tip of Africa. But tradition has it that he made the landing at Munro's Bay, a small inlet within the larger Mossel Bay. He is said to have handed out trinkets to the Khoikhoi before beating a hasty retreat back to his ship after an unfortunate incident, of the type the South African authorities would more recently refer to as an 'unrest situation'.

The situation arose as Dias and his companions were filling their casks with water from a small spring that still runs just next to the beach. The Khoikhoi, for reasons that have never been explained (but, one is tempted to surmise, may have stemmed from a sense of presentiment), began hurling stones at them from the hillside above. Upon which Dias, in a fit of temper, grabbed a crossbow and shot one of them dead with all the off-hand brutality with which the descendants of South Africa's indigenous population have become only too familiar in their dealings with whites.

Perhaps understandably, that 15th-century killing did not feature in the modern-day pantomime. The high ground on this occasion was occupied by the pudgy figure of President PW Botha, resplendent in his State regalia and black homburg hat and flanked by the South African cabinet. Which was only one of many details of the proceedings that the early Khoikhoi might have found discordant with their experience of Dias' landing.

Out in the bay a replica caravel, built in Portugal at a cost of some £300,000, was a seemingly brilliant reconstruction of the early vessels of its type, but contrasted oddly with the modern ships of the South African navy, including a submarine, which surrounded it. Munro's Bay had been cleared for Dias' return, being patrolled ostentatiously by coloured soldiers packing R4 assault rifles.

An adjoining beach was fringed with the graceful sails of beached catamarans, the playthings of South Africa's privileged few, scores of whom – some muscular, some paunchy, but all bronzed – played in the surf, their ethnic purity protected by signs at the pathway entrances that declared, paradoxically in the circumstances: 'Beach area for whites only.'

The station bomb

'This is the African Resistance Movement. We have planted a bomb in a large brown suitcase 20 feet from the cubicle above platforms 5 and 6 on the concourse of the new Johannesburg railway station. On the handle of the suitcase is tied a label bearing the words 'Back in Ten Minutes'. It is not our intention to harm anyone.

This is a symbolic protest against the inhumanity and injustices of apartheid. The bomb is timed to explode at 4.33 pm. Clear the concourse by using the public address system at once. Do not try to defuse the bomb as the suitcase is triggered to explode if it is opened.'

In an unpublished manuscript, *The Station Bomb*, writer Kenneth Mackenzie described the building at the time: 'The new concourse of Johannesburg's Park Station is high-ceilinged, modern and elegant, with plenty of glass of various colours and mosaic facings over the concrete construction. Round the edge there are shops – milk bars, chemists, bookstores. There is a restaurant at the mezzanine level. Arches lead to the outside, through which one can see trees, a car park and bits of curving motor bridge. In the centre of the concourse there are the stairs leading down to the various platforms. At the head of each of the stairs is a wood-and-glass shelter containing benches and display windows advertising goods from the shops.'

Perhaps the most striking aspect of the station building was, by virtue of some architectural trick, its quietude. But the air of tranquillity was shattered at 4.33 pm on Friday, 24 July 1964, when the hour hand of the Zobo pocket watch in an abandoned suitcase closed the circuit. A sheet of flame rose to the ceiling, followed by a thunderous noise.

'People with burning hair and clothes were running about,' recalled Magdalena Lombard, a waitress working at the station restaurant. In total 23 people were injured, one of them fatally – 77-year-old grandmother, Mrs Ethyl Rhys.

31/7/64

My darling Ann,

Things don't look too bad for me, so please don't worry too much (and pass this on to my parents) I think of you so much, my dearest one. And of course of our little David (I'll think especially of him on the 9th). My love, sweetest Buz. I long so much to see you, but don't expect that it will be for quite a while.

You know how much I love you, lovekin.

Your John

P.S. I'm keeping your letter near my heart – just to look at it, let alone read it, makes me happy for hours.

All's lost and found

– *Let's sit in that corner and I'll tell you a story. A bottle of Allesverloren?*

– *What does it mean?*

– *All is lost.*

– *That's lovely.*

– *I had a friend who lost her husband. Well, the husband really lost her. I always think of them when I hear the name.*

– *Go on.*

– *She met her husband at a party and they fell totally in love with each other. I think they went to bed on their first night. And they were married within weeks. After a few years the marriage got into a bit of a rut, like marriages do. So, anyway, she used to have this thing about having been cheated out of a courtship. She was always saying that it had been too quick, that they'd gone to bed too quickly and got married too quickly and she hadn't been wooed. She used to say it like that – wooooooed! Sort of wailing. It was said as a joke; but you could hear there was real regret in her voice. Then one day she turned to her husband and said she wanted an affair. She wanted a lover who would woooo her and listen to her and hear all her complaints and give her secret kisses at hidden-away places. Of course he was taken aback.*

– *I can imagine.*

– *But she said she was telling him, because she was giving him a chance to be the lover. She'd thought it out and he had to court her and seduce her. They would make secret phone calls to each other and meet at all sort of romantic places and they would have an affair.*

– *And?*

– *And they did. She was very determined. He had to phone her from work, when her husband was not at home. He wasn't allowed to find out. And they started meeting, having secret lunches at places where nobody would know them. They had a lovely affair. I would see her sometimes and she'd say very mysteriously: 'I've got a lunch date.'*

She would put on her favourite clothes and wear garter belts and silk stockings. They would meet at restaurants on wine estates and occasionally they would go to a film together, arriving separately, but arranging to sit together in the back row and kissing and cuddling.

— *And making love?*

— *Yes, but only after months. She was determined it was going to be different this time. But because she was concentrating on her affair and, because she was falling in love, her marriage began to deteriorate more and more.*

— *Her marriage?*

— *Yes. She and her husband started having arguments. And when she finally started making love to her lover she began to hate making love to her husband. She would say she had a headache and make all sorts of excuses. But her lover began to get jealous and told her she wasn't allowed to make love to her husband anymore and made her tell him when she had last made love to him and he got very angry when she had.*

— *You're making it up.*

— *Wait. She had terrible rows at home with her husband. And she used to tell her lover about them when they met and he would console her.*

— *And then?*

— *They ran away together.*

— *Who?*

— *My friend and her lover.*

— *Eloped?*

— *Yes. One day she just didn't come home. She sent a letter to her husband, saying she was sorry, but she was in love with someone else and their marriage had been a mistake; that they should have known it was a mistake, because the courtship had been too short and he hadn't wooooed her. They found the letter in the house.*

— *In the house?*

— *Yes. Nobody came home, you see. And friends got worried and went through all the mail to see if there were any clues to what had happened. And there was this farewell message to her husband, to*

13

say she had run away. You can see the house, in Rondebosch. It's all locked up and the windows are full of cobwebs and the garden is overgrown. Testament to a failed marriage.

— It's not true!

— You always say truth doesn't matter, it's the story that counts. And I suppose it's what she would have said.

14/9/64

My own darling Ann,

I'm writing this (or at least beginning it) an hour or so after your visit. How happy it made me to see you, to talk to you properly (or reasonably properly!) Again & again & again I appreciate your golden qualities – in fact, to use the word rather differently, it's my good fortune to be married to a wife of such quality.

I think quite objectively of how your marriage to me has on occasion placed burdens on you – our time in England was largely unpleasant for you, the loss of our first baby – now this. And although I know you know no suffering or difficulty I've ever caused you, directly or indirectly, has been the slightest indication of lack of love, nevertheless in this sort of way (& in little ways, like losing my temper & general thoughtlessness) there has been – call it selfishness …

Your truly loving, John

The assassin

The man sitting in the lunatic asylum had been incarcerated for longer than Nelson Mandela, in conditions worse than Mandela, for a crime that arguably delivered a more telling blow against apartheid than any single blow delivered by Mandela.

Dimitrio Tsafendas was to be found in an armchair on an enclosed veranda at Sterkfontein mental hospital outside the town of Krugersdorp. Dressed in a maroon tracksuit and towelled slippers, he gazed past the eucalyptus trees across the hospital grounds.

A youth in pyjamas ambled across, his body stiffening like a hunting dog's at the sight of a pheasant as he spotted the chocolate. Accepting a piece, he strolled away, munching, circled and then returned, going rigid again as he peered once more into the plastic bag. The assassin stirred and reached possessively for the chocolate.

The others, a multiracial audience in this rainbow bedlam, watched with an intent air of incomprehension before busying themselves with obscure inconsequentialities; a ballet of the mind played out in slow motion, choreographed by the pills handed out from the trolley, which could be heard rattling its familiar way around the corridors on its mission of tranquilization.

Dimitrios Tsafendas was mad. There may be argument about degrees of madness. And, more importantly, the dates of his madness. But the official record showed that he had been mad since he was defined, declared and condemned as such by Justice Beyers a little more than a month after that moment of bloody violence when he stabbed to death the Honourable Dr Hendrik Frensch Verwoerd on the floor of Parliament in 1966.

In fact Judge Beyers put it a bit more trenchantly than that when he consigned Tsafendas to the dustbins of society and of history. The Judge President of the Cape prided himself on being a straight-talking man; he was known to bring barristers close to tears, never mind the helpless wretches he routinely savaged in the dock. And the words he used were as pitiless and dismissive of a man's humanity as if he had delivered them with the black cap on his Minotaur's head. 'I can as little try a man who has not at least the makings of a rational mind as I could try a dog or an inert implement … He is a meaningless creature!'

The land of Scotty Smith

The old lady, Evelina de Bruin, was wiping tears from her eyes in the dock. A psychiatrist slipped a tranquilliser to Kenneth Khumalo. The boxer, Xolile Yona, was leaning into the public gallery, embracing his weeping girlfriend. Justice Bekebeke was reading Du Toit's *Punishment in South Africa*. Justice wants to be a psychiatrist and was studying by correspondence; Du Toit rules that out on death row.

A deep voice started and the 14 condemned stood in the Upington courthouse and sang 'God Save Africa', the riot police watching impassively. As they finished, a policeman called for order. The judge, Justice Basson, took his seat beneath the South African flag, bolted to the wall.

Upington was an unlikely setting for such a courthouse drama. It was a quiet little town, situated on the banks of the Orange River in the remote Northern Cape, near the border between South Africa and Namibia. It was not always quiet. Named after a former Attorney-General, it was something of an outlaw capital in the mid-19th century, home to such legendary desperadoes as 'Captain Afrikaner' and Scotty Smith, the Robin Hood of South Africa.

The town settled down under missionary influence and developed into a centre of a thriving agricultural community, producing crops and livestock ranging from peaches to peas and the prized karakul sheep. It was a conservative community and in the late 1950s Upington itself became something of a model apartheid town – the whites living in the suburbs, the coloureds dumped on the outskirts and the blacks, who had previously coexisted happily with them, hived off into their own township of Paballelo.

Much became known about Paballelo because the Defence team in the trial commissioned several sociological studies as part of the battle to persuade the judge to find extenuation.

This was a community of about 10 000 people living in deprived circumstances. The unemployment rate ran at about 31 per cent and those employed had minimal incomes: at least 92.4 per cent of breadwinners earned little more than £100 a month, according to a survey, and 47 per cent less than £40. There was serious overcrowding, most of the small block homes – rented for about £10 a month – housing more than one family.

But despite the deprivation, the people of Paballelo were, like their white counterparts in Upington, fairly conservative. And it was not until more than a year into the 1984–86 townships rebellion that that euphemistic term beloved of South Africa's securocrats – 'unrest' – first began to be heard in connection with the township.

There was some trouble in the local high school early in 1985, students boycotting classes over the standard of teaching. A students' council was formed around the issue and in November 1985 the youths pushed the older generation into calling a public meeting to discuss broader community issues, including rents, the abuse of alcohol among schoolchildren and the activities of a recently established municipal police force that was earning an ugly reputation in the township.

The meeting, in the local community hall, passed off peacefully, but afterwards police fired tear gas at groups of youths who had allegedly thrown stones at them. It was the first recorded incident of 'unrest' in Paballelo.

Amid rising tension a second community meeting was called three days later. It was widely claimed in the township that the meeting was called by the police themselves to discuss residents' grievances. The police denied this. Whatever the truth of it, about 3 000 residents gathered on a local football field on 13 November. Riot police dispersed them with tear gas.

What followed was an incident tragically familiar to South Africa at the time. Some 300 members of the infuriated crowd fleeing the soccer ground turned on the home of a member of the municipal police force, Lucas 'Jetta' Sethwala. The policeman opened fire on them with a shotgun, wounding a child. He then fled the house, was tackled, hit over the head twice with his own gun – one of the blows killing him – and his body set alight with petrol.

The trial that ensued was strikingly similar to the world-famous case of the Sharpeville Six, with one distinction: in Upington the actual killer was identified in the person of Justice Bekebeke, aged 28, a male nurse who was found to have struck the fatal blows with the butt of the shotgun. But they were all convicted, as in the Sharpeville case, under 'common purpose' – that controversial doctrine imported from English Law and applied with such unfortunate enthusiasm by the South African judiciary.

The presence of the 'actual' killer in the Upington case made the grounds for the other convictions even more startling. Twenty-five were found guilty of murder for throwing stones at the policeman's house, the judge in effect claiming that they were taking part in a conspiracy to drive the policeman out and to his death. A 20-year-old girl was convicted of murder for shouting that she had seen the policeman in his house and a labourer for attacking the dead body.

A striking aspect of the Upington case – mirroring, as it did, a surprisingly common attitude among black South Africans in general – was the confidence the accused appeared to have in the legal system. They showed bitter contempt towards the trial judge. As the findings of 'no extenuation' were handed down, the 25 convicted of murder ostentatiously shook hands with each other, in sarcastic congratulations.

But, speaking to them during a tea adjournment, they were

confident of the final outcome. 'We've got faith in the appeal,' said the man who struck those fatal blows, Justice Bekebeke. The judge nodded to the No. 1 accused and the Xhosa interpreter invited Kenneth Khumalo to say his last words to the court.

The rest of the condemned were dressed in tracksuits, supplied by the Defence; even Evelina wore a tracksuit jacket. But Kenneth was dapper in a dark suit and tie, as was befitting a one-time mayor of Upington's Paballelo township. He told the court that the case against them was based on 'fabricated lies'. The trial would 'act as a scale which will measure justice in the legal system of South Africa'.

And so it went, the accused rising one by one to their feet to make their appeals, to express their hopes, and give vent to their anger. None of them appeared to have prepared for the moment and they spoke hesitantly.

Justice Bekebeke, the 28-year-old scholar, was the most articulate. He made an appeal for racial harmony and told the judge: 'I would like the Lord to give you many years so that one day you can see me walking on the streets of a free South Africa. May the Lord bless you.'

Evelina spoke of her children: 'I feel very sad for my children and my home. I've been taken away from them for something I didn't do.' Her husband, Gideon Madlogolwane, went on at length, criticising the trial in detail. He was listened to with the deference due to a father of 10 who was being sent with his wife to the gallows, until the judge interrupted to say that the merits of the case could be argued by his counsel on appeal.

Xolile, the boxer, asked the judge to reconsider. 'You are taking me away from my family,' he said. 'I grew up without a father. Now my child must grow up without knowing a father. I would like to be a boxer. I would like to be a good boxer. I'm asking for a last chance.'

The last of the condemned, Albert Tywilli, struck a note of defiance. 'If I had come before a clever judge he wouldn't have found me guilty,' the 27-year-old former policeman said contemptuously. 'Congratulations on your brilliant judgement.'

The grim ceremony of the death sentence – 'You will be taken from here to a place of execution … ' – has long been abandoned in South Africa's courts. Judge Basson was anxious to get the formality over, so he called out the numbers of the accused and added, perfunctorily: 'You are sentenced to death.'

He rose quickly and slipped out of the courtroom, leaving the condemned milling about uncertainly. The court was cleared to give relatives 15 minutes with each of the accused. It was their last chance to kiss and embrace.

As the relatives left the court they began to sing and dance with friends and supporters waiting outside. The growing crowd moved around the side of the building to see the 14 go, harmonising the haunting melody, 'Senzeni Na?' – 'What have we done? What have we done? Our sin is kindness.'

Then the youths among them broke into the toyi-toyi, the 'soldiers' dance of the Spear of the Nation, the military wing of the ANC. The big yellow police van with its barred windows raced out of the courtyard and the 14 condemned and the people of Paballelo waved their goodbyes to each other over the heads of the riot police and their growling Alsatians.

A year later South Africa was utterly changed, the ANC unbanned and Mandela freed. In May 1991 the appeal court overturned the death sentences and 11 of the 14 were released from death row. Justice Bekebeke was the last one out in January 1992. The trial had given him a new ambition. He always wanted to be a doctor. Instead he became a respected lawyer.

Jetta

At the human rights violation hearing in Upington, Ms Sethwale said:

'On the 13th November 1985, it was a Wednesday morning. My son was driven out of the house by a crowd of people who were stoning the house. We were in the house, 405 Philani Street. He was driven out of the house, and shortly afterwards, he was killed and burnt.

Briefly, what I would like to say is that the effect of my son's death has been great. I have been scarred by my son's death. Shortly afterwards, I had to remove my children from Upington, and I had to place them at schools elsewhere.

In 1986, December, I went back to my home, and I tried to pick up the pieces of my life again. Thereafter, I had to hear from the people in the Paballelo community that I had shopped my son to the police, that I had betrayed him to the police and that I had been paid for doing so – that I had been paid for my child's murder.

I went through a great deal of pain through all these years. It is now ten years and ten months and forty-three days ago that he died, but the pain is still with me. It still lives inside of me because the 'whys' and the 'wherefores' I still don't know. Although there are some people who pretend that nothing happened; there is a peace on the surface. The pain which I suffered, well I think my second eldest son, the one just after the deceased, I think his drinking problem is the result of the death of his brother.

During the time that I suffered so much, I felt like I had been banned from the community, that I had been rejected by the people. I felt that I could not look the world in the eye. I should just accept things as the world accepted me. It was a great pain for me to move in amongst the other women in the women's associations and groups to go and pray. It was always, it felt to me as if I was accused of this 'Upington 26' case. It didn't matter to them what was happening to me. Their prayers were always plaintive. I always had to hear about the food that they were dishing out to their loved ones, never mind the ones who had died. Even the ministers were the same. Not one, I didn't hear one minister praying for the deceased's mother who had also suffered a loss, who had also lost a son. The pain has been living with me through all these years.

The court case was a long protracted one, and I had to suffer a lot of prejudice, and people swearing at me, insults that I had to endure. But the fact that I am sitting here today does not mean that I want to accuse anybody in Paballelo of anything. I was quite sincere when I spoke to you during the Court case after I gave evidence. I was given the opportunity to speak to you and I am, I still say to you, I am extremely disappointed in you people of Paballelo community. Paballelo is a small community. We know each other. We know each other very, very intimately, and when we speak of each other, we immediately know who is being referred to and I still say to you, 'I am disappointed in you.' But there is nothing in my heart. I thought I just had to endure the pain and suffering that I was going through, but I still maintain that my faith in my fellow human beings has been scarred for life. I will, can never violate anybody else's rights because you knew my son, Tsenolo Lukas. Some of you were his friends. But that means nothing. Talk will not bring him back.

My pain and suffering is still a reality, and that played a major role in that household because I don't have a child in the Paballelo school. I would also have wanted my child to go to school there. I had to remove my children, and I had to go and live with other people. The hardship, the songs that you sang for me, that really affected me badly. It happened not that long ago. The last song was u-Jetta and that was such a bitter thing for me because some of you who sang that song, you go to the same church as I do, and some of you have very high posts, as you sit here. Some of you didn't know what exactly took place that day, but you just felt that you could just ride roughshod over my feelings. You felt that you could sing that song, but when you saw me walking across the street you started singing this u-Jetta song. I laughed at you. I answered you and said Jetta didn't hurt you, he is dead and that is nothing less than the truth.

Paballelo community, the community killed my child and they burnt him to death. That is the truth. Lastly, I would like to say thank you very much to the South African Police (SAP) who looked after me and my children as well during that time. Thank you very much. For the 'Upington 26' group I want to say it was a low blow, it was a heavy blow, but I picked myself up again, I survived. Thank you ...

(VOL. 5 P362 TRC FINAL REPORT)

The boxer

The African National Congress was the 'terrorist' organisation the world loved to love. Its cause even cut across the Cold War divide. Morally, as well as racially, it was a black-and-white issue; the goodies and the baddies were unmistakable. Like eating people, apartheid was wrong. And the ANC was the organisation decent people backed to beat it.

But there was something particularly tragic about the young men and women who joined the journey into exile in southern Angola during the Apartheid War.

They had fled South Africa and the neo-fascist goons who posed as the security forces – 'with the aspirations of a jumped-up South American junta' as the great advocate, Sydney Kentridge, once described them – to risk torture and death. They did so on a voluntary basis and with no expectation of reward, for their own liberation and that of the masses back home.

But when they got to the ANC 'camps' in the neighbouring country they found themselves being treated with suspicion, as potential spies. Instead of fighting in the high cause of liberation they were treated by commanders in much the same way as the goons back at home had treated them.

People like Ben Lekalake who, sickened by the 1976 slaughter of schoolchildren in South Africa's townships, left his job as a newspaper telex operator and abandoned his title as Transvaal lightweight boxing champion to join the struggle. As he explains in an affidavit, he found himself not in the struggle, but in prison, his jailors the ANC. 'I was part of a group of 14 at Nova Catenque (southern Angola) who refused to undergo further training, or follow orders because we demanded to immediately be sent back home to partake in the armed struggle.'

It is worth recording that in its formal submission to the TRC on deaths in exile, the ANC records that 34 cadres were executed 'by order of our military tribunal' in Angola, while 41 committed suicide.

The abbatoir

The prisoners were unlocked, we searched them. They were then identified in terms of photographs, they were placed in row or in a queue so that the first person due for execution would be in front. We then took them one by one to a table … where they again compared their thumbprints and looked at their photographs again … After they took the fingerprints … we accompanied the people to the church. There would then have been a brief church service. Some of the people would receive Communion for the last time and at about half past six … the Ministers would then move out … Their [the condemned's] hands were cuffed behind their backs and they had to remove their shoes. At about ten to seven or there about, we would then move with them down the passage and by then it was deadly quiet. They still sang and prayed, they greeted their people, their friends, then we moved to the gallows room, through the various gates until we were in the first reception room before the gallows. They would then stand against a wall with their faces towards us. They were then identified again against their photographs and then the executioner would come them and ask them about their last wishes. They sometimes thanked us, they sometimes said to us, 'God bless you', and after the entire story, we would then put the caps on. You accompany the person [to the gallows room] ... Between the trapdoors there would have been a pipe railing. The person who was due to be hanged would go on the left of the railing and the person accompanying would go on the right. Then on the trapdoor there would be two footprints painted, and you had to make sure that the person was standing on that mark. [The] man who was going to execute the people came and he placed the rope around their necks and he would then pull the flap on the hood ... and he pulls the lever ... When I looked down, I noted as the people were swinging from the momentum and had their spastic movements, I noted how they moved ...

(VOL. 2 P173 TRC FINAL REPORT)

The human abbatoir 2

The Maximum Security Prison in Pretoria was a prison designed for death. Its sole purpose as an institution was to imprison persons condemned to death, clothe them, feed them and keep them whole until they were killed. However, from the first time a prisoner arrived at death row, elaborate mechanisms were put in place to ensure that he or she would not kill themselves. This was a job reserved for the State and no one would take it away.

The lights were on 24 hours a day; prisoners were watched from a grille above their heads, they wore no belts. After the suicide in 1987 of Frikkie Muller, who gouged his wrists with a shoe nail on the day before his execution, all the condemned wore soft shoes …

No studying was allowed, and the prisoners were often taunted with the fact of their impending death. What do you want to study for? Why are you exercising? What is the point of improving your body or mind when you are going to die?

The routine was ghastly but familiar. The Sheriff would arrive at Pretoria Maximum Security Prison with a batch of notices in his hand … The prison warders would walk down the silent corridors between the individual cells, and footsteps would stop outside.

Those that were, in [the opinion of the State President] no longer fit for this world were sent to the 'Pot'… It was there, in the waiting cells, the hourly countdown began. It was also here that the traditional silence of death row was broken – with singing day and night. Singing mostly of traditional and religious hymns but sometimes of freedom songs where those to be hanged were guerrillas.

During the week that they waited to die, they were measured for the hangman: the thickness of their neck, their height and their weight are all measured to ensure that the length of the drop is calculated correctly.

On the night before the execution was to take place … each of the condemned prisoners [would be given] a whole, deboned chicken to eat and R4 to buy something from the prison tuck shop …

The bodies would be taken in the coffins … to unmarked graves in one of the segregated graveyards around Pretoria … No family members were allowed to accompany the coffins or to pray while the bodies were interred. At a later date families were handed a grave number.

(VOL. 4 P214 TRC FINAL REPORT)

Fighting for life on death row

The news came through on the South African wires shortly before 10 am. Three men had been hanged at Pretoria Central Prison at dawn. Which wasn't bad for Shucks. He'd done better and he'd done worse. But to save two lives in one week is something worth doing in anyone's book.

'Shucks' was an execution monitor. Every week he went out to bat for those miserable people who live on South Africa's death row and used every trick and talent he had to try to save them.

It was a terrible job in more ways than one; terrible having to go and talk to those guys, knowing that next morning they're going to be corpses; terrible having to tell the families that the next morning their sons are going to be corpses and, above all, terrible because to the world they are nothing but corpses – you know, 'another three hanged in Pretoria yesterday … Forty-five have died so far this year on South Africa's gallows.'

Shucks was not his real name. His name was Huggins Sefanyetso, but everyone knew him as Shucks. He wasn't sure where it came from, but it suited him. 'Cool, man, cool,' he was always saying, half listening to the telephone clutched to his ear, his other hand frantically scribbling instructions for a barrister or an announcement to the press. He looked a bit like Sammy Davis Jnr, with those quick, nervous, yet graceful movements.

He landed this terrible job almost by chance. Shucks had always wanted to be a lawyer and he did study law, at the University of the North – one of the 'bush colleges'. But his studies were disrupted by political unrest on the campus and he never got started again. Instead he became an articled clerk and later was taken on by Lawyers for Human Rights, which was set up in 1979 by some of South Africa's top barristers. It was a noble organisation that tried to promote black lawyers.

The organisation became closely involved in capital punishment when they heard there was a man on death row who was about to be hanged although his lawyers had not got around to filing a petition for clemency to the president. They decided to try for a stay of execution on the grounds that the prisoner had not explored all legal remedies open to him. The director, Brian Currin, asked Shucks to handle the application to the Supreme Court. He did and won the case and then another one, and so the process snowballed until Shucks found himself working full-time on the job.

The great scandal of the apartheid legal system was the inadequacy of legal representation. Legal aid was virtually nonexistent, so the vast majority of people who appeared in South Africa's courts – who were of course black and poor – were sent to jail without the privilege of a professional defence. In capital cases, however, pro Deo lawyers were provided. But the fees paid for such work was so pathetic that the briefs were usually picked up by newly qualified youngsters or old hacks. The accused in capital cases were, for their part, usually uneducated. They frequently thought that their lawyers were acting for the State, rather than God. All of which gave rise to such as people being hanged without anyone bothering to exhaust the appeals procedure.

Since he began working as South Africa's 'execution monitor' Shucks must have saved more than 50 lives. The way he did it was to hang around Pretoria Central Prison waiting to hear when notices of execution have been issued, giving a prisoner seven days until his death. Then he banged off a request to the Justice Department for the dates when the prisoners' various appeals were dismissed.

If the reply showed that any of these lines of appeal had not been tried, Shucks hared off to the Supreme Court with a barrister to stop the execution on the precedent he had set.

Sometimes he used other strategies, as in the case of Almond Nofomela, a Security Branch officer who had murdered a white farmer. Nofomela received his notice and sent word to Shucks that he had a story to tell about political killings. Shucks sent a young white barrister in to hear the story. The barrister came back and said Nofomela had a long story about how he had not killed the farmer. Shucks was impatient – almost everyone on death row says they didn't do it – and he sent the barrister back.

Meanwhile, Shucks was fighting for a second prisoner, Freddy Dreyer, a young coloured killer. Dreyer had not filed a petition for clemency, so Shucks sent in another barrister to get his permission to go for a stay. The lawyer came back, disconsolately, with a scrawled statement from Dreyer: 'I, the undersigned, Freddy Dreyer (23 years of age), declare hereunder that I am not prepared to make a petition for clemency to the State President, because I don't know about and I don't believe that I did commit the offence for which I find myself here. That's all. I have made peace with the Lord.'

Shucks had no more time for that case – Freddy had to be left to his God now – and he raced around to nearby chambers to see the barrister who had just got back from Nofomela. The barrister was looking shaken – the policeman had confessed to nine murders as a police 'hit man', including that of the civil rights lawyer Griffiths Mxenge.

The two men argued strategy. Shucks wanted to go for the jugular – a court application and press conference; the State couldn't afford to be seen to be covering up on the Mxenge killing. The barrister wanted to negotiate; the precedent for a stay on these grounds was dubious. Shucks conceded and the barrister went to see the Attorney-General.

The day before executions was always frantic for Shucks and so it proved on that occasion. Nofomela was demanding all his attention. Dreyer was a goner. There were three others due to be hanged – Harry Ncqobo, Khalewayo Gumede and Mfanozi Mthethwa – but there was seemingly no hope for them.

In mid-morning the wife of an ANC prisoner on death row came into Shucks' office and said she had managed to have a few words with Ncqobo while visiting her husband earlier; he had said that he had not heard from his lawyer since the last stay of execution. Shucks flicked through the papers littering his desk, looking for the Department of Justice briefing, which showed that all three men had their petitions rejected on specified dates. How could they have petitioned without being consulted? Frantically they start trying to locate the pro Deo lawyers in the cases.

At 11.50 am they get through to the Durban office of the lawyer who represented Ncqobo. He was out, but the secretary promised to fax the petition. At midday the fax came through; the petition was no more than a rehearsal of the trial. At 12.55 pm the lawyer confirms he did not even send Ncqobo a copy.

There's hurried debate in Shucks' office. He was also worried about Nofomela – there was still no word from the Attorney-General.

At 1.14 pm they agreed on a delicate call to the Durban barrister; they needed an affidavit from him saying his client was inadequately represented.

By 3.25 pm there was still no sign of the affidavit and they were getting frantic. It arrived at 3.45 pm. The face of Lucretia Seafield, assistant director of Lawyers for Human Rights, fell as she read it. The thrust was that Ncqobo had a comprehensive defence. The co-director, Peter Mothle, was pulled in. He urged them to go for it.

But Shucks had vanished – he'd gone to Nofomela's barrister. At 4 pm he was back triumphant. The Justice Minister had capitulated and Nofomela had his stay. Now for Ncqobo. Shucks set up a judge at home for a 6 pm hearing.

At 5.30 pm they were packing to go when I ask Lucretia about the other two men She looks bewildered. Ncqobo had said he did not think the other two men had heard from their lawyers either, I point out. Lucretia says she would check it.

The outcome is on the wires: Dreyer, Gumede and Mthethwa were now corpses, so Ncqobo was saved. Had Gumede and Mthethwa seen their pro Deo lawyers about their petitions?

I could have telephoned Pretoria and asked Shucks. But I wasn't going to. He had another six to bat for the following week. Solomon Ngobeni was the last person hanged by the State on 14 November 1989. A month later Shucks died when his car was struck while reversing out of a parking lot. 'And so it goes.'

Spencer Tracy and Madame Defarge

But let me digress for a moment, in this account of man's inhumanity to man, in tribute to the real innovators where the death sentence is concerned. The Americans of course introduced 'Old Sparky' – the electric chair – to the world and then they started using lethal injections in an attempt to make the ultimate act of inhumanity more humane. To this record there must now be added the Predator, the flying, killing machine that brings some confusion to the business of execution.

For those who do not know of the Predator, it is a pilotless aircraft, or drone, which has been deployed in conflicts in the Middle East and Asia, supposedly in order to hunt down and exterminate 'terrorists'. It is the ultimate in execution machines.

It putters through the sky at about 80 miles an hour, with two Hellfire missiles slung under its wings and is equipped with a highly sophisticated and powerful camera, looking for those under sentence of death. With the help of satellite links, it can be flown over the Middle East and its missiles fired from CIA headquarters in Langley, Virginia. The US army, navy and air force also use them. So why is this an execution machine, as opposed to a mere weapon of war? The answer would seem to be twofold. Firstly, because a weapon of war is used in a time of war and, secondly, because the Predator gets personal. Typically, when Paul Tibbets dropped the atom bomb on Hiroshima it was in a time of war and it is assumed he did not know anyone on the ground. It was, needless to say, horrendous, but nothing personal. If his mum had been down there, for example, he would not have been expected to do it (his mum was in the air with him, at least in the spirit – Tibbies having named his bomber, the *Enola Gay*, after her).

Executioners, on the other hand, kill people because of who they are. Sometimes they might even be told what they have done, although this is not necessarily a prerequisite for execution.

State assassinations raise a slightly fuzzy area of definition – after all, they are carried out in times of both peace and war; so what is the difference between them and executions? Possibly the distinction is that nations using the death sentence tend to boast of executions – seeing them as a social duty – while trying to conceal assassinations, feeling vaguely guilty about them.

There are a number of conundrums arising from the use of the Predator, notably to do with jurisdiction. Where is someone executed if the button is pressed (executioners apparently use joysticks) in Langley and the condemned man dies in Yemen or Pakistan?

But the most puzzling issue to me is how a country with culture and conscience rooted in Hollywood and such great films as *Judgment at Nuremberg* – that classic on German depravity and American principle – could carry out executions without a fair trial. The answer, no doubt, is that such proceedings are played out behind closed doors, for reasons of national security, on a 'need-to-know' basis. We can but hope that one day a need to know will be recognised on the part of the public in whose name the executions are carried out.

Shortly after the machine started killing people the US air force boasted that a 23-year-old girl had launched a Predator missile that had executed 12 Taliban. Unfortunately we do not have her name, but one day it will no doubt emerge. In the interim let us think of her as Madame Defarge.

Medal of honour

The record has it that Constable James Farmer was beaten to death by an angry crowd at Salt River, near Cape Town, despite an unsuccessful attempt by a Muslim clergyman to save his life. The clergyman, Moulana Faried Isaak, was hailed for his heroism.

In its bare bones, the story was true. Constable Farmer did die at the hands of an enraged mob and the *moulana* (priest) did make a heroic effort to save him. But there was another, ironic dimension to the tale.

Constable Farmer was killed by Muslim mourners attending the funeral of Ebrahim Carelse, a 31-year-old father of three who had himself been shot dead by a policeman near Cape Town. The constable made the mistake of getting too close to the funeral procession – keeping it under surveillance with a colleague, both in plain clothes. They were challenged by the mourners. One policeman ran for it, but Constable Farmer panicked, pulled his pistol and opened fire, hitting a 51-year-old man, Yusuf Lakay. The wounded man survived and many said later that he deserved to be shot anyway – he had identified himself with the white cricketing establishment.

When the crowd surrounded him and began punching and kicking Constable Farmer, Isaak – who had been leading the funeral procession – fought his way through and shielded the constable. The attackers did not stop. Isaak began to take some of the blows, which is where the unreported dimension to the story begins.

There were shouts at Isaak to get off, that the man he was shielding was 'a cop' and he had shot Yusuf Lakay dead. The priest asked Constable Farmer whether he was a cop and when he said 'no', began to go through his pockets looking for identification. But there was nothing in them.

At this point, the priest was quite willing to die for the man. But then another clergyman shouted that he was a cop and he had seen him shoot Lakay. The priest, who studied theology for eight years, remembered a principle that for anyone to be held guilty of a crime at least two witnesses had to be found. When a second witness was produced and attested to the shooting, Isaak was satisfied. He pretended to faint and was dragged away while the life of Constable James Farmer was brought to its end.

Later Isaak went to address a public meeting and was greeted by shouts of *'Hulle lieg!'* (Afrikaans for 'They lie!') The liars, to the crowd, were the press for their reports that Isaak had tried to save the life of a cop. They all knew that their priest would never try to save the life of a cop. Both at that meeting and other rallies, Isaak had to explain that he did not know the man was a policeman and, no, of course he would never try to save a cop.

It was difficult to get hold of Faried Isaak to get the real story of what happened during that march in Salt River. He was reluctant to take telephone calls, because someone from the office of the state president had been trying to contact him. He heard they want to give him the Woltemade Cross for Bravery, the equivalent to Britain's George Cross, or America's Congressional Medal of Honor. He didn't want it.

Law–abiding killer

There was a young insurance salesman among members of the public milling around in Pretoria's Palace of Justice. Gerhard van Wyk, aged 21, had taken time off work to show his support for a man he did not know very well, but whom he considered to be a friend. He was casually dressed; in a bomber jacket, a khaki shirt and jeans he looked like any other white South African on the streets of Pretoria.

The friend Van Wyk had gone to support was Barend Hendrik Strydom, the mass murderer who had trotted through the streets of central Pretoria in November 1988, smiling with apparent happiness as he shot 22 black people, killing seven of them.

'He did what many people in the country would do,' said Van Wyk, during a break in the proceedings. 'I have much respect for him. He had guts. I wouldn't do the same, but I approve of what he did.'

Most people in South Africa were horrified at the time by the massacre. And the blanket coverage given to the trial by the local press had about it a sense of incredulity. Privately most people wrote him off as a 'lone nutter'.

But the court found, on psychiatric evidence, that Strydom was not insane. And the supportive presence of Van Wyk, coupled with that of two rows of fellow right-wing extremists in the public gallery at the Palace of Justice, suggested he was not alone. All of which raised the question: If Strydom was not insane, was he not at least a product of an insane society?

Strydom's background was not untypical in white South Africa. He was to some extent a creation of Christian National Education, a system of education designed to inculcate the values of Afrikaner supremacy.

The son of a policeman, he first took an interest in politics at school. 'We were taught to be proud of our country,' he recalled. His *volktrots* (pride in one's country) was shaped at *veldskole* (field schools) – weekend camps attended by children at government-controlled secondary schools in what was then the Transvaal. Run on paramilitary lines, under a rigidly Calvinistic ethos, the children were imbued with right-wing claptrap along the lines of 'evolution is a communist plot'.

By the time Strydom reached his fifth year at secondary school he was writing letters on Christianity, communism and apartheid to the likes of Margaret Thatcher, Ronald Reagan, PW Botha and the leaders of the South African homelands. The homeland leaders were seemingly unimpressed, because – by his account – they tipped off the police and the schoolboy was visited by the Security Branch who advised him 'to fix my attention on other activities'.

The Security Branch seemingly failed to open a file on Strydom. He was admitted into the police force on leaving school in 1984. And he took with him the attitudes instilled at school. The 'enemy' he had to fight as a policeman was communism – 'a satanically inspired movement ...'

But communism was not the only obsession for Strydom;

there was also the survival of the white race. 'Each black person threatens the continued existence of whites, even an 88-year-old woman,' he said, referring to an 88-year-old hawker who was among his victims. 'It is often the innocent black who causes the most problems,' he added. 'Scientists have shown that the oxygen is decreasing. This is the fault of blacks. They are threatening the life of the entire planet.'

It was a weird perspective, even within the context of the South African Police, and it led him into trouble with his superiors. In 1987 a photograph found in his room shows Strydom holding the head of a black man in one hand and a knife in the other. His intention, he explained to court, was to have the photograph blown up into a poster with a slogan across the bottom: '*ANC, pasop*' ('African National Congress, watch out.')

Strydom said he was held in jail for a weekend and then dismissed from the force, but subsequently reinstated without explanation. But the 'humiliation' was too much for him and he resigned.

After a brief flirtation with the Oranje Werkers – a group of die-hard Afrikaners attempting to establish a 'white homeland' – he hit on his final mission 'to show the world there were boers on the southern tip of Africa who would fight'. He prepared with prayer and training. He made a pilgrimage to the Voortrekker Monument, the holy-of-holies in Afrikanerdom. 'I prayed and asked God to do his will and not mine and, if he was not pleased, to deflect me from my path with some visible sign.' The sign failing to materialise, he headed off to a black squatter camp and shot two black women, killing one of them, in 'an exercise to see if I was physically capable of killing people'.

Evidence led on this first killing was that Strydom, dressed like a policeman, had attacked two women living in a shack on a farm at De Deur, south of Johannesburg. One of the women, Lizabeth Tsotetsi, described how they had been woken up by someone banging on the door and shouting, in Afrikaans, 'Open up!' She had opened the door and a man dressed in camouflage uniform had walked in, searched the room and then ordered them outside. 'He told us to lie on our stomachs. We kneeled, but he again told us to lie on our stomachs,' Ms Tsotetsi said. 'While we were doing so, he shot me in the left shoulder and I fell. My friend ran off and as he tried to shoot at her, I got up and ran off as well.' Ms Tsotetsi hurdled a barbed-wire fence, banged on a neighbour's door and, when they refused to open it, crawled into a dog kennel. She said she was unable to identify the gunman because it was dark.

Satisfied that he was capable of killing people, Strydom made his dreadful, smiling appearance in central Pretoria.

Why did he smile?

'The victims did not realise the seriousness of the situation,' he explained. 'They smiled at me and, since I am a friendly person, I would smile back at them and carry on.'

A horrific picture was painted by state witnesses of the massacre when Strydom, dressed in camouflage uniform, ran along the pavements in the centre of the capital shooting at random. A hawker described how Strydom had rubbed her cheek with the barrel of his gun and then shot the woman standing next to her.

One man, Hendrik Bantjes, had run up to him. 'I asked him: "What's your problem?"' recounted Bantjes. 'He said: "Are you a *kaffirboetie* (lover of blacks)? I will shoot your head off as well."'

He was eventually grabbed by four black men and taken off by police without resistance. An arresting officer said that he had appeared completely calm after the massacre. Told how many he had killed, he had commented: 'I must have been shooting shitly.'

Gert Beukes, a constable working at South Africa's police headquarters, told the court that Strydom had been living with them in the city. He had had a meal with Strydom in the city a few hours before the Pretoria massacre, during which Strydom had asked him: 'What would you say if I told you I was having an affair with your wife.'

Constable Beukes said he had replied by telling Strydom that it was time he found alternative accommodation. He had suspected his wife was having an affair with Strydom, whom she used to call 'Wollie'.

Mariana Beukes told the court that Strydom had asked her to have an affair with him while they were taking a walk together two days before the massacre. She had refused. About an hour before the shooting had started he had arrived at the estate agency where she worked with a packet of letters for her. Beukes said he appeared 'a bit broken-hearted' and seemed to be on the verge of crying. Later in the day she had given the letters to her husband. They included a poem that made reference to Blood River, the 19th-century Boer victory over the Zulus.

Evidence to the court was that, when parking his car prior to the massacre, Strydom put money into the parking meter. He was, after all, a law-abiding man.

The castle of the white wolf

The Rautenbach family proudly call it their 'castle'. They spent 12 years building it, with their own hands, to avoid taking a housing loan and – as they explained it – risk placing themselves in the debt of 'international Jewish finance'.

The front door was made from the wood of ammunition boxes. There were opaque windows, instead of curtains, to minimise the threat of fire from petrol bombs. And over the front entrance stood a tower from which the family could look out for the black mobs they believed will one day advance upon them.

A monument to paranoia though it may have been, the crenulated monstrosity in a sense represented an ethical headache as South Africa tried to move into a new era of national reconciliation and, in the process, tackle a question that had so troubled successive Secretaries of State for Northern Ireland: What is a political prisoner? Apart from the execrable taste shown in its construction, the 'castle' was something of a local landmark because it was home to the Rautenbachs' only daughter, Karen Strydom.

On Pretoria's death row, Karen swore to love, honour and generally devote her life to Barend Strydom. The headache for the authorities came in the form of a 1 000-page application submitted to them by Strydom's lawyers, demanding that he also be recognised as a political prisoner and – in the company of hundreds and perhaps thousands of others who do belong to that category – be pardoned for his crimes.

The process of pardoning and indemnifying political prisoners used to be seen as one of the major obstacles facing the ANC and the government of FW de Klerk in their efforts to negotiate a peaceful settlement to the South African conflict. It was an issue tackled at the very first of the 'summit' meetings between Mandela and De Klerk, when the two sides agreed to create a mechanism for the release of political prisoners and the granting of immunity for political offences. A joint working group was set up to arrive at a definition of a 'political offence'. They failed to produce a definition per se, but 'guidelines' were agreed for De Klerk to use in judging individual cases. A 'consultative body' was set up both to advise him and to act as court of appeal, and a general invitation was gazetted for fugitives and felons to apply for forgiveness. Strydom took up the invitation.

The offences for which Strydom sought forgiveness were notorious. He was subsequently condemned to death eight times, the eighth sentence relating to the prior death of the black woman in the squatter camp outside Pretoria, whom he had killed in a 'practice run'. On the face of it the killings were unpardonable.

But, after a visit to Karen Strydom in her 'castle' at Hartbeespoort Dam, north of Pretoria, one was left with the uneasy feeling that judgement as to the criminal or political nature of Barend Strydom's crimes was not going to be so easy. Both the Rautenbach and Strydom families laid claim to a noble tradition of Afrikaner resistance. Karen herself was a direct descendant of one of the most celebrated of Boer War commanders, General

Christiaan de Wet. Barend's family similarly claims ancestors who fought and suffered in the Boer War and in the 1914 Afrikaner Rebellion – the earlier, less-successful counterpart to Ireland's Easter Uprising.

Framed pictures of these bearded patriarchs of more heroic times for the *volk* decorated the 'castle' walls, together with a fuzzy photograph of Barend himself and a flag of the latter-day, neo-Nazi Afrikaner Weerstandsbeweging (AWB). The couple met as fellow members of the AWB, although it seems their relationship was no more than that of nodding acquaintances. Which led to much speculation that an ulterior motive lay behind her decision to marry him, a suggestion that Karen emphatically denied: 'There are a lot of stories that I married him because of the publicity, some say because of the money. I don't know where the money is. But it is all nonsense,' she said. 'I just married him because we love each other … After a year we are still very happily married.'

Why did he do it? 'Africa is a hard country,' said Karen 'and to survive in this country you must act hard, because only the strongest survive in Africa. He did it to show the ANC that if they kill our people – innocent people – the boers will also act,' she says. 'Barend acted because there was a lack [of will] on the side of right-wing leaders to act strongly enough for their people.'

But to shoot dead seven individuals at random, laughing as he did so? 'Barend told me he never picked out individual blacks. He just started running and he shot everyone that was before him. He didn't look at that one and say: "Yes, I want to shoot that specific one." There was no personal contact or anything … I know there was a story that he was laughing, but the press made that up. Because he told me he never laughed at anyone while he was busy doing his thing. He just did his thing, and went on; and the next one, and went on. He wasn't laughing at anyone.'

Karen stressed that Barend has since given up his 'armed struggle'. He submitted a formal statement to the government, repudiating the use of 'political' violence. 'He wants to give the talks a chance to develop and to give peace a chance,' she explained. It was all chilling stuff. But in a disturbing way many aspects of the story echo that of another multiple killer at the other end of the political spectrum.

The story of Robert McBride was also given widespread publicity. An ANC guerrilla and a 'coloured' man in terms of South Africa's race laws, McBride was sentenced to death in 1987 for a bomb blast outside a crowded bar in the coastal city of Durban, which killed three women and injured more than 80 people. Like Strydom, he also claimed heritage of noble rebellion – as a descendant of Major John McBride, who actually fought in Ireland before dying in the executions that followed the Easter Rebellion. McBride was also allowed to marry on death row and he, too, repudiated political violence.

On the face of it, the only apparent difference between their actual offences – apart from argument as to the 'legitimacy' of their respective causes – is that Strydom faced his victims, while McBride used a timing device to remove himself from the scene of the blast. But there is another distinction between their cases in that behind-the-scenes pressure was placed on Pretoria to save McBride, from quarters as varied as the British government and the trial judge who condemned him. In Strydom's case, on the other hand, even abolitionists found themselves pondering whether there were not some instances where capital punishment can be justified. But under the new dispensation what would be their ultimate fate?

When I questioned the ANC leader on the issue, before he became president, he declared with passion in his voice that the ANC did not seek retribution against any individuals. Mandela is said to have told De Klerk at one of their meetings that he wanted to see everyone with a claim to political motivation freed, 'even Barend Strydom.' To which De Klerk is said to have retorted, with reference to Strydom: 'But I don't.' Mandela's position was understandable; he did not want to risk black liberation on the altar of vendetta. And De Klerk did not have his way. In 1992, as part of an amnesty for 150 political prisoners, both Strydom and McBride were pardoned.

Another extremist, named Cornelius Lottering, was jailed for 20 years. He had killed a black taxi driver, again as a 'practice run' – this time for the planned assassination of black leaders. Evidence was that he held up the taxi driver at gunpoint and stabbed him as 'part of my personal training' in the use of a knife. He put the wounded man in the boot of the taxi, drove around for a while, stopped in a deserted spot and resumed his 'practising'. His victim was kneeling in front of him when Lottering decided to try a stab through the jaw and into the brain. 'The angle of attack was not 100 per cent,' he said. The taxi driver tried to run. Lottering stopped him with a shot to the torso and, as he lay on the ground, finished him off with a shot to the head. 'Because the black was my natural enemy … the deed did not bother me in the least,' he declared.

And then there were the state killers in the police hit squads and the army's Civil Co-Operation Bureau. The latter was so enamoured of murderers of blacks that it even went out of its way to hire one as its in-house accountant. All of them would claim political motivation. All, or most, have benefited from the political trade-offs that have taken place behind closed doors in the name of national reconciliation. It makes one hanker after the Nuremburg Trials; not the punitive element, but the educational. Because surely it is time that society thrashed out once and for all the question: Do the Barend Strydoms represent an acceptable face of politics?

'She had no enemies'

For a boer, a farmer, Nick Pretorius made a frail figure, as he stood on the roadside, waving the car down. He leaned down to the passenger window, his skull shining brownly through his thinning hair under the Free State afternoon sun. 'I just want to say that she had no enemies.' He paused, as if uncertain about the point he was making, and then repeated it: 'She had no enemies, that's all I want to tell you.' With that he stepped back, waved and trudged over to his van, on his way to start digging a grave for his 81-year old mother.

Her name was Jani Pretorius. A widow, she lived a few kilometres outside the small town of Verkeerdevlei on the property she had farmed with her husband for most of their life together. The police didn't give much away about the killing, even to her son. But it appeared she was shot. Although there were items in the house, such as the television set, which would have attracted the attention of a burglar, nothing was stolen except her pistol.

What made the killing of Pretorius significant was that it was the latest of a series of murders of whites, which took place in the *platteland* (farmland) of the Free State. Six white farm people were killed, in addition to several other attacks in which the victims escaped with their lives. The baffling aspect was that, as in the case of Pretorius, there was no apparent motive.

Verkeerdevlei was a town of tumbleweed boredom, a tiny farming community served by a couple of churches, a handful of stores, a police station and not much more. The name translates directly as 'the wrong swamp', but it would translate more appropriately as the 'swamp of wrongs' – because to an outsider, at least, it seems haunted by an unarticulated sense of injustice.

It was a feeling first brought home at the police station, where a fresh-faced young constable was manning the charge office. The station commander was away, he said; he was the only officer available and he knew nothing about the murders. But he offered to call the local farmers' leader on the station's Citizens' Band radio and he began intoning the man's call sign. But the farmers' representative was not interested in making representations to the press. 'They owe me nothing and I owe them nothing,' he said cryptically, chiding the constable with the threat that he would switch off his receiver if he did not leave him alone.

The constable refused to give the name of the farmer. Part of the reason was possibly that the local press had previously identified the farmer as the leader of a lynch mob that killed a black man in the area earlier in the year. The killing took place when a group of farmers came to the rescue of an elderly couple who had been attacked. Three of the attackers were caught, one was beaten to death, the other two surviving to make a battered appearance in court on charges of attempted murder. Police said they had opened a murder docket on the mob killing, but although the identities of those who participated are seemingly well known, nobody was immediately charged.

The anger – and fear – of the farmers of was tangible. At the local Afrikaner Protestant Church, the elders were just leaving a council meeting. One of them gestured to his colleagues, dressed up in their Sunday-suited best, saying: 'They are all carrying guns; you don't walk in Verkeerdevlei without guns anymore. Every night we patrol … '

A neighbour of the murdered Jani Pretorius, Chris Roux, was the commander of a reaction unit set up by the local commando (army reserve). Standing outside his home – his mother shouting imprecations at him from behind the heavily barred windows of the house for daring to speak to the foreign media – Roux was insistent that, although the killings might not have been 'directly political' murders, they were inspired by the ANC. 'For us it is very clear that it is not accidental,' he said.

In fact the belief was widely shared among the white farmers of the Free State that the murders are part of a strategy by the ANC to drive them off their land. Chris Hani – the former Chief of Staff of Umkhonto we Sizwe, the military wing of the ANC – gave personal assurances that no such strategy was being pursued. Needless to say, the assurances were little believed on the *platteland*. But if a story lying behind the worst of the murders was anything to go by, the farmers were faced by something more alarming than conspiracy.

Gabriel Mahakoe was under mental observation in Bloemfontein on the orders of a Supreme Court judge, after an extraordinary performance during his trial on charges of multiple murder. The 42-year-old farm labourer faced the death sentence for killing four members of a Verkeerdevlei farmer's family – Willem Engelbrecht, his wife, daughter and granddaughter.

Mahakoe was sent for psychiatric observation after three days in the dock, during which he shouted insults at the judge and his assessors, demanding that he be tried by a black man and represented by black lawyers. South Africa, having at the time only one 'black' judge (an Indian) and the Free State, to its shame, having not a single black barrister, the case proceeded in the face of the accused's continued protests.

Apart from his shouts at the judge ('Hangman! … Boer!') Mahakoe did not have the opportunity to explain why he carried out the murders. But he did offer something of an explanation in a statement at an earlier magistrate's court hearing, in which he confessed to the farm massacre. It made bizarre reading.

Working as a labourer on the Engelbrecht farm, he described how he entered the house while the family was away and searched for a gun and ammunition, which he found. 'After that I sat down in the sacred room where a kaffir never sits and waited for them. The devil helped me and they came.'

The Engelbrecht family walked into the house and Mahakoe confronted them, with the rifle levelled.

'Mauloje Afrika,' he greeted them. 'That means "Africa comes back",' he explained to the magistrate. 'Then I went on with my work.'

'What do you mean when you say you went on with your work' asked the State prosecutor?

'I killed apartheid. I wanted to chop off the hand but I only succeeded in chopping off the fingertips …'

'How did you go about it?

'I started shooting. I said: "I am not shooting you, I am shooting the name: dog, baboon". That is what we are called. They also kill us. Show the tribe of Africa we can do it anytime. We are tired of being slaves …

'When they had all fallen, I saw that one was not dead. So I hit the one lying under her mother with the butt of the gun. She should also have been dead.'

'What did you do after this?'

'I put the gun down, because its work was finished … I should have killed 20 to 50. Africa has become embittered. I have no regrets.'

On the basis of the confession, it might appear that Mahakoe was insane. But those who watched him in court said he was a strikingly intelligent man who reserved his rancour for the white court officials. In his dealings with blacks he was calm and gentle. The courtroom was packed with black spectators for his appearances. They crowded around him during adjournments to shake his hand and talk to him; on one occasion a frustrated crowd locked out of the overcrowded court building threatened to riot and were dispersed by police with tear gas.

Mahakoe became a cult figure in the townships of the Free State, having seemingly come to represent a deep-seated sense of grievance in the black population at past wrongs, whether real, or imagined. In the tiny black township servicing Verkeerdevlei, residents talked of unmarked graves in the area containing the remains of labourers murdered by white farmers over the years. 'Even here, in the township, we have three people buried without identification,' said the local branch chairman of the ANC, Neo Banyane. 'We don't know who they are. They are people killed by the whites. The problem is the treatment the white people have passed on to the black people.'

Driving out of the township, a van could be seen across the fields, parked alongside Verkeerdevlei's white cemetery. It was Nick Pretorius, digging a hole for a mother who had no enemies.

The Shishita Report

I have in front of me a curious set of papers entitled: 'Documents submitted to the TRC only by the African National Congress.' There is a comma missing, after the word 'only'. The ANC's intention was to restrict their circulation to the Truth and Reconciliation Commission; 'only' the commissioners were meant to read it.

There are 13 documents in the set of papers, starting with the Shishita Report itself, or what is formally known as the 'report on the subversive activities of police agents in our movement'.

The Shishita Report is famous in the ANC. The security department in particular takes great pride in it, claiming it is a record of how they 'dealt a heavy blow to the enemy when it uprooted its most prized network of infiltrators'.

Among other incidents it records is 'Black September', an iconic incident in the folklore of the ANC when an attempt was allegedly made in 1977 to poison 500 cadres in one of their Angolan camps.

Unfortunately the Shishita Report offers little by way of forensic evidence to explain how it was established that it was a murderous plot. Some veterans of the camps, when quizzed about Black September, are likely to mutter something about 'food poisoning'. Certainly the cadres were fortunate; not a single person died as a result of the poisoning.

Perhaps that statement should be amended to: not a single person died as a 'direct' result of the poisoning. Because 'Vusi Mayekiso passed the four capsules of poison to "Tiny" who was working in the kitchen and actually poisoned the food.' The identity of 'Tiny' or his fate are not known, but that is not true of Vusi. In these papers, Vusi is listed as being among 21 'agents executed on order of tribunals'.

The composition, or qualification of those tribunals is not known. One senior ANC official who was in a position to know, Mac Maharaj, has observed that it is doubtful whether the condemned enjoyed any trial at all, much less a legal one.

From the few details recorded, Vusi Mayekiso (real name Derrick Lobelo) was a very active spy. He 'got around', as the expression goes.

Before he was executed he managed to 'name' 64 other suspected agents. Apart from nearly wiping out approximately five hundred soldiers with four capsules of poison, 'missions' he carried out – at least by the ANC's account – included:

'Spreading discontent in the African National Congress camps over problems of food and tobacco shortages and generally whipping up an unstable political situation in the organisation.

'Stealing army property and medicaments from the clinic.

'Attempted or planned to blow up logistics stores (this had to be postponed due to failure to obtain sufficient quantity of TNT).

'Character assassination, especially of the camp administration, but up to national level.'

Another of Mayekiso's 'missions' according to the Shishita Report was to start a campaign against the ANC's Cuban allies 'saying, for example:

'The Cubans were promoting prostitution in the camps.

'The Cubans were discriminating in one way or another.

'The Cubans were causing damage to African National Congress property.

'The Cubans were receiving preferential treatment.'

The final denouement of Mayekioso is that 'he stole a number of articles with the aim of causing artificial shortages of particular items, especially cigarettes, at a critical time.'

A deadly assassin.

Excuse the sarcasm.

Rites of passage

– *I saw my first naked woman there, in that block of flats.*
– *She's probably gone by now.*

- *That's funny.*
- *Sorry, go on.*
- *I must have been about 11 years old – just coming through puberty, I guess. There used to be striptease joint called La Boheme on the ground floor – it looks like it has gone now. Word went around our school that you could go up onto the first floor of the flats and peep through a fanlight and watch the strip.*

    So my best friend and I went on our bicycles to see. I remember it so well – it was an old block of flats; you know, with open-air corridors built around a square in the middle formed by the roof of the nightclub. There were fanlights in the roof and when we got there, on the first floor, there was already a whole bunch of kids bunched around the, peering down. I can almost smell it now. Cigarette smoke, the tang of beer, the buzz of conversation rising up from the crowded tables, waiters in white uniforms and red fezzes padding around the tables. Then it began to fall quiet as the manager signalled to the waiters to get out – black men were not allowed to see a white woman naked. We were right above the stage. We couldn't believe our eyes. She came on and did the usual bumps and grinds standing in front of the audience. But when she was down to her underwear she went over to a stretcher on the stage – a camp bed. You know how, when you lie down on a camp bed, it sags, so your body is just below the edge? Well, that's what she did. She lay there and teased the audience, out front, by lying there and undressing, just out of sight of them – lifting one leg and languorously rolling a stocking off and so on. But of course we little boys were looking down on her and we could see everything. Off came the stockings, off came the bra, off came her panties and there she was, laid out beneath us. Like a feast for little boys. Oh, the excitement, gazing down at her; running around the roof bent over double, bumping into each other, gasped whispers of 'Did you see that, did you see that?' before running back to the fanlight again to have another look.
- *Little Peeping Toms.*
- *I'm sure she wouldn't have minded; if she had known what an*

impact she had on those little boys and how she would be remembered
so vividly by them down the years. She must be in her sixties now,
the stripper – a grey-haired granny, maybe. But in the minds of her
audience at the fanlight she still has long brown hair, firm breasts,
lissome legs, flat stomach … an immortality of a kind.

London town

My earliest recall of London, as a name at least, was as a child
going on holiday to a resort near the coastal town of East London
in the Eastern Cape. 'If we're going to East London, could we go
to the west a bit and visit London itself?' I asked my parents in the
front of the car. 'I wouldn't mind seeing London,' I said wistfully
before returning the saga of Robin Hood.

It was an ambition I nursed, like so many other colonial kids,
into adulthood when I finally made it in 1974 at the age of 27. It was
not simply a career move. My wife, Marianne, and I were trying to
catch the eddies of the revolution that had already, unbeknownst
to us, sailed on by. Bob Dylan had sung 'The Times, They Are
a-Changin'; from Berkeley to Berlin there were riots and riotous
fun; images of those long legs and mini-skirts in Carnaby Street
tantalised the world. In a word, liberation. But I had missed all the
fun and my frustration was compounded by what was happening at
home. Time there had atrophied into a stale culture of censorship
and repression. I had to find fresh air.

But when we discovered London, it was hardly the city of
our dreams. Heathrow – 'the world's largest airport' – was just
a collection of prefabricated buildings all bolted together. And
then we got onto a bus to London and it trundled through these
little streets, lined with pokey little houses. 'Look, all the windows
are closed,' I called out in wonderment to Marianne. At first
everything seemed a disappointment. St Paul's was much smaller
than I imagined. Westminster Abbey seemed so squashed, all those
tombs of kings and queens crammed together in little corners.

And then I got to Trafalgar Square where I had imagined a huge, dramatic space but it was barely the size of a cricket field, grimy with all these goddamned pigeons messing it up. But that's when I discovered England. Or London, at least. I was standing there, looking at Nelson's Column and wondering why the heck they'd put the statue up there. Statues are meant to be looked at, so why put it more than 100 feet above people's heads? I looked it up in my guidebook and it was then that I started falling in love with England. It said the statue was erected 'by the grateful citizens of London, to afford Lord Nelson a view of the sea'.

The Duke of Edinburgh's mistress

I've really been pretty good, only telling the story at the occasional dinner party. So I've decided to go public and tell the tale of myself and the Duke of Edinburgh's mistress. My only concern is that people will not believe what even I must admit is an extraordinary story. This story is true. I promise.

After a short stint with a Welsh newspaper, I had joined what was then the South African Argus Group's (now the Independent Group) London bureau.

It was said to be the largest foreign newspaper bureau in Britain. The staff, of about 35, were mostly ex-editors of newspapers and magazines sold or closed by the Argus Group and put out to pasture, if you like. The Argus Group was then (I think I'm right in saying) the biggest newspaper group in the southern hemisphere. It was beginning to contract, so there was plenty of demand for the pastures of semi-retirement.

The head of this bureau, the editor in chief, was Sandy Noble. He used to come to work in a pinstripe suit, brolly and bowler hat and was that sort of a man, a true-blue conservative.

I don't know how true it was, but it was said that Noble had two fears in life. One was that he or a member of his staff would inadvertently do something to antagonise management in South

Africa, imperilling his life in happy exile. Management was God and any request from them, or supported by them, had to be met literally, instantly and with respect.

I tended to handle requests from the *Tribune* newspaper in Durban. So they would telex the bureau asking if we could ask Prince Charles for a tip for the Durban July Handicap, South Africa's premier horse race. Instead of telling them to go take a running jump, in terms of the Noble Doctrine, I had to phone Buckingham Palace, put the question, take whatever abuse the press spokesman wanted to hand out and then compose a polite message saying something to the effect of: 'Buckingham Palace declined to comment on Prince Charles' favourite for the Durban July.'

The other fear that apparently loomed large in Nobel's mind was that he, or his staff would antagonise the Royal Family, who might complain to South African management, and so on and so forth. On this particular day these two fears came into conjunction and seemed about to be realised over the (one of many) Duke of Edinburgh's mistress.

I was summoned into Noble's office where I found him staring at his fabulous view up Fleet Street with the melancholy air of a man who knew his time had come. I coughed and he turned. 'Ah, Beresford, I've got a difficult assignment for you,' he said and, picking a piece of paper up from his desk, presented it to me. It was a telex from the *Tribune* asking us to find out if it was true that Mrs Jane Gilbey (the name is fictional, largely because I've forgotten her real one) at an address in Kensington had had an affair with the Duke of Edinburgh.

I gulped. 'Now what I want you to do,' said Noble, 'is go to this address, put the question. You will probably get a 'no comment'. Now I don't want you to come back to the office,' he continued. 'I want you to go to the nearest public telephone and phone me and tell exactly what happened.' The poor man's terrors had finally caught up with him.

So I caught a black cab and headed off for the Kensington address.

'Do you want me to wait, Guv?' asked the taxi driver.

'If you don't mind,' I said. 'And keep the engine running,' I muttered to myself.

The address was a Regency house with a big brass knocker. I knocked. The door swung open. It was a balmy English summer's day and the sun was shining brightly. I remember the weather, because it was all darkness behind the young woman who answered the door in her uniform of an English housemaid.

'Can I help you,' she asked?

'Uh, yes, is Mrs Gilbey in?'

'Yes. Who shall I say is calling?'

'David …'

'David! David Beresford!' came a cry from inside the house and a middle-aged woman I had no recollection of ever having met before brushed the maid aside and threw herself into my arms. 'David, how wonderful to see you.'

This story is true. I promise.

'Come in, come in!' She led the way into what turned out to be a grand vestibule with a sweeping stairway down which was coming a gorgeous blonde.

'Charlotte, look who's here. David, David Beresford,' trilled Mrs Gilbey, to who was evidently her daughter. 'You haven't seen each other since you were so big,' she said, making a gesture indicating knee height.

'What are you doing. How did you know where to find us? How did you know where to find us!' At this stage it was becoming clear something was wrong. I must have been giving a fair imitation of a dying fish, mouth opening and closing without a word emerging.

Fortunately I had the telex, by now a sweaty ball in my hand. Wordlessly, I held it out. She took it and unrolled it. Her nose swept up and the atmosphere turned glacial.

'Come with me!' she commanded, leading me into a sitting room.

To cut a long story short, she had been my mother's best friend in South Africa, some 20 years before. She had emigrated and they had lost touch. Back in the old days she had met the Duke of Edinburgh – then little more than a Greek prince and naval officer who still had to become famous by marrying the Queen – when his warship briefly docked in Cape Town and a shore party was held for the crew.

In later years her aged mother, feeling her family's achievements were not publicly appreciated, telephoned the *Tribune* to inform them that her daughter had bedded the Duke of Edinburgh. The *Tribune* had telexed the Argus London Bureau and, in a city of millions, I had come knocking on the door.

She had me out the door in five minutes – I never even had a chance to say goodbye to my childhood friend. The taxi was waiting and I asked him to take me to the nearest phone booth, from which I called Sandy Noble. 'Fraid it's a no comment,' I said.

The Wizard of Oz

I returned to South Africa in 1984 as *The Guardian's* correspondent in Johannesburg and in 1991 I was sent to cover the first Gulf War, intending to write the *Naked and the Dead*. I returned trying to understand the *Wizard of Oz*. When I left, my family bade me sad farewells, assuming there was a good chance that I was not going to return from this assignment. Chemical warfare was certain; the only question was whether the Iraqis would use their biological weapons.

On the eve of the Allied ground offensive, I was looking for souvenirs in a bazaar near the town of Hafar al Batin on the Saudi frontline with a couple of Americans and a Canadian colleague. We ran into a member of the Special Boat Squadron – the maritime equivalent to the SAS – a captain, if my memory serves me. He was a friendly guy and agreed to join us for lunch back at our small hotel. I am a former Irish correspondent and should have known better; the SAS don't talk unless they have an ulterior motive.

Over the meal he was able to give us extraordinary detail on the Iraqi chemical warfare capability in Kuwait – down to the types of chemical agents they were planning to use against Allied forward and rear positions (a distinction that had to do with the dispersal rates of the chemicals). He explained that all this was known to him as a member of 'special forces', because units like his own had been able to infiltrate Iraqi positions at night and actually inspect their stocks of chemical weapons while the enemy troops were asleep. Desperate for copy to liven up the wait for the ground war to start, we could hardly believe our luck.

But it was luck that was to be repeated when we similarly ran into a young Kuwaiti man who had been studying at an American university at the time of the Iraq invasion. Patriotically, he had volunteered and, because of his language ability, had been drafted into 'signals', listening into Iraq radio transmissions. He was able to pinpoint sports stadiums that were being used as torture centres. Again, we could hardly believe our luck.

But any doubts were swept aside by the pundits – the television networks in particular, pumping out to the world not only confirmation of the chemical weapons threat, but details of the immense and sophisticated fortifications prepared by the Iraqis in preparation for the Allied land invasion; the massive underground labyrinths constructed to protect the heavy armour against aerial bombardment; the giant artificial sand dunes making miniature Maginot lines across the desert; the huge canals of oil that would be set ablaze when the tactical moment came.

I finally went to war, with the Egyptians. We swept right across Kuwait, through the battlefields. Maginot lines there were none. There was one oil moat – which I jumped across. The only underground fortifications I saw was a single line of trenches, the sophistication of which would have had a World War I combatant scoffing. An American communications expert who examined their equipment shook his head, saying he did not think the Iraqi radios were capable of transmitting to neighbouring trenches, much less headquarters

One sorry deserter did have a chemical warfare suit, or at least that's how he described the rolled-up, throwaway raincoat he was carrying. He was carrying it in anticipation that the Allies would use chemical weapons.

The 'ferocity' of the fighting was such that the only Allied casualty I came across was a GI who had got his arm caught in the door of his armoured personnel carrier.

As it transpired, of course, not a single chemical warfare weapon was discovered in the Kuwaiti theatre of operations, or in the weapon heads of any Scud missiles.

I helped 'liberate' Kuwait City, after being captured twice – by the US 7th Army Corps and then by the US Marines who had little else to fill their time.

I arrived in the city in the company of hordes of other journalists and we were all mobbed as 'liberators' (the Allied armies were waiting to make sure all the television cameras were there before they actually marched in). Most of the liberated were extremely anxious to recount their tales of atrocity (remember the stories of how Saddam Hussein used to push critics of his government into vats of acid?).

I had had experience of atrocity tales in South Africa and knew the dangers of exaggeration inherent in second-hand accounts, so I kept asking: 'Did you see it yourself?' None had and, unfortunately, the first-hand witnesses from whom they had heard the stories were recovering from trauma in a mental hospital … had disappeared … had …

The next morning the world's newspapers were stuffed full of atrocity stories. 'Kuwait Liberated – Horrors Revealed.' Cursing myself for missing the 'angle', I determined on the next day to find myself some atrocities.

As luck would have it, as I headed out on my quest I spotted, in the foyer of the huge and abandoned five-star International Hotel in which most of the journalists had dossed down for the night, a large Arab in flowing robes sitting at a desk, a notice on the wall above his head announcing: 'General Tours – You name it and we will show it.' They were offering atrocity tours!

The tour offered to me by the guides was a visit to the 'torture chamber', where, I was earnestly assured, blood was to be seen on the floors and indescribable steel instruments could be inspected. The torture chamber turned out to be the Naif, an old palace on the central square of Kuwait City, apparently used by the Iraqi security services as a base. As far as atrocities were concerned, it offered poor pickings. 'Hey, Ron, there's a smell here,' cried one American journalist to another as he picked his way down a darkened passage. 'It is the smell of death,' replied his colleague. But the dead were not to be found, smelly, or otherwise.

I left the guided tour increasingly anxious to get myself an atrocity in time for the day's deadlines and went in search of the 'incubator story'. The incubator story is probably the most famous of the Kuwait atrocity tales, given credence by President Bush himself: that Iraqis had thrown newborn babies out of hospital incubators, which they then stole, leaving the babes to die.

The incident is meant to have occurred at the Al-Sabah Maternity Hospital, reportedly the biggest of its kind in the Middle East. When I introduced myself there, several doctors smothered smiles. A gynaecologist, Dr Narges Faleh, explained that there had already been six parties of journalists to see them. No, the Iraqis had not dumped any babies or stolen incubators. The staff had no idea where the story had originated. The only baby she personally had lost to the war had been a boy who died when a bomb destroyed the local power station, cutting off a suction machine needed to clear the child's breathing. 'I nearly cried, because I could have saved him,' she said, biting her lip. She added pointedly: 'I don't know who bombed the power station.'

It subsequently transpired that the incubator babies story was dreamed up by Nijirah al-Sabah, a member of the Kuwaiti royal family. It had a certain amateurish quality about it, a 'one-off', so to say, rather than the ring of a professional propaganda operation. In that respect it sounds rather like the account by Parisoula Lampsos, Saddam Hussein's self-proclaimed mistress who later claimed that the dictator was on Viagra and enjoyed watching videos of his political opponents being tortured.

The captain of the Special Boat Squadron and the translator I found more worrying, not simply because they were serving members of the armed forces and presumably acting with military authority, but because of another peculiarity of press coverage of the war.

Before the Gulf War, Saudi Arabia was, media-wise, one of the most tightly controlled regimes in the world. The Allies set up a pool system for the war, a system by which a limited number of correspondents were given facilities to cover the fighting and were then expected to share their reports with the rest of the media. There were about 400 pool positions, and yet four times as many journalists – some 1 600 – were allowed into the country. Correspondents who were not on pools were strictly prohibited from entering operational areas, and yet no action was taken against reporters like me who openly did so.

If one assumes there was a coordinated effort to manipulate the press and, through them, mislead the public, it all makes a certain sense. The pool positions, although much fought-over, would have been distrusted by editors, in that they were completely controlled by the military. So let loose 1 000 more 'irregulars', make them feel that they were independent and feed them with lies.

Whatever the morality of the Gulf War, it must rank as one of the most one-sided conflicts in world history: a small Arab nation up against 34 countries, one of them a superpower. It was the equivalent, in sporting terms, to an international squad playing a primary school. Victory was guaranteed, but open to ridicule unless the spectators could be persuaded that the school kids were in fact some sort of super-dwarves in disguise.

With the help of such as my special boat captain, they seem to have succeeded in that goal. One of the most experienced of Middle East correspondents, Bob Fisk, asked me shortly before the ground war began what my prediction as to the outcome would be. When I hazarded a guess, in my naivety (it was my first time in the Middle East and my first conventional war) that the Allies would win within three days, he pulled out a map to show me where the Allies would be evacuated, from Aden, and confided how he had persuaded his employers to have his and his colleagues' bodies flown back to England for burial.

I left the Gulf suspecting that the real story of what I had experienced was not war as such, but a massive psyops exercise in the deployment of what Churchill referred to as a 'bodyguard of lies' on a scale and with a sophistication the world has quite possibly never previously experienced. Certainly it had me questioning whether journalism – our attempts to 'tell it like it is' – does not in fact render society a disservice by misleading the public into the belief that 'the truth' is actually discoverable, particularly when governments are determined to conceal and mislead.

The thought brings to mind a column in the Spanish newspaper, *El Pais*, by Gabriel Garcia Márquez in the aftermath of the Falklands War. The article purported to tell the inside story of that miserable little conflict – including hair-raising accounts of the savagery of the Gurkha troops who, according to Márquez, spent their time chopping people's heads off, as well the perversions of British officers whose predilection for sodomy had, again according to Márquez, landed large numbers of young Argentinean POWs in hospital nursing their rear ends.

My initial indignation at this obvious travesty of the truth began to fade as it dawned on me that Márquez had come closer than any journalist to communicating the 'truth' of the Falklands. With the magical power of caricature and parody he had encapsulated the essential savagery and obscenity of war. It was, of course, 'magical realism', the art of war.

War memoirs

'It's a funny kind of war,' said Sergeant James Horton from Montana. And that is perhaps the best epitaph for it, although there was not much in the way of fun.

When the Iraqi prisoners tried to surrender to us and we had to tell them to go away because we were too busy, it was kind of sad. When we surrendered to the infantrymen in that highway graveyard of burning tanks, pulverised trucks and flattened cars it was just frightening.

And there was nothing funny when a Texan medical officer, Charles Russell, shook his head, stopped the heart massage and finally gave up his three-hour battle for the life of the emaciated Iraqi POW.

But at least it started with a bit of fun: somewhere a tape recorder was playing the Egyptian national anthem and a group of soldiers stood cheering on top of the 20-foot berm marking the Saudi Arabian front when we burst through together with the tanks and armoured personnel carriers.

On the other side the heavy armour streamed across the desert, the command pennants fluttering from their radio masts like knights galloping across an ancient battlefield. Tanks, mobile bridges, tracked recovery vehicles, camouflaged ambulances and even a municipal-style omnibus to carry the expected prisoners raced on for nearly 12 miles before the first battle began.

From behind, heavy Egyptian artillery guns were thudding their shells high over our heads. In front a few puffs marked Iraqi shells falling short. A butterfly fluttered around my head. Batteries of multiple rocket launchers mounted on trucks moved into position and a fearsome four-hour bombardment ensued in a light rain.

'Ten kilometres to Iraqi troops, but no resistance,' called out a captain. It was a phrase that was to characterise the entire ground war for Kuwait: 'no resistance'. The Egyptian 3rd

Armoured Division drove on northwards and then turned east, angling towards the Kuwaiti capital. The route provided a study in military wretchedness far removed from the propaganda that Allied commanders had been pumping out in the build-up to the war.

Conditions in the trenches were miserable. They stank of faeces. Scattered belongings showed the panic in which they had been abandoned. The inscriptions on ammunition boxes reflected the variety of Iraqi arms suppliers from Jordan to America, Russia to Saudi Arabia.

The panic among the Iraqi troops was understandable considering the one-sidedness of the fighting. An American tank commander complained his men were beginning to feel immortal in their state-of-the-art Abrams tanks. He described one incident when a mine ripped one of his tank's tracks, forcing it to a standstill. An Iraqi tank had fired four main rounds at the sitting target, scoring direct hits with them all. His crew had climbed out and walked away unhurt.

His men had destroyed 14 tanks in a single action, at ranges of between 1 500 and 3 000 yards. 'They never saw us. All the hits were total kills. They just burned and blew up. To the best of my knowledge, not a single shot was fired at us.'

The horrors of life for the conscript Iraqi soldiers over the last few months showed in the faces of hundreds of prisoners sitting in abject groups on the side of the convoy routes, waiting for transportation south. Two prisoners, aged 45 and 50, looked more like men of 70. Both had fought in the Iran-Iraq war.

At one stage, when the Egyptian column halted, a group of 11 Iraqis materialised out of the desert driving equally emaciated camels before them. Again their belongings on the backs of the animals were pitiful, but they did include comprehensive protective clothing against chemical warfare. The column stopped in mid-afternoon some 40 miles west of Kuwait City. Travelling south with three American correspondents, we picked up an

Egyptian commando unit, including a Saudi Arabian aristocrat, Prince Fahd, serving on attachment as a captain. We were invited to follow them to Kuwait City.

Their jeeps careered eastward towards the Gulf across a desert that became increasingly eerie in a fake twilight created by a smog of mist and smoke from burning oil wells. In the sepulchral light the desert looked surrealistic, littered with glinting silver canisters of cluster bombs, the green casings of high explosives and here and there in the distance the skewed and broken barrels of Iraqi artillery and tanks.

The commandos joined the front of the Egyptian 4th Division as night fell. The commanders apparently considered driving on to Kuwait City, but decided to halt. The US Marines had dug in on the outskirts of the city. Their reputation for killing their own men with 'friendly fire' made it too risky to advance through them in the dark. We drove on another six miles to the south to a main road running from the southeast into the capital. The road turned out to be a super-highway and the drive along it belonged to the imagination of Francis Ford Coppola, a blasted landscape limited to the headlamps' angle of light. Every few yards on both sides the grotesquely twisted wreckages of saloon cars, tankers, trucks and armour loomed out of the dark. Two blasted tanks were still burning.

On the other carriageway, figures of Iraqi soldiers could be seen ghosting by. One suddenly ran across the centre island and waved us down, begging by sign language to be allowed to surrender, waving at seven others drifting across behind. We shouted to them to lie down and wait for dawn. The lead soldier suddenly broke into cries of 'Thank you thank you', close to happy tears at having a decision taken for him.

A few miles on we stopped. Out of the dark came the ugly rumble of an armoured vehicle. We dived for the verge, away from the car. We could faintly see troops fanning out, and desperately strained to pick up the language of their faint shouts, eventually hearing with relief the cursing of GIs under hair-trigger strain. 'Americans, British,' we screamed. They were the 'tiger brigade' of the 2nd Armoured Division, General Patton's famous corps.

They congratulated us on our survival, explaining we were within a few hundred yards of entering a Marine 'killing sac'.

Waiting for permission to make another try for Kuwait City we met two doctors working with the division.

There were three patients in their ambulance – critically injured Iraqi prisoners, including one whose brain had been penetrated by a shrapnel splinter. As we stood in the ambulance the heavily sedated prisoner suddenly rose up on his cot and groaned, in a seizure.

Charles Russell, the Texan, began pumping the man's chest in a heart massage. 'Come on,' he urged in a hoarse whisper. 'Heartbeat is almost nonexistent,' replied his colleague, Dr Kazamore Yamomoto, and then folded his stethoscope and walked out abruptly in final judgement. An orderly, Raymon Gonzo, moved to the dead man's side, put his head on the cot and began to pray.

James Bond

Parkinson's gets one down from time to time – times that tend to be marked by my shuffling around in querulous search of a battered booklet published by Stanford University's Hoover Institution on War, Revolution and Peace.

I am slightly embarrassed by this confession, because old political instincts urge me to deny it, rather than publicly discover it. For a start it is written by someone called James Bond Stockdale, which smacks of ridicule. A naval pilot on the 'wrong' side of the Vietnam War, he is transparently an 'American patriot'. He concludes the booklet – entitled *Courage Under Fire* – with the cloying final lines of WE Henley's 'Invictus', familiar to public schoolboys of sentimental bent: 'It matters not how strait the gate/

How charged with punishment the scroll/I am the master of my fate/I am the captain of my soul.'

In other words, Stockdale (a Vice-Admiral and, it should be mentioned, a one-time vice-presidential candidate of conservative hue) runs the gamut of my personal and political prejudices.

I stumbled across this thin publication by accident. Despite the prejudices, I quickly became engrossed. Based on a speech delivered at King's College, London, in 1993, it is a brief account of Stockdale's eight years as a POW after being shot down over North Vietnam. He spent four of the eight years in solitary, two years in leg irons and was tortured on many occasions.

I do not have a taste for tales of noble suffering. But this particular account was intriguing, because Stockdale had done a postgraduate course in philosophy at Stanford before his capture and developed a passion for the Stoics. As the subtitle 'Testing Epictetus's Doctrines in a Laboratory of Human Behaviour' suggests, Stockdale relied on the teachings of Stoicism to survive his subsequent ordeal at the hands of the Vietnamese.

What particularly intrigues about the booklet is not Stoicism, but why I should be embarrassed by its authorship. Stockdale is, on the face of it, a fairly admirable human being. He holds the Congressional Medal of Honor, which means presidents have to salute him, out of respect, when they find themselves in his presence.

Whatever his taste in poetry, Stockdale is seemingly – at least to the extent his booklet stands as evidence – a brave, intelligent, thoughtful and articulate man. So why the grudging recognition of it?

The answer that comes to mind is that my prejudice against Stockdale was as a 'Cold War Warrior'. Even now, looking back over the Cold War years, I suspect I have not come to a full appreciation of how that conflict warped my view of the world. I say that as one who prided himself on being a professional sceptic. I was frankly astonished by the power of the totalitarian lie and the confusions of perspective it gave rise to. The extent of those distortions was brought home to me in Mozambique.

Renamo had long enjoyed a special place in my catalogue of infamy, for a record of hideous atrocity seemingly confirmed by allegiance – heads planted on supermarket shelves ... children made to butcher their own parents ... founded by Ian Smith's illegal regime ... ties with South African military intelligence ...

The devilish nature of Renamo was a 'truth' over which I had often waxed indignant in print. Which led to a simple paradox confronting me when I visited Maputo for the country's first democratic election: that these 'bandits' – having sustained a long civil war supposedly only on the basis of sheer terror, which was the antithesis of populism – enjoyed sufficient support to be credibly challenging for power in a democratic ballot.

While puzzling over this conundrum, my sense of journalistic angst was compounded by a reminder of my earlier opinions. It came in the form of an editorial from my newspaper in London – the views of which I had helped shape by my reporting – advising the UN to abandon the democratic process and have no further dealings with Renamo on the grounds that their record of atrocity outdid even that of Pol Pot.

Familiar with the images of piles of skulls erected as monuments to atrocity in Cambodia and ignorant of such in Mozambique, I hurried off on a long overdue trip to test rural sentiment in a war-time 'hot spot' well removed from the capital.

The picture I returned with offered no claims of atrocity as such, but a bitterness at being visited by the hardship and brutality attendant on war – a bitterness nursed towards Renamo and Frelimo with an impartiality reminiscent of the curse called down upon the Capulets and the Montagues.

How had my misapprehension arisen? Government manipulation of the media might have had some impact. But I remain convinced the West outstripped the Soviets in the closely related black arts of propaganda, psyops, public relations and spin-doctoring.

Besides, the Cold War involved delusion on such a scale that even governments fell victim to it – notably Western governments, which so memorably fooled themselves with regard to the economic and military strength of the Soviet Union up to the moment of its collapse.

Looking back on the Cold War period, at its mad landscape of competing hysterias and collective self-delusions – one cannot help but marvel at the failure of our species to recognise our inability to reliably inform ourselves. It impinges most seriously on leadership. All men being born equal in their capacity for self delusion, none are fit to lead – at least in anything more than a nominal capacity demanded by the notion of sovereignty and the need to have someone to dress up on festive days.

Looking back on the 20th century, the factor most destructive in its impact on the social order is the conceit of political leaders that they enjoyed a wisdom given recognition by leadership. Even Nelson Mandela was threatened by the syndrome, to judge from a brief flurry of presidential pronouncements after his release on such as the need to enfranchise children, but in the end was saved by his apparent understanding of the theatrical nature of politics.

Some (believe it or not) judge the Reagan Administration the best in US post-war history. If so, it was made so by his appreciation that all the presidential role properly demanded of him was to maintain his vacuous grin for the cameras. Plato advocated rule by philosopher-kings. From our vantage point in time we can see this to have been a contradiction in terms. The great thing about princes and kings is that they are so richly inbred they are wont to reassure subjects by shaking hands with trees, rabbiting on in the cabbage patch, or playing polo. Only in comic roles are kings nowadays to be exalted.

Who will rule us? But why do we want rulers? Rule is best understood as contractual and we have the law to rule us in that respect. Not statutory law – representative, as it so often is, of the tyranny of the day – nor even the 'quick fix' of constitutional law, but the common law, the evolutionary nature of which most closely mirrors if not the purpose, then at least the apparent process of creation. Surely the mere development of such a body of law points to the need to put the rule of man beyond the rule of man. To do otherwise is to acquiesce in the rule of such as us, whom time will inevitably expose as fools. Such are the diversions of Parkinson's.

The death of Rambo

'These children, the Comrades, were looking for this man called Rambo,' said the black building contractor as we sipped tea out of porcelain cups in Johannesburg's northern suburbs.

'All of us were in fear of him in Soweto. I don't know why he killed people. What we know is that he killed 22. But there are those that we don't know. He just used to go on killing.

'I remember one Sunday when he killed seven at the very same time. Seven! One stab and you die! One hole, it's enough! I think this was *muti* [magic] as well, because most people get five or six stabs and they're still alive.

'They said it began when he killed an 11- to 12-year-old child with a knife, holding him up and cutting him like this. And thereafter he said he wants to kill all the youths.

'But then it was not only youth: even if he met me, or a father, or whatever, then he killed. Each time and every time he met you: "I know you're looking for me," even when you're not looking for him. Then, pow! He stabs you and you die.

'But most of those he killed were youths. At last he killed a young child, a very young one, and the youth got too angry. Since then they've been looking for him all the time.

'Sometimes they caught him and suddenly he would disappear. Sometimes they are only left with his cap. The police were looking for him, too, but he even disappeared from the police. I mean even in a place where there is nothing you could hide yourself. *Aaiyh!* It's strong *muti*.

'So the Comrades went to a *nyanga* ['witch doctor'], so that they could get him.

'He went away from Meadowlands, because they were looking for him too much. His mother was sick. She was sick in hospital. Before he left he said to each and every one that if his mother dies, then each and every mother in Soweto must also die. All the mothers in Soweto.

'He was hiding himself in Brakpan. It was early in the morning – about 2 o'clock – that these children went house by house, getting cars. They just knock at your door and they want your car. You'll say, "Yes, let's go." So they got two Combies. They were all full, these two Kombis. They went there where he was in Brakpan and they just kicked in the door.

'He was still asleep, and his belts were not on him. The *muti* belts. He woke up with a knife and he tries to stab them. The knife fell down. Then he took a *panga* and the cuts one of the youths in his hand – these four fingers.

'One of the youths had a gun, but they were all scared to shoot him. But there was one who didn't care and he took the gun and shot at him, just one shot. He lost balance. Then one took the knife and stabbed him once. Then he loses balance again.

'Thereafter they took him and put him in the Kombi with all his clothes. All his *muti* belts – everything. Then he said to them: "Please man, just let me go. Just take me to the hospital and I'll give you R85 000." But they didn't mind about getting that R85 000.

'They put him in a blanket, because they didn't want blood to splash on the seats [of the Kombi]. You know, if they take something from you, though harshly, they will be very careful with it.

'They took him back to just near where he used to live in Soweto. Then they called all the people to come and see the Rambo. They were shouting.

'I was asleep. I thought I was dreaming. Then I looked out the window and there's people running. I asked what was happening. "Hey, man, they've got the Rambo. They've got the Rambo today."

'When I arrived he was just lying there on the ground, still exhaling and inhaling, but he wasn't saying anything.

'The Comrades were singing slogans and freedom songs and all that. They were calling the people: "Come and see the Rambo," while others got four tyres ready for him.

'I went away, but then my wife wanted to go and see him. When we got back they were turning him, just like when you're braaing [barbecuing] the meat. They had put the tyres around him, from here to here [neck to feet] and put his *muti* and all his clothes on him when he was burning.

'They cut his head off and one foot to show the people. We said they were stupid, they should have done it before, because you're going to show something that has been burnt. People don't know who it is.

'But one group went one side, one group went the other side, showing each and every one that we've got the Rambo today.

'The youths who had got the head, they went straight to the police station to show the police. Man, the police chased them away! They caught one youth who couldn't run very well.

'The other youths went school by school, house by house, with the one foot, showing it: "This foot is for the Rambo." Some said: "Today we got PW Makhusha. So we're still left with [President] PW Botha to get a necklace."

'Then here comes the police with these mellow yellows [police lorries] and a Land Rover and they throw tear gas and the Comrades just ran away. Twenty-two were arrested.

'The Comrades burnt a very fat woman in Soweto once. They made her lie down and put tyres around her and put her on fire. You can still see the fat there on the ground where she was burnt. She was SB [Security Branch].

'You know, it was a strange thing, but the wind was blowing when Rambo was burning.

'And the smoke went straight up into the air.

'Straight up.

'That was a very strange thing.'

'More tea?' she asked.

'One cup and I must go,' said the storyteller.

'Yes, please.'

Duncan Village

He nursed a secret terror that he would find himself present at a necklacing. Would he take refuge behind journalistic 'detachment', or would he intervene at risk of being roasted alive himself? How will he live with himself if he does not? It becomes something of a phobia; which way will he jump? He begins to worry, knowing he is ducking assignments in the townships.

One day he goes to Duncan Village, near East London in the Eastern Cape, for the funeral of 19 people who have been slaughtered by the police. About 50 000 pack into a football ground on a hilltop.

When they dance the toyi-toyi, the earth itself seems to be heaving in the rising dust from pounding feet. In the centre of the crowd is a raised platform on which a handful of clerics sit in comfortable chairs, exchanging greetings and observations with studied aloofness.

His stomach lurches as he arrives to see on the outskirts of the crowd a roving band of ululating youths jogging to their own rhythm, led by men holding aloft car tyres ready for impromptu executions by fire. But he has forgotten them, concentrating on the funeral service when it is interrupted by pandemonium a few yards to his right.

Two men, their necks garlanded by tyres, have been driven through the packed ranks of mourners like gargoyle figureheads at the front of a human battering ram, to within a few feet of the raised platform. 'Burn them, burn them,' rises the chanting.

'No don't,' he shouts, waving a helpless hand, his cry as lonely and lost in the roar of the mob as the call of a seagull in the thunder of waves. 'Burn them,' roars the mob, matchboxes brandished helpfully towards the two 'informers' bleeding in their torn clothes.

One falls forward onto his knees, looks up at the men who have risen to their feet on the platform above him and then extends his hand in a beseeching gesture. The clerics draw back from the fury of the crowd and hesitate until one hand reaches down and pulls them, dazed, to sanctuary.

After the funeral he drives through the departing crowd, faces smiling friendship at the whey-faced stranger, self-important 'marshals' running alongside his car, enthusiastically clearing a passage. Eventually he accelerates clear of the mourners into the dusk, the anxious refrain – 'You tried, didn't you? You tried?' – beating in his head when he is brought to a halt by an open-top police Casspir squatting in the road.

A youth is being driven by shouted curses to clamber, like a monkey, up the steel flanks of the armoured vehicle.

A policeman on the top gestures the youth to the floor. Staring down at the waiting car he makes pounding motions with his rifle, as if grinding a body at his feet. The obscenity of the moment extends to the masturbatory rhythm of his movements.

Frozen in the policeman's knowing stare he finds himself face to face with that complicity of inaction he has feared all along.

Returning to his hotel in East London he learns that two white men, test-driving their new car, had ploughed into the same funeral crowd through which he had been happily guided earlier. About 11 people had been injured in the accident. The crowd had retaliated by setting the car ablaze and tossing the two whites into the fire.

The blue dress

The ANC in Angola was celebrating the 25th anniversary of Umkhonto we Sizwe (MK), its military wing. An argument started over lunch between Johnny Makhathini and a new recruit over necklacing – the barbaric means of execution, prevalent in the townships in South Africa, by which victims were made to swallow petrol and then set on fire with a petrol-soaked tyre around their necks. Makhathini, who was a guest of honour at the celebrations, and the ANC's rep at the UN, was critical of the practice. Portia, aged 17, was not.

'Give us guns and we will eliminate the *izimpimpi* [informers] nice and cleanly,' said the teenager. 'Yes, Comrade Makhathini, necklacing is cruel, but it's helped us put the traitors to flight … What the *izimpimpi* have done to the people is even more gruesome.'

> She was held in a small concrete chamber on the edge of the small forest in which she was buried. According to information from those who killed her, she was held naked and interrogated in this chamber for some time before her death. When we exhumed her, she was on her back in a foetal position, because the grave had not been dug long enough, and had a single bullet wound to the top of her head, indicating that she had been kneeling or squatting when she was killed. Her pelvis was clothed in a blue plastic packet, fashioned into a pair of panties indicating an attempt to protect her modesty.

> The girl's nom de guerre was 'MK Zandile'; her real name Phila Portia Ndwandwe. One tends to think of her simply as 'Portia'. By the time she vanished she had a baby son.

> One evening she had asked a neighbour to keep the baby while she went out for a few minutes to meet a contact. The baby and his mother were never to see each other again. A story went around that Portia had turned informer herself and joined the South African security forces. In the absence of any other explanation even her family in the coastal town of Durban believed it.

That was until her body was found in that concrete tomb by the TRC, naked except for a plastic bag. Ironically the contact who lured her to her death turned out to be one of those collaborators whose gruesome end she had urged so passionately two years before in that memorable argument with Johnny Makhathini.

She didn't put up any resistance. There was not much point – there were too many South African Security Branch men in attendance. They bound her hands in masking tape, ushered her into a van and later transferred her into a minibus, travelling to a farm in Elandskop. There they interrogated her.

She seems to have answered them with trite information and it quickly became clear that their high hopes of 'turning' her had no chance. When they put the offer to her she flatly refused. So they hit her on the head with a club and fired a single shot into her skull.

It was at least a 'clean' way of doing it. Better than poison. Better even than the hangman's rope.

A judge, Albie Sachs, commissioned an artist to do a painting for the Constitutional Court in memory of Portia. The artist, Judith Mason, chose to do a triptych of a beautiful blue dress, reasoning that such a girl would want to be remembered in such a dress, rather than a plastic packet. The painting hangs in a place of honour in the Constitutional Court gallery.

(VOL. 2 P543 TRC FINAL REPORT)

V677
Pretoria Central Prison
Private Bag 45
Pretoria

18/9/64

By now they have a pretty good overall picture and their firm opinion is that there is only a small chance that I will not be hanged … My brave lovekin, I want you to face this likelihood. I am not going to write reams on what you mean to me … Rather I want you to hear some of the thoughts on the future, on the assumption that you may be permanently without me.

1. As little as possible withdrawal from the world, both literally and figuratively. The happiest, fullest life you can manage, dearest, sweetest heart. My love for you means that I profoundly want you to have as much happiness as possible for your entire life. And there is the quite separate (but dependent) very important point – that David must have happy surroundings.

2. Although this is terribly hard to say, I must do so. You must not exclude the possibility of remarriage, both for your happiness and for David's. There is no question of disloyalty to me or anything like that. Keep in the forefront of your mind that I want your happiness – and it may well lie in this direction.

The angel of death

The announcer, clutching his microphone and cataloguing the latest shootings, was beginning to seem like an angel of death in mufti. He plucked a tatty track shoe out of a plastic bag and brandished it. 'They brought us this shoe,' he bellowed over the giant loudspeakers. 'If you've got a relative or son or whoever is missing, you can come up and try and identify the shoe.'

A few yards away stood four coffins on the white lines of the 100-metre athletic track. On each side stood the guard of honour: ranks of four girls and boys standing stiffly with clenched fists in the Black Power salute, many wearing yellow sweaters with the names of the dead emblazoned across the front, and on the back the legend: 'They served, they were sacrificed, they were selfless ...'

Behind the packed stadium facing them a column of smoke climbed into the cloudless sky. Appeals had been made for the owner of the car to identify it; when he or she failed to do so, they had set it ablaze, assuming it was a police vehicle.

It was the sports stadium of KwaThema township, about 25 miles east of Johannesburg along the gold reef and the centre of the latest bout of violence to affect South Africa. During the night police firing pistols and birdshot killed seven blacks who they said were rioting. The next day it was the scene of further death as a crowd of some 20 000 packed the grounds for an emotional funeral service for four youths killed in disputed circumstances a fortnight before.

Halfway through the service, shots rang out a few hundred yards from the stadium. A section of the crowd rushed outside to find two youths aged about 10 and 17 lying in a patch of open ground with bullet wounds to the head. Both appeared to be dying, but a saloon car and a minibus raced off with them to hospital. According to witnesses, the boys had been stoning the nearby home of the mayor of the township. Two black policemen had emerged and fired three shots at a range of about 50 yards. As the victims were taken off, a heated debate started about whether to make a concerted rush on the house.

The Bishop – suffragan of Johannesburg East, the Right Reverened Simeone Nkoane – who was attending the funeral, intervened, telling them it would be suicidal. The youths accused him of being a sell-out, arguing that some of them might die but that the policemen had to run out of bullets. As the cleric harangued them, they gave in, vowing to return after the burials.

Inside the sports ground the funeral service continued uninterrupted, with an extraordinary display of mixed jubilation and anger. As the green, black and gold flag of the outlawed African National Congress was brandished, student leaders urged the mourners to make the country ungovernable. Every few minutes the crowd burst spontaneously into rhythmic dancing and thunderous rebel songs. After more than three hours the funeral procession, led by four black cars packed with wreaths and followed by 61 minibuses and trucks filled with mourners, finally started the journey to the cemetery.

Maki Skosana

I did not see Maki die, even on television. Thank heavens. It was bad enough being there when her mother, Diana Skosana, tipped the bloodstained contents of the plastic carry-out bag from a local supermarket onto the kitchen table. We stared wordlessly at the little pile: a piece of faded blue T-shirt, a headscarf, handfuls of earth and some broken sticks.

She was keeping them for burial with her daughter, Maki Skosana, a name that is not well known, although the last minutes of her life were witnessed by millions of television viewers around the world.

Maki was the girl who was beaten and burnt to death in front of cameras at a funeral in the township of Duduza. The story behind her death is a long and complex one: of eight young men who died trying to 'strike a blow against apartheid'; of their Russian grenades, which did not work properly; of a mystery man 'from Lusaka' who supplied them and who may or may not have been a provocateur; and of Maki who may have been his agent. Or may have died simply because of her name.

It seems to have all started sometime early in June, when a mystery man made his appearance in the townships of Duduza and nearby KwaThema and Tsakane. He introduced himself to student leaders belonging to the Congress of South African Students (Cosas), as having come from Lusaka and being a member of the ANC's Umkhonto we Sizwe.

He said he had a supply of weapons and he had come to arm the Cosas executives in the townships. He seemed flush with money, telling them he had R10 000 for them and would pay the commander of a proposed operational unit R2 000 and others R1 000 apiece.

After a number of delays the students agreed to cooperate. But they decided they would not all take part – for fear if anything went wrong it would wipe out the entire leadership – instead deputing some of their more militant members.

One Monday in June, a group of them were collected by the 'ANC' man in a minibus and driven off to a derelict mine in the bush. He produced two grenades and explained how they should pull the pins, count to three and then throw them. They threw them and they exploded. Duly satisfied, they returned to the township, agreeing to meet again the next night at three collection points, including a church in Duduza and a shebeen (illegal drinking den) in Tsakane.

The targets were to include the homes of two security policemen in Tsakane and KwaThema and the limpet mine was to be used on a power substation at KwaThema. At their collection points the 'ANC' man distributed the grenades, reminded them again how to use them and left after instructing them to try to coordinate the attacks at midnight.

In KwaThema three of the students headed for the home of one of the policemen. They were early, so they went to a friend's house nearby and waited. Then at about midnight they marched out and, as they approached the target house, heard the blast of the limpet mine in the distance.

The first student took out his grenade and pulled the pin. It exploded immediately, killing him. Police appeared down the street and the other two students ran for their lives. It is not known what happened in Tsakane, where two died in similar explosions, or at the power station, except that the limpet mine obviously exploded prematurely.

In Duduza the picture was confused. By one account a group of students was seen talking outside the church, behind a security gate. Then police were seen at the back of the premises and the students began to run. As they bunched to get through the gate there was an explosion. One dropped dead and several appeared to have been injured. The survivors ran for it, taking refuge at a house some distance away.

More police arrived at the house and in a melee that followed there were further explosions in which another three students were fatally injured. In Duduza the bodies were left lying in the street and a large crowd began to gather.

The scene was described by a black journalist, Rich Mkhondo, in a report subsequently published in the Johannesburg daily newspaper, *The Star*: 'We joined about 2 000 residents who had gathered around the bodies of the youths who had died at about midnight. The most horrifying moment of my life was when I was shown the bodies of the youths. I had never before seen the body of a man without a head. Nor had I seen pieces of human flesh scattered around and people trying to put them together again.

'As I was trying to gather information about the deaths of the youths I noticed more hippos [armoured personnel carriers] and police vehicles had arrived. I heard residents shouting, refusing to allow police to take the bodies to the government mortuary and saying they had their own mortuaries.

'As I ran into a house with a number of residents I felt a burning pain on my right shoulder. I had been struck with birdshot. On looking outside I saw the bodies being loaded into police vans. Some parts fell to the ground. A person inside the house said: "Look. They are throwing the bodies inside the vans like sacks of potatoes." A woman standing next to me was crying.'

It was confirmed that the grenades were Russian-made RGD5s, an egg-shaped device packed with TNT and with a fragmentation radius of 15 to 20 metres. The firing mechanism was quite simple. It had a conventional grenade lever, anchored by a split pin. When the pin was pulled out and the lever released, it unleashed a spring-loaded pin that hit a percussion cap, igniting a chemical fuse which took three to four seconds to burn before exploding the detonator.

They could have been doctored, simply by replacing the three-to four-second fuse with an instantaneous one. But accounts of the one explosion taking place as the pin was pulled suggested that if they were doctored it was done more elaborately. It was possible that these particular grenades were adapted, at the manufacturing stage, for use in booby traps – with a tripwire – and were supplied in error by a genuine representative of the ANC. Incidents have been reported of South African security personnel being injured in a similar way while testing such grenades.

But in the townships the residents had no doubt that the entire episode was a scheme hatched by police to wipe out the student leadership. And, whatever the truth of it, the events fuelled the hatred that led to the death of Maki.

Maki's precise relationship with the 'ANC' man is not clear. What is known is that he was originally introduced to the students by a girl and that by some accounts he did have a girlfriend called Maki, although it appears she was not Maki Skosana – she just had the same first name.

Whatever the circumstances, the story began to circulate in Duduza that Maki Skosana was a police agent. She heard the rumour – she even went to a local priest and told him about it. But she insisted she was innocent of any involvement in the hand grenade deaths and that she was not going to acknowledge guilt by running away.

Maki was a simple girl, aged 24, an unmarried mother with a five-year-old son, working in a nearby glove factory. She lived with her mother, a 54-year-old domestic servant, a brother and a cousin in one of those little four-roomed matchbox houses characteristic of South Africa's townships with their concrete floors and ceiling-less iron roofs.

Stubbornly, she not only insisted on staying in that house, but went to the funeral of the Duduza grenade victims, and to the funeral of those killed later.

Apparently there was an attempt, by one or two student leaders, to get her away from Saturday's funeral. But she refused again. And so the fury of Duduza was unleashed upon her. They chased her across the veld, they beat her, they stoned her, they tore her clothes off, they set her on fire, they put a huge rock on her so that she couldn't get up and they rammed a broken bottle into her vagina.

It was when she got to the broken bottle that Maki's mother began crying uncontrollably. The two black clergymen with me couldn't take any more and one of them lumbered to his feet and said: 'Let us pray.'

We stood there with heads bowed, around a plain kitchen table in the township of Duduza in the middle of the Transvaal. And her mother wept on and there were tears in all our eyes: tears for Maki, tears for the beloved country.

The mad chocolate eater

At one level, at least, hindsight says Judge Beyers was wrong in describing Tsafendas as a 'meaningless creature'. That right hand, which now fumbles to find his mouth, smearing chocolate across his chin, earned Tsafendas an unchallengeable place in the history books at 2.10 pm on the afternoon of 6 September 1966. Which was when, dressed in his parliamentary messenger's uniform, he strode between the green leather benches, shouldered aside a cabinet minister and plunged the knife four times into the prime minister with such precision that conspiracy theorists would say the wounds could only have been made with training.

It is a matter of record that Verwoerd was succeeded by John Vorster – a prime minister who, whatever his other sins, began the process of reform in South Africa that was carried on, however falteringly, by PW Botha and brought to fruition, however unintentionally, by FW de Klerk. Whatever the motivation, when that hand stilled the heart of the Hollander it can be said to have set in motion the retreat from ideological racism and set the country on the road that led directly to that moment, more than quarter of a century later, when Nelson Mandela walked out the gates of Victor Verster Prison to the adulation of an adoring world. Meaningless he was not, in the historical sense.

But it is, perhaps, more in the attempt by Judge Beyers to rob his life of personal meaning that the significance of this story of madness lies.

It is suppertime at Sterkfontein and I help an orderly shovel Tsafendas into a wheelchair for the procession to the dining room. He dribbles mashed potato onto the Formica tabletop and, mechanically, I wipe his mouth. 'Did you kill Verwoerd?' I scribble on a piece of paper. 'I killed Verwoerd,' he affirms in a stentorian tone of absent-mindedness. 'Why?' I write. He studies it for a few moments then nods solemnly.

The court established his madness, of course, by scientific means. 'He showed me eyes where I couldn't possibly see eyes and a nose and a mouth which were just not there!' indignantly complained clinical psychiatrist Johannes van Zyl of Tsafendas' performance on his precious Rorschach ink-blot tests. 'Modern paintings?' inquired Beyers from the bench to dutiful smiles around the court after the psychologist had explained the significance of his blobs.

The mind doctors did not come out of it too well. Van Zyl had already had some trouble explaining why there was a need for 'the New South African standardisation of the Wechsler Bellevue Aut Intelligence Test' ('it is standardised for white people and there are separate tests for coloureds'). And, hanging over proceedings, was a blunder by Dr Ralph Kossew, Cape Town's District Surgeon, who happened to examine the 'mad knifeman' for a disability grant three months before the assassination, finding him 'schizophrenic in the highest class' … but not certifiable.

But it was from his own mouth that he condemned himself as mad, at least as relayed by the mouths of others. 'I don't think I will be able to live in Cape Town after this, because of public opinion, you know,' one psychiatrist quoted him as saying in the immediate aftermath of the assassination. 'If I was ever offered a job in the House of Assembly again I do not think I would be able to face up to it!'

'There is an instance now where one hot day he tried to cool the fowls off, which proves to me he was also mentally deranged,' recounted Peter Daniels of the infamous lodger who came to stay with them for a few weeks in 1965. 'He got hold of the hosepipe and tried to cool the fowls down, because he thought they were hot too!'

And then there was the worm. It is an article of faith among most South Africans that an imaginary tapeworm ordered Tsafendas to assassinate Verwoerd. Except it did exist and it never gave him 'orders'. He seems to have had a tapeworm in his youth and a delusion about its survival appears to have haunted his later life – he has left instructions in his will for a post-mortem to settle the issue. But police interrogators, try though they did, never managed to get his admission that the worm talked to him, much less ordered the murder of the prime minister of the Republic of South Africa.

The fact is, however, that Beyers, on the best psychiatric advice of the day, found Tsafendas insane and, whatever the truth of the worm, there is no reason to dispute it.

In search of a diagnosis

In the face of unexplained ailments, one falls easy victim to quackery, including New Age therapists who ambushed me on the anxious path to diagnosis.

One was an old woman in her late eighties who was recommended as a masseuse. She quickly had me stripped down to my boxer shorts and pegged out cruciform in the converted garage that was her 'clinic' behind her home in Johannesburg. My knees, ankles and elbows were bristling with acupuncture needles and she had neatly planted four large crystals: one each on the palms of my up-turned hands, one in the middle of my forehead and one on my bellybutton. 'Now say "Ummmm" while I go and make myself a cuppa tea,' she said, tottering out the door. 'Ummmm,' said the war correspondent hopelessly.

Another New Ager was a reflexologist in Johannesburg's luxurious northern suburbs. The high-security gate guarding the driveway rumbled shut behind me. She led me shyly into her husband's sumptuous study. After we had stood in mute tribute before a picture of the two of them posing next to their racing bikes – testament to their burgeoning good health – she ushered me to her husband's chair, inviting me to bare my feet as she disappeared into the kitchen.

'David,' my mother once said thoughtfully while inspecting my feet as a child, 'when you grow up perhaps it would be better if you do not let women see your toes.' Reluctantly I took off my shoes and socks as my therapist staggered in with a bucket. 'Nice?' she inquired, softly stroking the soles of my feet in the warm water.

'Mmm, but does it work?' I asked. 'Must do,' she said, looking up at me solemnly. 'Nobody has ever come back.'

I glumly contemplated my toes.

The flying pen

To be fair, 'qualified' doctors can be even more alarming than the so-called quacks. Like the one who, abandoning a medical diagnosis, put an arm of sympathy around my shoulders as he led me to the door. 'I had another patient who suffered what you have got,' he declared, with a confiding air. 'He's a company director. There was nothing wrong with him, until you sat him down at a table, put his chequebook in front of him and gave him a pen. At the moment he was about to start writing, as pen was about to touch paper, his hand would leap up into the air,' the doctor declared, giving emphasis to the description by waving at the ceiling. With a clap on my back and a chuckle, he closed the door behind me.

Black busker in cloth cap

He was just a black busker in a cloth cap. But for a few minutes Danny Khobo captured the spirit of the national defiance campaign challenging the authority of the South African State.

Danny, once a tea-boy in the giant De Beers diamond-mining corporation, was playing his saxophone along a shopping mall right in the middle of Cape Town, as he has been doing for the last nine years. He saw a crowd marching purposefully towards him from St George's Cathedral, wearing the black gowns of graduates and lecturers and the crimson of PhDs. The 90-or-so academics came to a halt in the middle of the mall and formed a ring, brandishing yellow placards declaring, 'We demand the right to protest', and appealing, 'Stop repression.'

A crowd of lunchtime shoppers began to gather and Danny stopped playing, drifting over to join them. The academics were tense, waiting for the police. They had just seen the brutal wounds inflicted by the big bull whips on a Catholic priest and others who had earlier tried to protest outside Security Branch headquarters in the city. One of the academics saw Danny and asked him to play them a tune.

So Danny walked forward in front of them and his sax sang a song he first learned to play 36 years ago, at the age of 10, on his pennywhistle. The academics and the gathering crowd sang with it, the words of the haunting hymn that has for so long been identified with the decades of suffering and struggle by the blacks of South Africa: 'Nkosi Sikelel' iAfrica.'

As the last notes faded the police made their appearance around a corner, brandishing the fearsome whips, and their commander immediately began reading the Emergency regulations, declaring it an illegal gathering and ordering the demonstrators to disperse. But it was as if the sax had woven a mood of defiance in the crowd of bystanders, now numbering hundreds, and they greeted the police moves with jeers, mixed with ovations for the academics – which seemed to worry the police, because an officer began moving among his men, collecting their whips and hurrying to hide them in a nearby vehicle.

Then they began – peacefully – leading the academics to the waiting prison vans. The scene was to be repeated in some respects later, but it was completely different from the earlier demonstration outside the Security Branch offices.

There a group of about 20 men and women, including the chaplain to the Catholic Justice and Peace Commission, Father Peter-John Pearson, made their stand with their placards. The police vans roared up and officers leaped out to seal off the street and drive away press cameras before thrashing the protesters to the ground – including Father Pearson and others, men and women wearing thin T-shirts with slogans on the back proclaiming them to be 'Christians defying unjust laws'. Something of a principle was being established by the Mass Democratic Movement – that where demonstrators in the defiance campaign meet with police violence their leaders will immediately move in to repeat the demonstration. So, in the early afternoon, Archbishop Desmond Tutu arrived at his cathedral to join other community leaders, including Professor Jakes Gerwel, Vice-Chancellor of the University of the Western Cape, and Franklin Sonn, rector of a local polytechnic.

After a brief strategy meeting at the back of the cathedral, they said a prayer: 'We commit ourselves to Your care as we take this action. Abide with us that there may be justice in our land.' Then they marched out towards the Security Branch building, with hastily scribbled placards saying 'Stop beating our people' and 'This is a peaceful protest'.

This time the police were waiting, forming a uniformed barricade across the road. The proceedings were perfunctory: the warning was read, rejected and the protesters hustled into another prison truck. As the truck's steel doors were slammed shut on them, the protesters were singing 'We Shall Overcome'.

Danny was not there to lead them this time, but then they had their own leaders.

Conspiracy

The ANC was paranoid about conspiracies, although not very good at tracking them down. Ten pages of the 51-page Shishita Report are devoted to 'The Assassination Plot of 12 March 1981'. They seem never to have found it.

The authors of the report explain their interest in this plot: 'We are convinced that assassination plot(s) constitute the most important, the central element of the overall strategic plan of the racist regime which is the total destruction o the national liberation movement in South Africa, led by the African National Congress. This conviction is based on all the statements confessions and activities of all the confessed agents ... Their recruits and collaborators as well as those "malcontents" whose activities, viewed objectively, furthered the aim of creating a suitable climate for the execution of assassination plot(s).'

Unfortunately, concludes the Shishita Report after an

exhaustive (and tediously exhausting) analysis of the information at their disposal, 'the date of 12^h March 1981 is not supported by the evidence already in though further investigations may still substantiate this.'

Death of a small hero

… We only found out that it was a bomb blast when we arrived in Durban in the hospital. I can't remember the name of the hospital. They told us that my son's not there, but they know of a little boy who was in the mortuary. By that time it was very late; the mortuary was already closed, and I went to my uncle's house …

We went to see him the following morning, but I didn't want to believe that it was my son that was lying there. I asked them to take him out of the glass case so that I could see his chin. Under his chin, he had a small little cut which he got when I accidentally dropped him when he was a child. I still really didn't want to believe it, and my wife and my father had to convince me it was my child. Then after that, we came up to Pretoria. We buried him in Pretoria. I told newspapers that I thought my son was a hero because he died for freedom for people that … (I would prefer to speak Afrikaans). He died in the cause of the oppressed people. A lot of people criticised me for this. They thought that I was a traitor, and they condemned me, but I still feel that way today …

(VOL. 5 P375 TRC FINAL REPORT)

Do you know …?

Van Eck: Chairman, I'm here today to talk about what happened on the 16th of December 1985, on the farm Klerkshoop in the district of Messina. Chairman, the result thereof of this landmine where I was also involved, four children that died and their ages range from three to nine years. Two women, they also died at the same time and four persons were wounded. One kid was not injured and one woman died immediately thereafter because of this bomb … On the 18th of December 1993, the newspapers told us that Ncube [a perpetrator] got an award for being a hero, which actually took place in a meeting in Soweto. And it was awarded to him by Nelson Mandela … Do you know how it feels to be blasted by a landmine? Do you know how it feels to be in a temperature of between of 6 000 and 8 000 degrees? Do you know how it feels to experience such a blast that is so intense that even the fillings in your teeth are torn out? Do you know what trouble reigns if you survive the blast and that you must observe the results thereof? Do you know how it feels – how it feels to look for survivors, only to find the dead and maimed? Do you know how it feels to see crippled loved ones lying and burning? Do you know how it feels to look for your three-year-old child and never, Chairman, never to see him again and forever after to wonder where he is? … Chairman, do you know how it feels to try to cheer up a friend while your own wife and two children lie dead? Do you know how it feels to leave a baby of eighteen months behind to go and look for help …?

(NELSPRUIT HEARING TRC/MPUMALANGA)

The head of her husband

I was told that he was stabbed by a spade on his head, then they stabbed him several times. He was made to drink petrol, they put a tyre over him and then they ignited him. During this time my younger son was hiding under the car, some of the petrol got to him and when he was trying to escape somebody saw him.

Silumko was hiding in one of the shops at Mboya. He asked one of the businessmen to hide him under the counter. They took him and they ignited him alive in front of the shop. I am telling you as it is. They cut his testicles while he was still alive.

Then on Monday at the police station, the doctor told me that he was going to inject me, at that time I had not seen them yet … I will not be able to tell you about the head of my husband.

(VOL. 3 P108 TRC FINAL REPORT)

'Burn me!'

On the night of 28 April 1985, police officer Aubrey Jacob Fulani and his wife, Ms Nokuzola Carol-Anne Fulani, were abducted from their home at Uitenhage by UDF-aligned 'Comrades' because Fulani was a police officer. The Fulanis had been at home on a Sunday evening when a group of attackers broke into their home, shot and wounded Fulani, forced the two of them outside into waiting cars and drove them to a house in Soweto, Port Elizabeth. Ms Fulani told the Commission: 'They took him out of the house. They had black plastics and five litres of petrol and some tyres … Then I was made to watch him. I was made to look at him for the last time. During all this time I had only a nightdress on. I was told to stand outside and look as this dog was dying. Then I asked them to burn him with me because I could not endure to listen to his cries.

(VOL. 3 P110 TRC FINAL REPORT)

Fifty lashes

Motsoeneng told the Commission that the security police, including Major Stephenson, forced his father to beat him in front of the police. His father gave him 50 lashes. The victim was denied medical assistance after the beating. He said that his parents' marriage broke up as a result of the incident and his mother disappeared. He still did not know where she was.

(VOL. 3 P350 TRC FINAL REPORT)

The red-hot irons

In January 1996, three women were tortured and then 'necklaced' by UDF supporters in the Duncan Village township outside East London. These killings came after several months of violent unrest in the township, involving mainly clashes between UDF-supporting youths and security forces. Ms Nofikile Dikana (50) and her daughter Ms Zameka Dikana (29) (EC1967/97ELN) were accused of bewitching their son and brother, UDF activist Fudwana 'Giza' Dikana (EC0943/96ELN). Fudwana Dikana had died a few months earlier when an SANDF armoured vehicle drove into his car, an incident that was regarded in the community as a deliberate killing, since he had often helped wounded activists by driving them to hospital. The two Dikana women and a third woman were abducted by a crowd and taken into a house while a fire was built in the road nearby. A witness, Skonwana Mntuyedua, stated in an affidavit to police at the time:

'[A man] was placing iron rods approximately one metre long into the fire. He seemed to be handling two or three of these rods. When these rods were red hot they were taken and handed over to [another man]. All the time I could hear screaming and pleading for help coming from inside the house. These rods passed in and out for a period of about one hour. Throughout this the screaming and shouting for forgiveness never stopped ... The following morning when

I arrived there I saw a large crowd of people gathered there. In the road I saw the same three females I had seen the previous evening lying in the roadway. [Three men] were standing next to the bodies and were placing tyres on top of the bodies. [All] three of the people were dead.'

Two men were subsequently charged with the killings. Mntuyedua was stabbed to death a week before the trial was due to start and the case collapsed. The police reports on the matter indicated that UDF-aligned 'comrades' were responsible for the killings.

(VOL. 3 P113 TRC FINAL REPORT)

Kinross Rd
Parkview,
Johannesburg

My darling Ellen,

It has been pretty hectic since I last wrote, as you can imagine. I've developed something of a tan, for the perverse reason that I have stood in the sun at so many funerals. Somehow it is a contradiction – getting healthy attending to the dead. After Belfast surely I have seen more funerals than anyone else (no, I guess not). I have written so much about them for *The Guardian* that there is not much left to tell, except that every time I go to one I wish you were there, because you would so enjoy the music. I feel a little uneasy about it – the music, I mean, the sense of entertainment. The relatives don't join in, they sit there with a tremendously dignified air of restrained grief. If you try and talk to them they don't reply – it is obviously considered inappropriate. But the crowd sings at every opportunity and oh how they sing – those immensely deep and melodious voices, with the voice of some self-appointed solo – sometimes a woman's soprano, other times a powerful bass – weaving in and out. And they dance and they stamp and the earth shakes until you feel you are watching a huge beast and wonder how the hell white South Africa can restrain it. But restrain it they do – detentions are over the 1 000 mark; the old cycle of repression is turning once more. But it can't go on forever. The change is obvious each time I come out here and it is all going one way.

Love, David

Mandated territory

I was then in the military, you know in the paratroopers and the Special Forces, and I was decorated for a couple of operations in South West Africa. I don't know if I must apply for amnesty for Kasinga ... It was probably the most bloody exercise that we ever launched, according to me ... We were parachuted into that target ... it was a terrible thing ... I saw many things that happened there, but I don't want to think about it now, because I always start crying about it. It's damaged my life.

The first specific incident that I remember is chasing a SWAPO unit commander or political commissar. We picked up his spoor and chased him for two days ... This was typical of the style of contacts that I was involved in. Five Casspirs, 50 men chasing one or two people running on foot. We finally did catch him, hiding in a kraal. The unit commander ... lined up a bunch of Koevoet people next to the hut he was in and drove over the hut with the Casspir. Everyone then fired into the rubble ... The SWAPO commissar was pulled out and was given to me to keep alive. He had been shot in the arm and the leg and had been driven over ... because he was a commissar he would have been carrying a handgun. John Deegan (acting unit commander) started to interrogate him while I was putting up a drip. The purpose of this interrogation was to find the handgun ... We never found the handgun because John shot him in the head out of frustration while I was still attending to him. The incident and the face of this SWAPO commissar haunted me in dreams for years.

[The SWAPO commissar] was a veteran ... He would have been an excellent source of information but he was so fucked ... Each team had an army medic and Sean started patching up this guy while I was busy interrogating him ... and he was just going '*Kandi sishi*'.

Even at that stage he was denying everything and I just started to go into this uncontrollable rage and he started going floppy … and I remember thinking 'How dare you' and then – this is what I was told afterwards – I started ripping. I ripped all the bandages, the drip which Sean had put into this guy … pulled out my 9 mm … put the barrel between his eyes and fucking boom … I executed him. I got on the radio and said to Colonel X … 'We floored one … we are all tired and I want to come in.'

On their return to base the four [prisoners] were placed in a hole in the centre of the base 'approximately eight-foot square by about seven-feet deep' which served 'as a place of safe-keeping of all arrested terrorists'. [Kevin] Hall continued: 'They were the only ones in the hole. While I was guarding them some of the troops poured boiling water over their heads; another troop of whom I cannot remember the name jumped into the hole and cut off the left ear and centre finger of the right hand of one of the prisoners.'

(VOL. 2 P61 TRC FINAL REPORT)

Marching through the night

My son was normal and had a happy childhood and a successful career until his compulsory enlistment in the army for border duty. Here his problems started, i.e. serious drinking, trying like so many others to forget. He could not come to terms with the horrors of the war … His wife divorced him, leaving a seven-year-old son without a father …

One morning a 'bum' will be found dead – a child of God whose only mistake was to fight for his country … When you see the mothers sobbing for their children on TV you can understand how I feel. I hate the government for turning my son into a zombie. Somewhere, someone should start a place for such boys, because when he marches his troops through the night there must be many others doing similar things.

And then on Thursday, 9 March, I was confronted with the total shock of the news of his death. I was told that my son was killed a few kilometres from Oshakati. He was brought home wrapped in a thick, sealed plastic bag. The instruction was that the bag should not be opened. The only thing I know about the state my son was in is that all his limbs were intact. And this I heard from his uncle, who could only establish by running his hands over this plastic bag.

Again, I accepted this as a military law. You are not allowed to have the last glimpse of your own child – even as he lay there, lifeless. On the day of Wallace's funeral, his coffin wasn't opened. It is ten years since I last laid eyes on my child – nine years since he was laid to rest. But in these nine years, I have been struggling to complete the mourning of Wallace.

A part of me wonders if in fact it was him in that plastic bag. How can I lay him to rest within my heart, if I didn't see him go? When I lost my mother, whom I loved very much, I saw her, I touched her and therefore I was able to separate from her, release her and move on.

But with Wallace, there are so many questions that are still unanswered. In my struggle with my grief, I would like to know where exactly he died. How it had happened. Who was there with him when it happened? Did anybody help him to prevent it from happening? Who was the doctor who attended to him? I have never had the opportunity to ask these questions. Nobody has ever explained anything to me about my son's death.

I sometimes see Wallace in the streets. I remember two [distinct] occasions, when I thought I was seeing him. And it turned out to be somebody who looked like him. My grief becomes more intense on the anniversaries of my son's death and on his birthday. He would have turned 30 in January. I've an album of all his photographs, as a way of dealing with the many feelings I have about the loss. But it's very hard, when there are so many things you are not so sure about.

(VOL. 4 P239 TRC FINAL REPORT)

Nightmares

I really had bad dreams … I have dreams of bodies, or parts of bodies … like an arm … this is a recurring dream I still have now … an arm sticking out of the ground and I'm trying to cover it up and there were people around and I know that I killed them, whatever is down there and it's been down there for weeks … and it is this intense feeling of guilt and horror that this thing has come out of the ground again …

(VOL. 5 P284 TRC FINAL REPORT)

Rwanda's worshipful dead

The Holocaust was the defining moment of the 20th century and the accumulation of bodies represented by genocide, or its variant of ethnic cleansing, has become the correspondents' grail.

He had long wanted to confront it, to 'uncover' it and claim it with images and words designed to chill the heart and inflame the mind. He had the opportunity in a remote church, about 60 kilometres south of Kigali in Rwanda, just as the African genocide was ripening into memory.

The article he wrote was a triumph of indignation. Later, however, he could not help but suspect that he had been mocked. It was as if someone had lured him into an ambush. A set designer, maybe, of great, if perverse talent sporting bones for necklaces and skulls pendant from pierced ears, cackling her way around the stage and then retiring into the wings wiping spittle from her chin hairs in happy anticipation of his arrival.

She was Mademoiselle Death – the Great Jester in drag. He was Pilgrim fitted out in the safari kit of the modern foreign correspondent, camera jacket *de rigueur* from Banana Republic, binoculars by Zeiss, anxious to enter the valley of death in order to meet an early page deadline.

A trail of clues had been laid out by the Great Jester, degenerating from homely familiarity to obscenity in a distance of happy intimacy. A small, checked shirt lay innocently by the rutted and dusty road to puzzle the passing traveller. A herd of cattle grazed contentedly over there. A silver asbestos roof shone a welcome over a rise, covering a beige brick building partly shaded in turn by a grove of wattle trees.

The deliberation of it was almost insulting. On the path a single leather sandal. Nearby a weather-beaten identity card lay open on the ground. All that was legible on it was an entry recording ethnicity: 'Hutu' and 'Twa' crossed out, leaving the word 'Tutsi' standing reproachfully alone. Over the rise they waited for him.

On the threshold of the door through which worshippers used to file to glorify their almighty God, a blackened head plays the welcoming deacon, its mouth gaping in a never-ending scream. Inside, the congregation abide in pious silence, lit only by the gentle light filtering through stained-glass windows and a few more punched out by rocket-propelled grenades. It is a pandemonium of quietude. A jumble of blankets and bags, lonely limbs and decapitated heads piled between the pews and around the altar. Only one sits, a small boy with his head on the bench in front who seems to have fallen asleep, as if lulled by the rituals of Rome into the dreamland of childhood fantasy.

The door to the sanctum is burst open. Through it tumbles a river of meat and bones, charting a stampede of desperation into the open air. A young man grimaces through melting flesh.

In the sunshine where the devout used to gather in their Sunday best, exchanging the solemn pleasantries of those lately cleansed of sin, lies an obscene playground of battered white balls, skulls whose fractures testify to a harvest by machete blades. Scattered through the surrounding underbrush was the remembrance of those who nearly got away; legs and arms and heads and clothes, abandoned in the flight to mortality. A rib cage lies in a clearing like an oversized chicken picked clean and abandoned by thoughtless picnickers.

In the distance he seems to hear the knowing cackles of the crone, limping away from the Church of Ntarama.

The stone that crushes

In the aftermath of the Black September poisoning incident, the ANC decided it was time to beef up their security. They sent 'certain' cadres to countries, including the Soviet Union and the GDR, for 'specialised training' in counter-intelligence and security work.

These cadres completed their training between 1978 and 1979 and, in the words of the African National Congress, 'NAT began to take shape'.

Nobody seems to know the origins, or exact meaning of the acronym 'NAT', but it is accepted that it stands for 'the Department of Security and Intelligence'. 'The Department's main responsibility was to defend the ANC and protect its activities from external and internal enemies.'

Its popular name was the Mbokodo, which – as an ANC commission of inquiry observed – was a Xhosa word meaning 'a stone used for grinding maize and in some people's minds, a euphemism for the harshness with which the department treated its victims'. In other words, 'the stone that crushes'.

The abuse of ANC cadres by the Mbokodo was so brutal that grievances erupted into full-blown mutiny in December 1983. There have been three internal inquiries by the ANC into the mutiny and the camps scandal and the horror stories that emerged appear to be beyond dispute.

Briefly summarised there were accounts of routine and bizarre acts of torture: beatings with barbed wire, bicycle chains and iron bars, and food and water deprivation. Detainees were made to crawl through colonies of red ants with pig fat rubbed into their skin. A prisoner had his lips burned by cigarettes and his testicles squeezed with pliers; a detainee was buried up to his neck before being suffocated with a plastic bag; a woman had a guard masturbate over her because she refused sexual relations with security officials. A trainee had tried to commit suicide after his girlfriend was 'taken away'. People were locked up in goods containers, in suffocating conditions. And people simply disappeared.

When the magic died

- *A wizard lived up here, on the side of Table Mountain. A black magician. He lived in a cave. A wonderful cave, with a pool in the middle of it. Beautiful golden carp lived in the pool. And when the magician wanted dinner he held his frying pan over the pool and whistled and a carp leaped up and landed in the frying pan and was instantly cooked, with sauces and everything over it. And chips on the side.*
- *Go on.*
- *The carp never dwindled, in numbers, I mean — so they never died, even if they cooked themselves for him. It's a children's story, you see, so nobody is allowed to die in it, not even the fishes. This magician had all sorts of magic available to him, with which he could do all sorts of extraordinary things. But then one day he got the most terrible toothache and no matter what spells he threw, or incantations he used, he could not get rid of it.*
- *Toothache?*
- *Yes. Terrible toothache. The magician had everything he needed in the cave except now he had this goddamned toothache, which he didn't need. So in desperation he decided he had to go and find himself a dentist.*

He knew Cape Town existed, of course – he could see it from his cave way up there on the mountain – but he had never been into it. He wasn't sure what he should wear to go into town, to visit the dentist.

He realised his big magician's robes probably wouldn't do, with golden stars and moons and things all over it. But the only people he had seen close enough to know what they were wearing were the Bergies, in all their rags, who sometimes went stumbling past his cave an alcoholic haze. Or at least they thought they were in an alcoholic haze, because every time they looked inside there was this big black guy dressed up in moons and stars and things and throwing bolts of lightning around.

The magician conjured up a suit of rags and also a bag of gold coins. Because he guessed he would have to pay for a dentist and in his hazy memory – he'd lived up there on the mountain for centuries since wandering down from a magicians' place in North Africa – you paid for things with gold. Believing he was now well equipped to go and see the dentist he went striding off.

He walked down a path and over the hill way over there, straight for Cape Town. He lost track of the path after a while and had to blunder his way through the bushes and the fences through District Six, past the Castle and onto the Grand Parade.

By that time he was pretty dishevelled, his rags even more raggedy. But nobody took much notice of him; they just thought he was a Bergie down from the mountains, or a local more like, stocking up on methylated spirits to drink.

And then he got lost. Not in Cape Town. I mean, not physically. He found a dentist, but the dentist didn't much like treating coloureds, particularly bedraggled ones, and his receptionist knew that and threw him out.

Then a policeman wanted to know what he was carrying in his bag and when he saw it was full of gold coins he said, 'Come along with me, skellum. Where've you stolen those from?' And so he ended up in Caledon Square police station. But the cops got tired of trying

to figure out who he was. So they threw him out and kept the gold –
'For further inquiries, you see' – and he ended up on the blue train
and then he lost all his magical powers and that was that.

– *The Blue Train? To Joburg?*
– *No, drinking the blue train. Don't you know why meths is blue?*
– *No.*
– *They put a dye into it and a horrible-tasting chemical to try to*
discourage people from drinking it. So the Capies drink it through
bread, to filter it. And when you get drunk on it they say you're on
the blue train.
– *That's awful.*
– *I remember meeting a community of them once; in a car scrapyard,*
somewhere near Caledon Square. There was sort of a sense of
community about them. I was a visitor, a stranger in their place;
they were superior, because I was on their territory. And there
was no embarrassment. Most of them had bandages on their legs
and arms. I had the feeling they were suppurating; a suppurating
community. 'Yaah, does the Baasie want to come on the blue train
with us?' And they all laughed. That's where all the magic went out
of the magician's life. On the blue train.

The swordsman and the bomb

It must have been the most audacious act of sabotage ever carried
out by one man. And yet the TRC devoted just 14 words to it in
the seven-volume Final Report. Even the ANC shows a reluctance,
when evoking the glories of the struggle, to make much of the day
it bombed the Koeberg nuclear power plant outside Cape Town.
It is almost as if it is too shocked by its audacity to acknowledge
the act.

The almost unbelievable attack was carried out by a swordsman
– South Africa's one-time national fencing champion – who
dropped out of university and joined a commune near Koeberg in
the late 1970s. In other words, he was a hippy.

The operation was born of chance. When the community ran out of money, Rodney Wilkinson, who had studied Building Science as well as Politics, reluctantly took a job at the plant then under construction. He worked there for 18 months.

Encouraged by his girlfriend, Heather Gray, a speech therapist, he stole a set of the building plans. The couple took them to newly independent Zimbabwe with the idea that they could be used by the ANC to attack the French-built nuclear installation. It was suspected at the time that the plant would be used by South Africa to produce plutonium for the construction of atomic bombs.

The ANC, which had recently had one of its agents jailed on charges of nuclear espionage, was initially suspicious of the white South African who pitched up on its doorstep, claiming to have penetrated what was assumed to be the most secure installation in South Africa.

After lengthy delays, during which the stolen plans were authenticated by Soviet and Western nuclear scientists, and Wilkinson was vetted, the ANC invited him to carry out the attack himself. He was taken aback by the request, but agreed and returned to South Africa.

To his surprise, he gained fresh employment at Koeberg, with the task of mapping pipes and valves at the installation for use in case of emergency.

The ANC appointed a guerrilla commander in Swaziland to act as Rodney Wilkinson's handler. Once a month he visited the mountain kingdom – a favourite resort for whites in search of illicit pleasures not available in puritanical South Africa – under the pretence of enjoying a 'dirty weekend'. There he and his handler thrashed out strategy, designed to maximise embarrassment to the South African authorities while ensuring the minimum risk to human life.

They honed down possible targets to the two reactor heads, another section of the containment building, and a concentration of electric cables under the main control room. The choice of the reactor heads, which would be used to control the nuclear reaction, was to maximise the propaganda impact. Made of 110 tons of steel, they were unlikely to be seriously affected by the blasts, but they would demonstrate the ANC's capacity to hit at the heart of the plant.

The other two targets were chosen to cause as much damage as possible. Wilkinson established that nuclear fuel had been moved into the plant ready for loading into the reactors, but was in dormant storage, which minimised any risk of radioactive fallout.

The date for the attack was set for 16 December. White South Africans marked the day each year with a public holiday celebrating the battle of Blood River, a 19th-century victory by the Boers over the Zulus. But the date had another significance: the ANC commemorated it as MK Day, in honour of the founding of its guerrilla army, Umkhonto we Sizwe.

Rodney and Heather dug up four limpet mines from a roadside arms cache in the Karoo, a remote area of the South African interior. Hiding them in wine box decanters in their Renault 5, they drove back to their home in the Cape Town suburb of Claremont, where they hid the devices in holes conveniently dug by their puppy, Gaby. From there Wilkinson smuggled the mines one by one, in a hidden compartment of the Renault, through the perimeter security fence at the nuclear installation, depositing them in a desk drawer in his prefabricated office. He then carried them hidden in his overalls through a security gate into the main building.

The build-up to the attack was marked by a series of near-mishaps. At one stage an accidental short circuit started a cable fire. The incident was reported in the press and the ANC's president in exile, Oliver Tambo – who was privy to the planned operation but not to details such as timing – released a statement claiming it as an ANC attack. The claim prompted a security scare that ended, amid much derision towards the ANC, when the true cause of the blaze was confirmed by investigators.

In November the firm hiring Wilkinson told him it was laying him off at the end of the month, but later asked him to stay for another month. He turned this scare to his advantage, telling the company that in the interim he had taken another job and would have to leave on 17 December, thereby obtaining cover for his planned disappearance.

As it transpired, Wilkinson did not make the target date of 16 December, but finished planting the bombs the following day, a Friday. Setting the fuses to a 24-hour delay so that they would explode on the Saturday, when he knew the target areas would be deserted, he was then forced to undergo a farewell party on the premises with his fellow engineers, mentally praying that the time fuses were not defective. That afternoon he flew to Johannesburg and was driven with a borrowed bicycle to a point near the Swaziland border, where he rode into exile.

The bombs detonated, but not quite as planned: the springs on the firing mechanism proved brittle and the devices exploded over a period of several hours instead of simultaneously. But the damage was devastating. The authorities put the cost at half a billion rand and the commissioning of the plant was delayed for 18 months.

The attack was a chilling demonstration of the vulnerability of an atomic installation to sabotage, as well as a reflection on the incompetence of South African security. The authorities at Koeberg have since made the extraordinary claim that they not only anticipated the attack but had pinpointed the date.

In a book on the history of the plant, a former executive, Paul Semark, is quoted as saying: 'We knew the ANC would not target Koeberg once nuclear fuel was there, and that they would try to attack at a time which would ensure the least loss of life. We even pinpointed 16 December 1982, which was a public holiday, as the likely date.' Their inability to counter the threat is not explained.

The apparent helplessness of the authorities is even more astonishing in the light of Wilkinson's background. He joined the workforce at the plant twice – on both occasions getting access to the most sensitive sectors of nuclear installation – but was never subjected to security vetting.

If his background had been checked they could have discovered that he had a history as a military deserter and involvement in the anti-nuclear campaign. Six years before, doing his national service, he had been hospitalised after wrecking an armoured truck while going AWOL with 12 colleagues during the South African invasion of Angola. Military police took statements but, apparently because of the illegality of the Angolan invasion, did not prosecute him.

He was also caught breaching security at the nuclear plant, but nothing was done about it. Alcohol was banned in the plant. Testing security by smuggling in a bottle of vodka – roughly the shape of a limpet mine – he was caught in possession of it while wandering, hiccuping, around the 'holy of holies', the main control room.

'I wanted to have a look; you see it in all the films – this great big room with all these banks of computers. But the tension must have been too much for me; I drank the vodka,' he recounts wryly. Detained in the guardroom, he was released after being given a warning by a security officer whom he knew from the local squash club.

Wilkinson says his worst moment was when he was on his way to plant the second mine in the Reactor One containment building and spotted a guard watching him with apparent suspicion.

'My legs were like jelly and I could feel beads of perspiration on my face.' He detoured and placed the device at an alternative target the ANC had identified – in another concentration of cables under the second control room.

A seemingly impossible obstacle he had to overcome was carrying mines into the 'clean' area surrounding the reactors, access to which was gained through an airlock where he had to strip and don protective clothing.

But he discovered that pipe tunnels leading into the clean area had plastic diaphragms to keep the air clean, and he was able to simply push the bombs through them, pass through the airlock himself, and collect them on the other side.

'When I thought of that I was on cloud nine. I had been having sleepless nights about it,' Wilkinson recalls. A pivotal figure in the operation was Mac Maharaj, an underground leader of the ANC in South Africa and subsequently South Africa's Minister of Transport, after whom the project – 'Operation Mac' – was named.

'They never got to know how it was done; until now they have not known the identity of this couple,' Maharaj said. In expectation of 'vicious' retaliation by the South African security forces after the blasts, Wilkinson and Ms Gray were placed under 'deep cover'.

There was a subsequent attack by the South African security forces in which a couple was badly injured, which was believed to have been a misdirected act of retaliation.

Wilkinson flew from Swaziland to Maputo, where he met Tambo in the ANC leader's office, the two men crying in each other arms at their triumph. Ms Gray, who had flown out of South Africa a week before the attack, joined Wilkinson there and they flew to Britain, where they were married in Woodbridge, Suffolk.

Kinross Rd
Parkview
Johannesburg

Dear Dr Marsden,

I have been referred to you by a neurologist in South Africa with whom I believe you are acquainted, Professor Temlett at the Johannesburg General Hospital. I have been suffering from what appears to be a progressive disability of the right arm. It has been variously diagnosed as RSI, Writer's Cramp and Parkinson's disease. Prof Temlett says he is fairly confident that it is Writer's Cramp, but has advised me that you are the world's leading authority on this sort of problem and he has suggested that I try and see you in London ...

I am told that you will require some details of my medical background. Unfortunately, as a foreign correspondent, I have rarely stayed still long enough to have a regular GP. But I have had no serious illnesses and have undergone only one operation under general aesthetic, for the removal of wisdom teeth. I have undergone a brain scan and am told there is no evidence of a tumour. Apart from such as aspirin and antibiotics I have not taken any drugs and have no history of alcoholism. I am, I suppose, a tense personality but am extremely happy in my work, in which I have achieved some success. My father died at the age of 69, from a brain haemorrhage (his third) and my mother is still alive at the age of 81 ...

I am managing to continue as a correspondent with the help of an assistant who does my typing for me. I 'edit' with my left hand. But I am sure you will appreciate how threatening the condition is to me in my profession.

Yours sincerely,
David Beresford

V677
Pretoria Central Prison
Private Bag 45
Pretoria

19/9/64

Darling, darling Ann

... This business of morale is really odd. I can feel myself dropping or rising over a few minutes, without any particular stimulus (usually) for the movement either way. I do have some techniques to combat drops – one of them is writing to you, which is something I always enjoy – what I really mean is that it's a sort of protective barrier.

Oh my darling Ann, my very dearest buz, my most precious – I love you immensely, but at the moment helplessly ...

Ha – food's just arrived (yours). The highlight is the chicken (which I'll discipline myself into spreading over 2 days). Other unusual features today include a naartjie, some Cote de Orr [sic] chocolates (this Toblerone is very welcome) & my name written by my wife on the plastic bag. This last is delectablest.

(Pause while I had a quick taste of the chicken, which I couldn't resist completely, though it's rather early to eat. I'm also having just one piece of choc.) ...

It's late afternoon now, on the first day of the trial ...

Your John

The boy under a train

She squealed an enthusiastic hello when I identified myself on the telephone, which came as something of a relief. I had been feeling twinges of guilt about her for many years, wondering whether I should have told her story in the first place. And there was further reassurance when I arrived at her house to find she was still living in a 'White Area' – it was, after all, what she had wanted. Her road is called Cecil Rhodes Avenue, of all things.

I had last seen Diana de Proft 17 years ago when I knocked on her front door in the white Cape Town suburb of Maitland. I was clutching a newspaper cutting, a brief report recording the findings of an inquest into her son's death. The court had decided it was suicide, 'while of unbalanced mind', or some such formulation. 'By reason of a society's insanity' may have been a better finding, but that is by the way. I made my apologies, showed her the report and explained that I wanted to find out what lay behind it. She immediately broke down weeping. But she recovered to take me through to the sitting room where she told me the story, sobbing intermittently.

Diana had made the mistake of falling in love back in 1949 with a policeman, Ray de Proft. His profession was not the problem, but the date was. The previous year DF Malan's National Party had come to power and it was busy setting up the machinery of the race classification system. The Population Registration Act duly became law and Diana and Ray received their notices of classification: he was 'White' and she was 'Coloured'. By law they could not marry, live together, or even make love.

Diana was the daughter of an Afrikaner woman who had died young. She did not know her father and had never seen her own birth certificate. But she was convinced that she was white and that it was just a bureaucratic muddle in Pretoria. After all, the Population Registration Act specifically defined a 'white person' as one who 'is generally accepted as a white person and is not in appearance obviously not a white person'. And all her neighbours and friends were white. But Diana was unable to get the ruling reversed and eventually the couple made the decision to 'play for white', staying in Maitland and pretending to be married. Ray left the police – whose job it was to arrest and jail people like himself – taking a foreman's job in a steelyard.

Ray and Diana had five children. The eldest, Graham, was also light-skinned and although he was classified coloured, like his mother, they were able to place him in a local school. Their younger children posed problems, however, so Diana simply kept them at home and tried to educate them herself. When neighbours came visiting during school hours the children were hidden in the backyard to avoid awkward questions.

Which is how life proceeded for the De Proft family until 1974 when fresh tragedy hit them. Graham had started dating a white girl, Sonia Shepherd, who fell pregnant by him. He was unable to marry her, because of the Population Registration Act, and was seemingly too scared to explain, for fear that she would reject him.

Instead he had a bath, got dressed in his best clothes and walked to the nearest railway station where he jumped in front of an express train. After which Sonia had a state-sponsored abortion.

At this point of the story Diana broke down weeping again. Unable to speak, she was gesturing at what appeared to be a vase in a glass cabinet in the corner of the room. It was long seconds before it dawned on me; it was the urn of her son's ashes. She hadn't been able to bury him: a white cemetery would not have accepted him and if he went to a coloured cemetery his friends would have wanted to know why.

When the interview was over Diana asked what I was going to do with the story. Publish it, I said. But that would mean that all their sacrifices had been in vain, she protested. It was the only way of destroying apartheid, I argued – publication of her story would bring home the suffering being caused by the system.

We parted with the agreement that I would put her case to

my editor and leave it to his decision. Which was when I had last seen Diana, tearful at her door. The newspaper I was working for at the time made what was perhaps an obvious, but inadequate compromise, publishing the story without names. A rival newspaper followed it up, however, interviewing Sonia. After that the identity of the De Proft family was quickly exposed and their tale went spinning around the world. It became one of the most well-known stories about South Africa's race classification laws.

Even Moshe Dayan became involved; he had been touring the country when the story broke and made an angry impromptu speech warning that Israel could have nothing to do with South Africa if it was true. South Africa took no notice and, as the historical record shows, nor did Israel.

In the years that followed, in other places around the world, I frequently recounted the story of the De Profts, partly for its shock effect, but also because the argument with Diana contained a classic ethical dilemma – how to weigh private suffering against public interest. Each time I debated it, I made the mental note that one day I would return to the story and discover the consequences. The repeal of the Population Registration Act, the very piece of legislation that caused the whole tragedy, seemed an appropriate time.

She was waiting at the front door and once again led me into the sitting room. The same glass cabinet was in the corner, but there was no sign of the urn. It was not the same house I had left her at all those years ago, but it was comfortable, a little matchbox home, which, as she explained, was enough for them with the children gone.

Ray got up from his armchair to greet me, but he did so without speaking – a stroke wiped out the speech centre of his brain two years ago, which Diana blames on accumulated emotional pressure. Yes, she said, when the story got out the world's press did come banging at the door. But so did the government; within days the four surviving children had been miraculously reclassified 'white'. Which meant they could all go to school, except her eldest daughter, Dawn, who was 16 and insisted that she was too old.

But, apartheid being a doctrine of perversity, the authorities refused to reclassify her. At the same time they made no effort to prosecute her and Ray for their blatant breach of the Immorality Act. Indeed the policeman who interviewed them after Graham's death just cried when they told him the story. 'He said he had never heard anything so sad.'

It was to take another seven years before the Race Classification Board finally relented and pronounced Diana a white person. The successful appeal was handled by the eldest son of the former Nationalist prime minister, John Vorster. When the news came through, Ray took Diana down to the church where, at last, they were married. 'I was prepared to wait,' she said, 'because I loved my husband and he loved me.'

Graham's ashes had stayed in the glass cabinet for two years. Then they took them to the town of Matjiesfontein and sprinkled them in the semi-desert of the Karoo, where he had played as a child. 'Sonia wrote me a little note in Afrikaans. She said she was sorry for all the things that had happened, but I knew why she had to do what she did.' Diana assumed she was referring to the abortion.

And should I have written the story? Diana nodded her head. 'I don't know what would have happened if you hadn't,' she said. And then she added, wistfully: 'We didn't bother anyone, you know. Nobody knew. The neighbours used to think we were perfectly happy. They used to ask us why we laughed such a lot.'

Showing me to the door, I told Diana it looked a nice area. 'Yes,' she said. 'But the coloureds are beginning to move in.'

'And my sex life?'

'I'm sorry, it is Parkinson's,' said Professor David Marsden. He paused and gave me an inquisitive look after he pronounced sentence. I did not know how to reply; after all, I had trekked across the world to get answers, not questions.

Feeling impelled, however, to fill the expectant silence, I groped in my mind to find something to say and could only come up with another question. 'Will it affect my sex life?'

He gave a half-nod, as if in recognition of something, followed by a look of puzzlement as the import of my question dawned on him. 'Sex life? No! I don't think so. Why should it?'

It was only then that I recognised that half-nod. I had read about it, but never seen it: the moment a doctor gives one the 'Bad News' – usually cancer – and diagnoses (or rather categorises) you by response. What did his nod confirm me as? A hysteric? A stoic? Or a sex maniac? 'No, I expected it,' I mumbled in embarrassed explanation, 'The Parkinson's, I mean.'

As I left Queen Square I felt I was failing to do justice to a monumental moment in my life. So I stopped off at the first pub I came across and, leaning against the counter with the battle-weary air of a war correspondent, ordered a double whisky. The whisky was OK, but the moment seemed strangely flat.

Judgement Day

When judgement day arrived, the lawyer, Ernie Wentzel, found himself sitting next to Ann Harris in court. 'She was very quiet, dignified as she had been as a witness. She had an air of innocence and goodness. After the preliminary statement of the facts it was soon obvious to me that a death sentence was coming. The judge spoke of John's denial that ARM was communist and threw doubt on it, pointing to its cell organisation. I should have thought that all organisations were arranged in similar manner, even the OB (a neo-Nazi Afrikaner organisation). As soon as I was certain the death sentence was coming, I said to Ann: 'They're going to hang him.' I took her hand and held it. She was silent and I could sense her fear. When the sentence of death was passed with its formality I could not look at John. 'Don't let those bastards see you cry,' I said to Ann as the court adjourned.

[Ann to John – no date]

I have just been telling David what a wonderful father he has. Most little boys think their fathers are wonderful but I think he will feel the same way for his whole life.

I have read your letter through and through. You say that our love must be 'strong and proud'. Mine has never been more so. Don't worry about me. I have myself well in hand and the remarks I am putting on the report (imaginary) I am writing about myself are really full of praise – although they are very mild compared with those I am putting on yours. Everybody is coming up to scratch. I wish I could send you a parcel of the friendship with which I am surrounded. Messages, and invitations and money, the most unexpected people are being really kind. Your parents are being wonderful. I have seen quite a few signs of your father's Rumanian blood. Mom is well and reacting in the same way (probably her Irish blood). They moved into the house yesterday and I went to help. Lena has been guarding everything marvellously and apparently showing her Rumanian blood to visitors she did not like the look of. Betty was thrilled to see us – threw her arms around Mom's neck.

On madness

Madness, of course, takes many guises. There are some who have said that Verwoerd himself was mad. An Opposition MP, Major Piet van der Byl, told him so to his face. Ordered by the Speaker to withdraw his description of the prime minister as a 'paranoiac', the major said: 'I cannot withdraw it; it is true. It is my duty to the country to say this.' Whether or not he heard voices, Verwoerd did consider himself on personal terms with the Almighty. He believed that he survived an earlier assassination attempt by virtue of divine intervention.

And was South Africa not a society gone mad? Listen to the Reverend James Johnston testifying to Judge Beyers on Tsafendas' insanity: 'I went to see him chiefly in connection with his racial status ... I asked him whether he was a European or whether he was a coloured man. The reason why I asked him that was because I was concerned about him being a foreigner and if he was a coloured man it was quite right for him to stay in a coloured home as well as going to services in a coloured home. But if he was a European, or a white man, I would ask him to go along to services that were held in a white home ... I must say I found him rather strange, or odd ...'

Dimitrios Tsafendas was not white. He was not a member of the chosen race turning madly on his own – a white messenger in a white parliament killing a white prime minister. There the watchdogs of racial purity at the very heart of the apartheid state got it wrong. And nor was he 'a dog', or an 'inert implement'. Evidence to the contrary has always been there ...

Within the hours of that bloody confrontation on the floor of the National Assembly, TE Dönges – hurriedly made acting prime minister – was on the air, crackling and squawking to the nation over the valve radios of the day. 'The Cabinet will leave no stone unturned to get behind the reasons for this dreadful act,' he declared. 'This is not the time for rumours, or speculation and still less for people to lose their heads.'

As Dönges spoke, orders were already going out to government agencies and the first of thousands of pages of reports were beginning to pour in from departments of state, the police and security services round the world, anxious to deal with the spectre of the assassin that haunts them all. The papers were released by Pretoria's state archives under the 30-year rule.

Demitrio Tsafendas was born in Mozambique, in January 1918, the son of a marine engineer of Greek extraction and a mother who was a servant of mixed race. Tsafendas does not appear to have known his mother, Amelia. He was farmed out, for his early years, to his grandmother who lived in Alexandria, Egypt. When Tsafendas was six his grandmother fell ill and he returned to Mozambique. His father, by this time, had married a Greek woman. At the age of 10 he was shipped off again, this time to boarding school at Middelburg, in the Transvaal. There he seems to have fallen victim to an early dose of racial prejudice, suffering the nickname 'Blackie'.

When he was 14 his father went bankrupt and Tsafendas returned to Mozambique to attend a church school. He seems to have been something of a solitary and, to his father, difficult boy. His stepmother was later to recount of this time: 'He was difficult to control and his father often had to punish him in order to get him disciplined. His association with other children at this stage was, however, good,' she said.

'He showed a particular interest in the use of gunpowder and explosives and at one stage nearly blew up our house. Also at this stage I often found him gazing in space and when I asked him what he was doing his reply was that he was thinking ...' It was at about this time that the skeleton of his own birth came tumbling out of the family cupboard, when he was told he was 'coloured' and illegitimate.

Psychology tests later gave him an IQ of 125. But he left school at the age of about 16, refusing to study further, and started work as a shop assistant, taking up boxing in is spare time. 'He became a particularly good boxer and took part in many tournaments,' testified his stepmother.

In 1936 he moved to South Africa, working for a while at a munitions factory. It was about this time that he apparently fell victim to the tapeworm, about which he was to develop his obsession. In 1941 he joined the Merchant Navy and began life as a wanderer.

It was during his foreign adventures that his mental instability became apparent. His travels are signposted by a litany of deportation orders and psychiatric reports from institutions he found himself in around the world. At one stage he walked across the frozen St Croix River from Canada into the United States. At another he presented himself at the Mandelbaum Gate, demanding entry to Israel from Jordan.

He was detained for six months on New York's Ellis Island, given shock treatment in Portugal, certified insane in England, baptised on a beach in Greece, given more shock treatment in a German asylum, passed through France as a refugee under the auspices of the Red Cross and, finally, in 1964, returned to South Africa.

His mental disturbance appears to have been acute. One psychiatric report, for example, from the North Grafton State Hospital in the United States, speaks of him hearing voices from radiators and smearing faeces on the wall. But his racial history was integral to his condition. The same report quotes him as saying he had loved a girl in South Africa, but would not marry her because he feared that he would produce a black child – a throwback. The report also says that he left South Africa, because the CID was pursuing him as a communist.

A silent god

Beyers de Klerk was an Afrikaner weightlifter, claiming Scottish, English and French Huguenot descent, who took his orders directly from God. It was an explosive mix. When I met him in the dying days of eighties' apartheid, De Klerk did not give the appearance of a man benefiting from divine intervention. He was having a terrible time getting the mayoral telephone to work and the mayoral secretary had gone home early, so he did not know if he had the authority to give out a municipal fact sheet. All of which showed that he was new to the job.

But of one thing he was confident: he had landed up in the mayoral hot seat in this small Transvaal town through the will of the Almighty. As he put it: 'I must either do what the world says, or what God says. I'm doing what God says.'

The guidance De Klerk appeared to have had from Heaven was essentially to put the black man in the place he has occupied for the last 300 years or so. Because, as mayor of the industrial town of Boksburg, he was leading the campaign by the extreme right-wing Conservative Party to put racism back in apartheid. Since the newly elected Boksburg town council resolved to start re-erecting 'whites only' signs, the Conservative campaign gave every appearance of snowballing.

Several other of the 89 local authorities controlled by the Conservatives in the Transvaal had already indicated they would follow Boksburg's lead in barring blacks from municipal facilities. It emerged that at least one town – Carltonville, in the Western Transvaal – was actively investigating the reintroduction of the old curfew laws by which South Africa's towns used to be reserved for 'whites by night'.

While the Nationalist government dithered in the face of demands by moderate politicians for immediate legislative moves to block the Conservative campaign, black South Africa reacted with growing indignation. In Boksburg's local black township of Vosloorus, it was announced they were teaming up with businessmen, taxi drivers and community leaders in a nearby coloured township to launch a retaliatory consumer boycott – in clear defiance of current Emergency regulations. They also announced plans to stage a mass sit-in in the 'whites only' park on the edges of a lake in the middle of Boksburg.

The lake and its surrounding park had long been a favourite place for the black, white and multihued hoboes of the town. To De Klerk, however – in his mayoral parlour up in a grey, pebble-dashed office block overlooking the park – it was a latter-day Sodom and Gomorrah. He gave a lurid account of how one night he had roamed the park with a gun in hand and seen unspecified, but shocking scenes. 'Homosexuality! We had to padlock all the toilets,' he said, indignantly.

Attempts to fathom the rationale behind De Klerk's apartheid mania proved frustrating, at least for a correspondent with little talent for theological disputation. Questioned about his political beliefs the mayor dived for a drawer of his desk. His wife, sitting with us, raised her eyebrows to the ceiling and murmured: 'He has a direct line.' He emerged with a much-thumbed and much-underlined copy of the Book and enigmatically offered Matthew 14:24 ('But he answered and said, I am not sent but unto the lost sheep of the house of Israel.')

And the Biblical justification for barring blacks from Boksburg lake? 'Oh dear, here we go again,' he muttered as he hunched over the Book and flipped through to Deuteronomy ('For thou art a holy people unto the Lord thy God: The Lord thy God has chosen thee to be a special people ...'). 'We just want what is ours,' the mayor said almost plaintively, in an abrupt departure from the Testaments.

Some 20 kilometres from Boksburg (pop. 152 626 blacks), the dispossessed were preparing to stake their claim to what had been at least partly theirs. The chairman of the township's management committee, Sidwell Mofokieng, was briefing the press on his council's plans to deal with their counterparts in Boksburg. 'They are denying our people God-given facilities, which we have the right to use,' he said. 'They seem to have forgotten that 80 per cent of the buying power in Boskburg is black.' Mofokieng was sensitive to the legal pitfalls of calling for a consumer boycott – an act punishable, under the State of Emergency, by 10 years' jail – insisting he was only suggesting a 'withdrawal of spending'.

And the sit-in at the lake would be nothing more than an opportunity for the blacks of Vosloorus to 'go there to relax'. 'We have had a hard year; we need to relax.'

The peaceable language brought to mind that it was the 150th anniversary of the occasion when a Boer leader, Piet Retief, was invited by the Zulu chief, Dingaan, to attend a tribal dance, only to be slaughtered with all his men. De Klerk happened to be the great-great-grandson of one of that ill-fated party. But the story does not feature in the Good Book, so Boksburg's mayor no doubt found little significance in it.

Story of an uncaged bird

In Johannesburg's northern suburbs there lived a lovebird called JB. He had no cage and was as free as a parakeet can be that has developed a passionate attachment to his owner. But his owner was less contented. He knew that he was in a cage, albeit one without bars.

The story of JB – which stands for Jail Bird – and his owner, Raymond Suttner, is a story of the meticulous perversity with which the South African authorities so often used to deal with their political opponents on the left. JB was given to Suttner essentially to help save him from going insane.

Suttner was a well-known South African academic and political activist. A senior lecturer in Law at the University of the Witwatersrand, he was a member of the Transvaal Executive of the United Democratic Front (UDF) – then the country's main anti-apartheid organisation, and effectively outlawed.

He was arrested at Jan Smuts Airport on 12 June 1986 under the State of Emergency that had been declared on that day. As an anti-apartheid veteran, Suttner was no stranger to prison. In 1975, after electric shock treatment, he was jailed for seven and half years for 'furthering the aims' of a banned organisation – distributing pamphlets for the African National Congress.

So when he was picked up again in 1986, and taken to the university to have his office searched, he managed to tell a colleague that he was being detained and that he wanted an urgent interdict against the authorities to prevent his being mistreated again.

The authorities agreed to give an undertaking to that effect to the Supreme Court. But they dealt out what some might regard as a more refined torture: prolonged isolation. Held first at John Vorster Square, Johannesburg's notorious police headquarters, and then at Diepkloof Prison before ending up at Pretoria's maximum security jail for political prisoners, he had completed more than a year in effective solitary confinement when JB arrived on the scene.

It was unfortunately not possible to ask Suttner what this experience was like. In terms of his banning order he could not talk to the press. Suffice to say that the authorities began to get alarmed. A succession of reports were submitted to the government by doctors, including a psychiatrist, warning of the consequences if Suttner's detention continued.

And so it was that JB and Suttner won at least a form of freedom. He had been in jail for two years and three months – 18 months in solitary confinement.

Despite the plethora of security laws in South Africa, no grounds had been found during that time to either charge or try him. But he was apparently still regarded as a threat to the State, because he emerged from prison to be hit by a comprehensive banning order.

South Africa's 'meticulous perversity' in dealing with the left finds perhaps its highest expression in banning orders. It is a form of bureaucratic imprisonment that many notable figures have suffered – Winnie Mandela, Helen Joseph and Donald Woods. In Suttner's case, the terms of the banning order applied under the

Emergency regulations were particularly ferocious.

He could not take part in any press interview. He could not leave the Johannesburg magisterial district; he could not leave his house between dusk and dawn; he could not attend a 'meeting' of four people or more; he could not enter any 'educational institution'; he could not take part in the activities of various named organisations, including the UDF, and he had to report to a police station two and half miles from his house at specific times twice a day.

The effects of the restrictions were that he could not continue lecturing, and for practical purposes he could not hold down a job at all. His day had to be structured around those two visits to the police station.

He also had to worry constantly about who was at the door, or at least how many. There have been successful prosecutions of banned people who attended 'illegal' gatherings, including a man limited to one visitor at a time who was caught playing bridge.

But obviously it was a better life than in prison, in solitary confinement, which is presumably what Vlok meant by a 'humanitarian' gesture. Now he was able to enjoy at least a degree of freedom and was to be seen wandering the streets of Johannesburg's northern suburbs; a haunted-looking man, with a mop of curly greying hair and a lovebird called JB sitting contentedly on his shoulder.

Sometimes a black person – occasionally a white – approaches him and quietly murmurs a thanks for what he has been through on their behalf.

Darling, darling John

Tomorrow is the anniversary of the day I really fell in love with you (that day at the swimming bath) 10 years ago. Ten years is quite a slice in our lifetime, nearly half, and the longer I've known you the more I have loved you, and the more I have realised how lucky I am to be married to you, the most wonderful person I know. The last little while has made me more sure than ever. D [David] and I are here together in bed telepathing our love to you. How I wish I could take a bigger share of the burden. It belongs to both of us after all, but you are having all the suffering. I thought of you especially on the 2nd. Did you get the heart-shaped cake? Here is what we send you each day in your food bag: 4 oranges, 1 pint of milk, cheese, bag containing dried fruit and sweets. The rest vary each day. For the past two weeks at least we have sent a 5-cent chocolate each day. Nor I am breaking it up and putting it in with the dried fruit and sweets.

David is growing well. Ad says he often has a definite Johnish look, especially around the eyes, but that his mouth is like mine. He is undoubtedly beautiful, a real picture-book baby and so good. Maritz apparently told his Mother that D is the only baby he has ever really liked. We found him yesterday standing next to the pram and he said, David really talks, doesn't he? For the past half hour he (D) has been lying on the bed, going away and waving his arms and laughing whenever I look at him. It is lovely to be able to send you food and clothes. When I see your things hanging on the line next to D and mine I feel I have some physical contact with you, and I do long for that so much, darling J. What we have no one can take away though it is all the things we share, the experiences and the love that makes us one. 'Our world is now' but it is shaped by the past, and so we share it. You said, as we have said before, it isn't events that matter but only their effect on us. I think if we keep that in mind we shall come through triumphant. Darling, darling John, please take as good care of yourself as you can. Hold on tight to the fact that we belong to each other, matter most to each other. PLEASE DO NOT CONSIDER MY FEELINGS ONLY YOUR FEELINGS, I know you will agree. I talk a lot to Mom and so I know that she is really on top of things, full of fighting blood and very proud of you. The little space left isn't nearly big enough to represent all the very special hugs and kisses of all sorts that I am sending you.

Your Ann

23/9/64

Darling

… I chose so well, ten years ago. It was an intuition that must have guided me as if to say, 'This is the girl you must marry.' And the happiness that has flowed from that – well I don't need to describe it to you, for it's been our happiness.

And now, in the present strain, I appreciate what a fine marriage we have. For the two of us to be able to feel an inner peace & happiness beneath the violent disturbances on & near the surface – this is marvellous, & yet it is so …

My ideals & beliefs have not changed in the least over the past months, Ann dearest. If anything I've come to hold them more clearly & strongly. On this score I know there'll not be the minutest wavering or hesitation. I know that at all times I've done what I believed to be right & still so believe. Actions may have been ill-judged in any one of a number of ways, but motives and intentions – about these I hold my head high.

I love you
John

God's messenger

'It must have been shortly before 11 am that a certain Von Egidy arrived in town,' recounted Justice Nugent. 'He was a most unusual witness who ascribed his prescience and his actions moments before the shooting occurred to his role as a missionary for peace.' To be precise, Ralph von Egidy believed he was a messenger from God.

The scene was downtown Johannesburg on 28 March 1994, the day of the 'Shell House massacre' when thousands of Zulu warriors supporting the Inkatha Freedom Party (IFP) marched past ANC headquarters and 19 died in an ensuing shootout. In the inquest that followed the massacre everyone blamed everyone else for it. In particular the ANC blamed the IFP, accusing them of plotting an attack on Shell House in an attempt to wipe out their leadership. While the IFP accused ANC security men of opening fire with live ammunition on a peaceful march of demonstrators who had been exercising their democratic rights of protest. In the circumstances, while there were masses of demonstrators, there was a perhaps understandable shortage of reliable witnesses. That was until Judge Nugent spotted a white man whose head kept on bobbing up in the viewfinders of police videotapes of the massacre. The judge asked who he was. With some embarrassment the police told him …

Von Egidy was an artist from the Johannesburg suburb of Lorentzville. He didn't have much work at the time except, as he put it, as a 'servant of God'. On the day before the massacre he felt 'very disturbed', he recounted. 'I believe that God told me that my faith was going to be required the next day.'

The next day he had an appointment with an advertising agency, to show them his portfolio of work. He was only there for about half an hour. Then he drove into central Johannesburg, parked his car and got out of it. 'I saw that there were people on the move,' he recalled.

'There were quite a few people trickling down from side streets. They were wearing traditional regalia. I saw armbands and so on. They had sticks, wooden clubs, iron poles, spears, knobkerries and shields. Some were running, jogging, trotting. There was lawlessness. They were knocking over bins. They were carrying sticks.' There was 'shouting and jeering going on – "ho, ha type of stuff"'.

Then he heard shots. 'I realised I was in the middle of people approaching from all sides … I saw people in khaki, camouflage, blue security guard uniforms with epaulettes and blue police uniforms. Some were standing, some were crouching, or kneeling behind concrete barricades. All had weapons in their hands and held in a ready state in a defensive posture.' He saw one man pointing a 'long gun' (rifle) at him. A policeman gestured to the gunman, who lowered the weapon.

'I stretched my arms, walked in a circle and screamed: "Stop! Stop all of you. Stop!

'"How dare you! Who gives you the right? Do you not know it is wrong to kill? *Het julle geen vrees vir God nie?* [Do you have no fear of God?] *Hoe durf julle!* [How dare you!] Stop!"'

Miraculously all three groups moving in on him stopped. 'The first row of the group from the north was hesitant and standing back.' He found himself staring into their eyes. There was a momentary lull. But then the body of marchers behind the hesitant group broke through.

'They descended on me with sticks, clubs and knobkerries.' One stick jabbed him in the side. 'They hit me with steel poles and knobkerries. They attacked me.' He did not resist. 'I stood at peace.' He stumbled and fell.

He was on his knees when he heard more gunfire – this time automatic fire, as well as single shots. 'As I was kneeling I saw the legs and torsos of marchers going past me and three to four seconds later the same legs and torsos coming back. As they were coming back bodies were falling all around me and weapons were clattering.'

Suddenly the shooting stopped. The intersection where he was kneeling was deserted. 'The only people there were the wounded and dead bodies and myself.'

It was an extraordinary story. In the minds of the police who later interviewed him, it was too extraordinary. Feeling they would look foolish if they presented a messenger from God as a witness, they failed to bring Von Egidy's account to the attention of Judge Nugent. But the judge was fascinated and ordered that they bring Von Egidy before him.

Impressed by the man's account, he asked him to testify before the inquest. At first Von Egidy declined, saying he felt that he had already discharged God's mission. But when the judge pointed out that, to be a messenger, one had to deliver the message, he agreed.

Von Egidy's evidence enabled Judge Nugent to track the movements of the demonstrators, security men and police, coming to the conclusion that there was no plot by the IFP, no plan of attack. That, at least, was seemingly the message from God.

Of dwarves, weightlifters and clerics

Popularity does not, of course, distinguish Pastor Ray McCauley from fundamentalist and charismatic leaders in other parts of the world. But there was, in the unique political role that had been assumed by the goodly pastor, perhaps something that distinguished South Africa from other parts of the world.

McCauley's ascent from a rough-and-tough childhood to heights of saintliness (at least in the eyes of his multitude of followers) is familiar to the 'born-again' tradition, although his particular story is unique to the man.

He was born in Johannesburg, his father a bookie and mother – seemingly as a consequence of the perfidy of horses – an alcoholic. Ray himself was a fanatical sportsman and (steroid-inflated) bodybuilder in his youth, taking third place in the Universe contest in London in 1974. He is a one-time nightclub-bouncer and hairdresser turned religious pop star and political mediator.

Legend has it that he 'found God' after his fiancé had run away with a dwarf from a *Snow White* ice show, Ray tracking them down to a gas-filled caravan – the man dead in a suicide pact, the girl half naked and unconscious.

But while acknowledging the experience was important to his spiritual development (he spent sleepless nights at her bedside, holding her hand and praying with apparent success for her recovery), McCauley insists that his conversion was a more gradual process.

Whatever its origins, McCauley pursued his calling to America, first marrying his fiancé (another one) and then spending a year studying at the Rhema Bible Training Center in Tulsa, Oklahoma. He returned to South Africa to found the Rhema Church and – with the help of his congregation – a family (his parishioners successfully petitioned for divine intervention in overcoming his steroid-induced infertility and the pastor was blessed with a son).

His rise in the ranks of the godly was meteoric. Starting, by his own account, with a congregation of 13 gathered in his parents' front room, he went on to claim 'the biggest multiracial congregation in the world' – 17 000 strong, a third of them blacks, attending his Rhema church outside Johannesburg. He became president of the International Fellowship of Christian Churches, an alliance he founded of 600 charismatic congregations dotted around South Africa.

Once accused of peddling a 'gospel of prosperity' and identified with the white right, McCauley's commitment to non-racialism and the disadvantaged was startling and impressive. Deciding, as he recounted it, that it was wrong that black and white children should mix at Sunday school, but not during the week, he set up 80 multiracial church schools around the country, several of which were fire-bombed by right-wing extremists. He published what he called a 'Christian Manifesto' which denounced the government as 'tyrannical' and corrupt, demanded an apology from FW de Klerk's ruling National Party for the 'sin' of apartheid and restitution of land 'stolen' from blacks.

Apart from his newfound enthusiasm for the anti-apartheid cause, McCauley owed his political influence to a large extent to the unity of the South African churches. It is a unity that can be said to date back to 1990 and the extraordinary Rustenburg Conference. The conference, a gathering of church leaders ranging from the fundamentalists through the gamut of the establishment to the Afrikaans churches, saw an orgy of confession and tearful forgiveness for sinful apartheid.

Since that emotional event every political crisis in South Africa has been attended by a flock of clerics, working to defuse confrontation with a harmony and disregard for doctrinal differences no less remarkable for the fact that it would no doubt have been applauded by the founder of Christianity.

As McCauley puts it, referring to the baptismal issue: 'We have no time to argue over sprinkling, dunking, or drowning.'

McCauley himself set out deliberately to develop relationships with political leaders several years ago, touring the country to meet them. His encounter with the right-wing leader, Andries Treurnicht, was something of a disaster. McCauley demanded how – if Treurnicht won power – he could order black congregants to leave the church. The political *dominee* replied by pointing out that Christ drove the moneylenders out of the temple.

McCauley found President De Klerk, who had been to pray at Rhema, insistent that apartheid was a practical, rather than a moral error – refusing to disown his father who, as a cabinet minister, was responsible for some of the country's most odious race laws.

Sitting in the luxuriously converted warehouse that is church and religious headquarters, McCauley looked unnervingly like the actor, Jack Nicholson – aside from the muscles bulging under a modestly cavernous shirt.

McCauley is enormously satisfied with his position and

achievements in life, although he is quick to deny any hubris. It would be, he says, as mistaken for him to glory in his role as it would have been for Christ's donkey to have claimed credit for the adulation when it tottered into Jerusalem with its holy burden.

V677
Pretoria Central Prison
Private Bag 45
Pretoria

25/9/64

My darling love

... There's a powerfully voiced rooster somewhere in the neighbourhood. He has a very clear and carrying croon, for he doesn't sound very near, yet I hear him clearly. Not a very intelligent bird, I fear, for on overcast days he's to be heard at any time, particularly late afternoon!

... Have finished reading *The Star* (which is a miserable newspaper, with the odd generally interesting article) & have had supper. Now I'm going to send your letter.

All my love,
John

Shaking 'n freezing

It is a strange disease, Parkinson's. The symptoms vary from uncontrolled shaking to rigidity of the limbs, often at the same time. My walk is reduced to a senile shuffle; I have been robbed of the physical ability to write – making do with one-finger stabs at the keyboard – and I am beginning to have difficulty speaking, slurring my words. On occasion I freeze into near-immobility when my partner has to calm me down as I tremble on the edge of panic.

The problem has been identified with the progressive deterioration of a small group of brain cells. The causes are not known, theories ranging from trauma to viruses and chemicals. Symptomatic treatment is available with a 'miracle' drug, Levadopa, which turns into a nightmare with time – after about five to 10 years – triggering wild gyrations of the limbs. About 30 per cent of people with it sign off into dementia.

Parkinson's gives one unusual insights. Take Levadopa, for example. It is an extraordinary drug, at least in its effect. It is like Popeye's spinach, or Asterix's magic potion; one moment I'm a trembling immobile wreck and the next – POW! – I'm striding off. The transformation can happen, literally, in mid-stride (or mid-shuffle). I'm allowed enough of the drug to give me about eight to 10 hours of mobility. But there is a price to be paid; after an hour or two I'm hit by such an overwhelming lethargy that I have sometimes fallen asleep in mid-conversation at the dinner table.

Take a walk with me to the kitchen to make a cup of tea. Arriving at my study door, I freeze and begin casting around for a piece of paper to crumple. Freezing is a symptom familiar to Parkinson's and it always ambushes me when I am approaching a doorway or, more accurately, a passageway from one space to another. Time otherwise wasted during these phases of immobility, I have turned to productive use by developing my Theory of Doorways. This holds that all people have a subconscious reluctance (rendered overt by Parkinson's) to pass through doors, a prejudice arising from the experience of birth and the painful lesson learnt as to what lies in wait on the other side of the uterus.

I have developed various mechanisms to break out of a freeze, involving use of the imagination to fool the mind. An early technique was to picture myself as having been born as somebody else; perhaps Jesse Owens exploding out of the blocks at the start of the 200 metres, or hurtling into the final bend on his way to yet another world record leaving his opponents flailing behind and Hitler grimacing in the stands. But this approach has been discouraged by near-fatal collisions with other members of the household unaware of my transformation into a track star and doubtful looks cast in my direction when I am caught acknowledging the adulation of the crowds and giving a finger to the Fuehrer.

I now find that an effective way of breaking through a freeze is to grab a small object – a crumpled piece of paper, or bunch of car keys that will slide or roll along the floor – toss it at my feet and proceed to kick it. Upon which I start shuffling forward again, dribbling the 'ball' to the kitchen, as the phone rings.

Speaking on the telephone – an activity I had thought to be as automatic as direct conversation – I discover to be inherently stressful if not downright hurtful. When I inadvertently take a call on a handset (as opposed to my personal headset) I frequently have to cut the conversation short as I begin involuntarily ear-bashing myself. Similarly a game of chess – which I had taken as a relaxing pastime – can be a problem, particularly when a checkmate is in prospect, the growing amplitude of the shakes threatening to scatter the combatants by way of a few heavenly biffs to the battlefield. Poker must be hell.

I am busily shaking the kettle (involuntary) under the kitchen tap when I feel a yearning, familiar to such circumstances early in the day, to take my drugs. This in turn brings the usual troubling thoughts to mind: Who am I and, perhaps more importantly, why?

I hesitate for fear of being misunderstood, of it being taken as a post facto rationalisation of a personal tragedy, the pleading of a 'victim' for the charity of respect.

I was first alerted to it, I think, by a throwaway line in a newspaper profile of Superman Christopher Reeve in which an activist for the disabled was quoted as saying that 'the problem' with Reeve 'is that he wants a cure'. In the apparent paradox, I was startled to hear the echoes of 'black consciousness' and liberation theology.

I heard it again, in an observation by a friend of Stephen Hawking, that he thought the Cambridge genius had been forced by his disability to develop conceptual tools that had given him a new line of attack on mathematical problems. I think I have sensed it in political prisoners who have been through long terms of solitary confinement or torture.

I saw it when a beautiful artist swept aside the gleaming wave of black hair covering part of her lovely face to expose a huge, livid birthmark. Recounting the social ostracism she had suffered as a child because of her 'disfigurement', she explained she had eschewed modern laser treatment to get rid of it 'because it is my badge of empowerment'.

It is a question of perspective, really – a perspective of one's surroundings and above all of oneself shorn of pretence, particularly as regards one's own mortality.

There are high hopes at the moment for a better treatment, if not cure, for Parkinson's, many of them based on the recent breakthroughs in cloning, genetic manipulation, neural cell regeneration and embryo transplants. But these techniques offer far more than a way of dealing with this one disease. They open a possible road to some form of immortality, which would represent a rebellion against the given order of life of near-Promethean proportions.

Soothsayers who nowadays pass themselves off as futurologists have predicted that consciousness will be immortal by the year 2090 – presumably because the brain will either be endlessly repairable, or our memory banks duplicable and therefore transferable.

We are like hatchlings trying to break out of an egg. If there were a superior form of life, their view of humanity would be that of a mother hen watching a chick pecking at the shell – desperately trying to get out of that claustrophobic little world. Our scientists are the hard beak and our research breakthroughs are the holes gradually appearing and widening. Waiting outside to greet us is, surely, a new reality.

Comrade Tsafendas

Tsafendas was, before the war, a paid-up member of what was then the Communist Party of South Africa. And he did have a pronounced social and political conscience. Among the records of the investigation into his background, conducted after the assassination, is a copy of an internal memorandum of the Mozambican security police stating: 'Demitrio Tsafendas, of mixed blood (a coloured), was recently in the company of persons of the Negro race (blacks) in the bar of the hotel of Gondola accompanied by other persons of the Negro race and was heard to say the following phrases of a subversive character, including the following: "This country is not called Portugal, it is called the United State of Mozambique. Its flag is of a blue colour, with a rainbow, that rainbow represents all the colours. We already have money and any day now all this will come to an end, because what is necessary is not to be fooled into saying that we are Portuguese, because we are Africans. Long live our country, the United States of Mozambique."'

He, himself, offered the racial issue as a motivating factor in the murder of Dr Verwoerd. A few days after the assassination, he told an interrogator: 'I was so disgusted by the racial policy that I went through with my plan to kill the prime minister.' Shortly before the assassination, Tsafendas – who had somehow landed up with documents defining him as 'white' – applied for reclassification as coloured.

Despite his record of mental instability, many who met Tsafendas on his travels were impressed by him. The personnel officer at a German engineering firm recalls, for example: 'He drove up here in a big, battered American car, dressed and well mannered, he was extremely courteous – a very pleasant man. He looked like a satisfied, successful businessman.'

He was also a considerable linguist. A measure of that talent was provided by a priest of German extraction, Father Hanno Probst, recounting a meeting he had with him in Manzini where Tsafendas was working in a sugar mill: 'He told me that he could speak eight languages. I tried him with a few languages and I found that he spoke them all perfectly. He asked me where I was born. I said I was born near Munich in Germany. He then started to talk in Munich dialect. I then tried him in Spanish, Italian, German, tried a few words in Czech and he answered me in Czech.' The exchange ended on a chilly note, a squabble developing between the two men over the role of the Catholic Church in Africa. The priest denounced Tsafendas as a communist and rushed off to report him to security at the mill.

A man who did not have the makings of a rational mind? A man who was 'no more than a dog, or an inert implement'? There is an affidavit among those government files, taken in what was then Lourenço Marques by one Anthony Maw, a neighbour of Tsafendas's father. It records that, two or three years before the assassination, Tsafendas called unexpectedly at his office. He told Maw he had been all over world and was in Lourenço Marques on a passenger steamer, trying to identify his mother and locate her grave. Is there an image more redolent of humanity than that of a son seeking to mourn a mother he never knew?

Fleeing Parkinson's disease

I must have been mad to have bought it. But there it is. Each morning it is parked for me in the shade, under a tree across the road. I sit here, pecking away at my keyboard with my left index finger and, when I get tired, look out the window and gaze at its lovely lines before returning to my writing with the thought: 'Just a few more hours.'

In the late afternoon I swallow my drugs, then I hobble across the street (buggered knee – nothing to do with the Parkinson's) and head for the hills.

And as I hum through the Constantia vineyards, or along a coastal road I listen to the throb of the V8 engine bolted on to my rusting 1.5 ton Mercedes Benz 450SL sports car and I come as close, I guess, as I ever will to religious ecstasy.

As can be guessed from that statement, my religious enthusiasms are somewhat limited no matter how much the Pope may apologise for the past. The only church I would ever consider joining, if she had got around to founding it, would have been one based on the teachings of the little old lady who famously informed Professor Stephen Hawking that the world was situated on the back of a tortoise and for the rest it was 'tortoises all the way down'.

I am also less than enthusiastic about the 'I think therefore I am' school of philosophic agonising. But I do regret that someone has not put together a basic manual to life of which I could take advantage, which I would have thought should be the prime task of the philosophical profession.

Not one that goes so far as justifying the taste of some of the acts with which the Cosmic Impresario attempts to entertain us in the vaudeville show called life. Not a collection of pious platitudes, but a hard-nosed manual for life. Something – a book, a machine if needs, or an Internet site – at which I could pitch the question: 'Listen, my bank overdraft is getting a bit out of control, as is my bald patch, my knee is buggered and I'm having trouble walking and I've got this ... well, they call it a disease, although ...'

At which point bells will start ringing and across the screen (or whatever) will come the words: 'No more! No more, please, I get the drift. What you need is a 22-year-old, rusting sports car.'

The nearest thing to such a manual seems to be the *Enchiridion* of Epictetus, the Roman slave who became central to the Stoic school of philosophy early in the first millennium. I was starting to become a fan of Epictetus and was sorely disappointed to discover he had not only overlooked Mercedes sports cars, but had failed to mention chariots, which would, no doubt, have been a great comfort to the sorely stricken of his day.

The closest I could find to what might be relevant advice was the following: 'With regard to whatever objects give you delight, are useful, or are deeply loved, remember to tell yourself of what general nature they are, beginning from the most insignificant things.

'If, for example, you are fond of a specific ceramic cup, remind yourself that it is only ceramic cups in general of which you are fond. Then, if it breaks, you will not be disturbed. If you kiss your child, or your wife, say that you only kiss things that are human, and thus you will not be disturbed if either of them dies.' This struck me as a canny move, but an evasion of responsibilities verging on the distasteful.

I then stumbled across a paragraph urging the help-seeker to shun conversations with regard to 'gladiators, or horse races, or athletic champions'. Never talk about the Springboks?

So where can I get reliable advice to deal with the process of entropy that sadly attends all our lives? 'Rage, rage, rage against the dying of the light,' suggested Dylan Thomas.

Bugger that for a lark. I'm going to enjoy the sunset.

The assassin on death row

Dinner is over at Sterkfontein and an orderly politely informs Tsafendas it is time for bed. The assassin is wheeled away in his armchair, clutching his bag of sweets. If he had not been insane when he appeared before Judge Beyers, the State did its best to make sure he became mad in the years that followed. When the judge found Tsafendas unfit to stand trial and committed him as a state president's patient the expectation was that he would be held in a mental hospital. Instead the National Party government exploited a loophole in the law to place him on death row in what can only be described as a living hell.

As well as suffering personal abuse at the hands of warders – who are alleged to have made a practice of urinating in his food and beating him up while trussed in a straitjacket – he was subjected to the sounds of the weekly proceedings in the human abattoir that was the gallows: the singing, the crying and the thump of the trapdoor as the hangman strangled his fellow prisoners in batches of up to seven at a time. The sounds left him, on occasion, 'howling like a dog'. The nightmare was to last nearly a quarter of a century, until he was moved to a lower-security prison in 1989 and to Sterkfontein in July 1994.

But that has no bearing on the central question posed by the story of Tsafendas: Why did he kill Verwoerd? Was it an act of mindlessness, or that of a man driven to insanity by the racism that dogged his life? Was it just a coincidence that a boy tormented at school by the chant of 'Blackie' was the man who plunged a dagger into the heart of a head of state who is remembered as 'the architect of apartheid'?

Dredging through the State documents that tell the story of the events leading up to that pivotal moment in South African history, the analogy that comes to mind is of a cruise missile. One can only guess at the formative experiences that effectively punched the fatal coordinates into the biological computer that is his brain. But it was with a sense of inevitability, almost of purpose that he moved ever closer to the Mother City until he struck with such explosive effect.

Some even believe the missile was primed. Right-wing extremists mutter darkly that John Vorster, who was in Parliament that day, seemed strangely calm for a police minister when his prime minister was being murdered in front of him. And there are some puzzling details among those documents in the state archives. Take that exchange with Father Probst in Manzini all those years ago, when the priest asked Tsafendas where he learned so many languages. Tsafendas, according to the cleric, 'told me that he was in Russia and that he had learned these languages in a training school in Russia.' Tsafendas, who took pride in his linguistic ability, has denied speaking Russian. Which is curious, because there is a document on file quoting the Greek consul in Beira as testifying how Tsafendas – back from his world travels – had talked fluently in that language to the crew of a Russian ship that happened to be in the port.

During that 1966 hearing on the sanity of Dimitrios Tsafendas, there was a particularly piquant exchange between his counsel and Justice Beyers. The Judge President asked: 'Did the accused tell you that history will judge whether he was right in killing the deceased?'

'I do remember him saying something to the effect that history will prove whether he is right or wrong,' said Dr Cooper.

A madman, or a man with a mission?

Perhaps Mary Shelley came closest to summing up the life of Tsafendas with the words she put in the mouth of Frankenstein's monster: 'Am I to be thought the only criminal, when all humankind sinned against me?'

26/9/64

My own darling Ann

… At about 2, I was told that I had a visitor, & I soon realised it was Father de Sylva. How good it was of him to fit in this visit to me (& he's hoping to visit you & he's tried, on my request, to see your parents & he's phoned my mother three times), especially as he'll be away in Mauritius for a week (from Monday) & then immediately thereafter in Durban.

He and I talked for one and a half hours, though it didn't seem anything like that, the time went so quickly. I could talk so freely with him, & in every way he tried to help (& in many he succeeded). I was rather upset, of course, at moments, but this didn't matter at all – & there are few people with whom I could have been so at ease, too. Whatever we discussed or mentioned he was *for me*, in such an unquestioning and humane way. If he was a parish priest – well the parish concerned would be a fortunate one, for he is so human-oriented.

One thing he said was: 'We're storming the gates of heaven for you' – he was saying how they're praying for me, various people here …

Every scrap of my very best love is always yours, darling Ann.

Your John

Oath

MKs National Political Commissar, Andrew Masondo, at a closed TRC amnesty hearing:

'... The other thing ... for instance ... you know ... if we were very, very – some people would go around, collect them and shoot them, and it would be in their right to do so because they took an oath, an MK oath. And in that oath, you actually say that should I contravene these things, I am willing to be punished, even by losing my life.'

Massacre at Sunday prayers

At about 19.30 on Sunday, 25 July 1993, two APLA operatives burst into the evening service at the St James Church in Kenilworth. They fired machine guns and threw two hand grenades covered with nails at a congregation of over a thousand people. Eleven people were killed and 56 injured. The attackers escaped in a waiting car, which had been hijacked earlier. The congregation was racially mixed and those killed included four Russian sailors ...

Ms Marilyn described the attack that killed her husband Guy: 'It was one of those evenings that we went to church the normal time, started the worship service and a couple were singing "More than wonderful". And it was just at the end of that song that the doors opened. And I saw that man standing there and I [noticed] that he had a gun in his hand and started moving from left to right ... And after a few minutes, we got up and – well ... and I called to my husband and he didn't answer. And I got up and he was still on his haunches, and I think I was a bit bewildered at this stage, everybody was milling around and, with that, an usher came down in front of me towards my husband. And he bent down to feel his pulse and I just said to him, 'Is he alive?' and he shook his head.'

Amongst those who were severely injured was a teacher, Paul Williams (CT00618), who was shot in his spinal cord and cannot walk without crutches: 'Suddenly these doors just flung open. I myself, I couldn't imagine that it was a possible or imminent attack. At first I heard a gun shot and immediately thereafter ... saw a hand grenade hurling towards a live audience. The second person (while this hand grenade was still airborne), he opened fire with what I will call a very heavy machine gun. And he was just spraying bullets, you know, randomly just across the congregation. And I was sitting at the end of the pew and that pew was rather full ... I curled myself up to sort of hide my face from the gun firing ... but soon after I just felt the thud of the bullet hitting my lower back and it was like – it was like a tension wire snapping and with that went a lot of pain. I just – I had stretched my body and my lower body just became very numb.'

(VOL. 3 P506 AND VOL. 6 P339 TRC FINAL REPORT)

Brotherly love

The occasion was the burying of the dead, a familiar enough exercise amid what many now see as a 'low-intensity civil war' raging in the country. But this time it was somehow different, when South Africa's 'mother city' gave them a send-off that must have had the five gunmen – who hurled grenades into a church and sprayed the 1 000-strong congregation with automatic rifle fire – wondering what they achieved. They were members of the Azanian People's Liberation Army, the virulently anti-white military wing of the Pan Africanist Congress. APLA's chief, Sabelo Phama, had just declared 'The Year of the Great Storm'.

The dead were four of the 11 killed in Cape Town's St James Church massacre in July 1993. And the first farewells were said in the parliamentary capital's old city hall, where well over 1 000 citizens gathered to demonstrate their disgust with the violence in the country. Most of them were sporting the white ribbons of a new peace initiative in the city as they packed out the hall and crowded the passageways to give standing ovations as the great and the good – religious leaders and the city's alderman – demanded an end to the carnage. Perhaps the 'greatest and goodest' of them all was the Nobel laureate and Anglican archbishop, Desmond Tutu, who gave an electrifying address to those he fondly describes as 'the rainbow people' – the intensively multiracial audience below him.

'They have reached the bottom of depravity,' pronounced the diminutive figure, his purple cap and gesticulating hands bobbing passionately above the temporary pulpit and phalanx of cameramen crowded in front of him. If the gunmen's intention was to divide the people, 'you have failed; you have succeeded in bringing us together,' he cried, his voice warbling up and down the register of emotion. 'We are going to have a new South Africa; we are going to have a South Africa where all of us, black and white, will be free … we are unstoppable, we are unstoppable … because this South Africa belongs to all of us.'

Members of the audience embraced as the crowd poured out into the streets – white businessmen in suits, coloured labourers in overalls, shop girls, uniformed traffic officers, students in their jeans and housewives with children in tow – clutching hands to form a human 'peace chain' around the Grand Parade, the old military parade in Cape Town's city centre.

Out in the suburbs, where the massacre had taken place, more than 2 000 mourners gathered in the St James Church for a memorial service. In the main hall the furniture is still pockmarked with shrapnel and bullet holes, the carpet shaded by the lingering stains from pools of blood detergents could not defeat and gaps in the neatly ordered pews where survivors tore them out to use as makeshift stretchers for the dying and the dead.

The Church of England in South Africa prided itself in its

eschewal of politics and the service was notably lacking in verbal statements of defiance for the killers and determination to create a new secular society. But the statements were implicit, particularly in the face of the Reverend Clive O'Kill.

The former minister at St James stood with his family in front of the coffin containing his son, Richard, the teenager who took a bullet in the head as he shielded two schoolgirls sitting next to him from the lead spray of the assault rifles. The boy's mother held a white rose. Her husband nursed a determined smile before he was called up to the pulpit and – standing over the blood-stained carpet where his son was killed – taunt death with the familiar words from Corinthians: 'Where, oh death, is your victory, death where is your sting?'

The other three coffins, bedecked with flowers, included that of Myrtle Smith, one of three of the 11 dead who would have been classified 'coloured' under the old dispensation and who made the St James atrocity unique as the first 'multiracial massacre' in South Africa.

The other two were the Harker boys, Gerald, aged 21, and Wesley, aged 14. The circumstances in which they died were not clear. But both police and their friends believed either they both tried to smother one of the grenades with their bodies, or Gerald – who had the most shrapnel wounds – tried in vain to shield his younger brother.

They are tales that make of the St James massacre, and its mourning, a triumphant story of South African liberation. Five years later the attackers were granted an amnesty by the TRC.

Nkosi Sikelel' iAfrica

Bokaba stated that he and a Warrant Officer Van Wyk recruited Jackson Maake sometime in 1986. Later, he handled Maake jointly with Hechter and Van Vuuren. Maake was sent to Botswana to infiltrate ANC networks but, on his return, Hechter suspected Maake of being a double agent. He was picked up, taken to a deserted property owned by the Pretoria Portland Cement Mine, some five to 10 kilometres outside Messina, and interrogated. Maake denied the allegation that he was a double agent, but after being subjected to electric shocks, confessed that he was working for the ANC and gave the name of Makupe as his MK contact.

According to Van Vuuren, they then went to the Security Branch offices and drew Makupe's file, which confirmed that he was a courier for the ANC. Makupe was abducted, taken to the mine property and interrogated. He told the Security Branch that Harold Sefolo was the MK operative who chose targets and acted as an ANC courier. Makupe was taken to a telephone box and instructed to call Sefolo in Witbank, telling him that he would be collected by some ANC comrades.

That night, Mamasela and another askari abducted Sefolo. His interrogation began the next morning. Van Vuuren described how Mamasela 'forced a knife in Sefolo's nose, after which he provided additional information. He also begged for his life.' In order to persuade him to provide more information, they shocked Maake to death in front of him. As they were preparing to do the same to Makupe, Sefolo 'asked if he could say something'.

Van Vuuren said: 'I agreed to it. He asked if he could sing "Nkosi Sikelel' iAfrica" ... Mamasela had an ANC flag present, which was with us then. He threw this over Maake while Sefolo sang "Nkosi Sikelel' iAfrica". We then shocked Makupe to death. Sefolo himself was then shocked to death.'
(VOL. 2 P238 TRC FINAL REPORT)

1/10/64

My dearest one,

About 11:15 – The morning has passed quickly. I've just had my exercise, showering leisurely & pleasantly. Morale is high – for absolutely no reason! That's how it is, & that's why I aim at what you're aiming at, I know – no pointless depression & despondency – chin right up!

Immediately after visit – My darling, you mustn't judge my general morale by my becoming upset when I see you and little David. I only see you 2 dear ones for half an hour in 72 or 96 hours, & this means unrepresentative behaviour on my part. 99.5% of the time I'm calm & reasonably all right morale-wise – *truly, truly …*

All of my best love

Panic attack

Chrissake, talk about the cosmic jester! Why does this always happen when I'm at my most vulnerable? God, the panic attacks I have to ride. Like gusts of wind roaring through the high Alps, I guess, tearing into the climber's tent.

Trapped and terrified he listens to the shrieks and moans, wondering if the puny defences of his mind can stand the onslaught, listening anxiously for the first rip that will allow in the forces of unreason.

1.35 pm, the clock soldiers on. And so do I. Only little more than two hours to go.

Fuck the panic attacks … Not a bad little shelter I've rigged up here. Maybe this could be sold as a new adventure game: 'Roll up! Roll up! Get your Parkinson's here. Visit the shores of unreason. Terrifying thoughts to be had. Experienced guides available.'

'I might be some time'

I am troubled by a word that is new to me: 'lability.' It was used by a French neurologist in a report on my condition, which said: 'There is no apathy and no depression, but he complains of emotional lability, which bothers him a lot.'

Webster's offered the definition: 'Readily or continually undergoing chemical, physical, or biological change or breakdown.' My suspicion was confirmed: emotional lability meant blubbing a lot. They had misunderstood, of course. Not about the blubbing, but my being greatly bothered by it. I was rather pleased with myself, really.

I had been puzzled for some time by fits of crying. They would hit at genuinely emotional moments, but they were a disproportionate response. I was told, for example, that a group of friends and colleagues had clubbed together to upgrade my air ticket to Grenoble for assessment as to my suitability for surgery. Obviously one feels a surge of warmth at such a gesture and perhaps brushes away tears of appreciation. But I found myself staggering around sobbing my heart out and gasping to my concerned-looking Ellen: 'I don't know what's going on … '

One of the many positive experiences of Parkinson's is the way it brings home the understanding that we are the product of chemical balances, or imbalances. So I suspected this inappropriate response reflected another instance of my neurons, or whatever, misfiring because of a dopamine shortfall. In Grenoble I checked my theory with the neuro-psychologist examining me. She confirmed it was a known syndrome among Parkinson's patients and mistook my pleased reaction, at having made the correct diagnosis, for relief.

On second thoughts, maybe she was right in detecting relief. No one likes to be known for breaking down in tears on inappropriate occasions. Besides, I must be sensitive to questions of courage; why else my interest in the polar explorers?

My attention was drawn to the polar regions by a photograph of a penguin I stumbled over on the Internet some time ago. The bird was seemingly greeting the photographer with the proud display of an egg at its feet. A text said it was from a glass negative taken by a member of the ill-fated Scott expedition to the Antarctic.

The fanciful thought passed through my mind that there was a sad, almost symbolic irony about the penguin's pose, as if the penguin was reminding the expedition – in anticipation of the famous, looming deaths – of the importance of life.

The Scott expedition and the self-sacrifice of Titus Oates are, of course, icons of English courage. Checking my schoolboy's recollection of the brave captain's farewell – 'I am just going outside and may be some time' – I found myself reading extracts from Scott's diary with fascination.

I was startled to discover that, at least on a literal reading, they were not Oates's last words. After they had been recorded, Scott went on to say, 'We knew that poor Oates was walking to his death, but though we tried to dissuade him …' The implication would seem to be that the famous line did not lead to his immediate departure, but to a discussion.

It was not the only such discussion on the subject. The previous weekend Scott is to be found recording that 'Oates is very near the end ... What we, or he will do, God only knows. We discussed the matter after breakfast; he is a brave, fine fellow and understands the situation, but he practically asked for advice.'

Discussions on the subject are also hinted at by Scott's almost quaint attempt to impose his authority on the story of Oates's death: 'Should this be found I want these facts recorded. Oates's last thoughts were of his mother, but immediately before he took pride in thinking that his regiment would be pleased with the bold way in which he met his death.'

Intriguingly, in these final days of their ordeal, there was also a row between the explorers relating to the possibility of suicide. Scott notes that the expedition's doctor was forced to hand over, from his medical chest, 'the means of ending our troubles' in the form of 30 opium tablets each.

Intrigued by these so-human dimensions (as opposed to the super-human) to the Antarctica saga, I found myself reading *The Worst Journey in the World* by Apsley Cherry-Garrard. A classic study of courage in the face of appalling adversity, it is an account of the Scott expedition told by its second youngest member who – while short-sighted to an almost comic degree – demonstrated exquisite insights into his fellow men.

Most memorable were his observations of Scott. 'He was strong,' the young man notes. 'We never realised until we found him lying there dead how strong, mentally and physically, that man was.' At another point he characterises Scott as 'the strong leader whom we went to follow and came to love', adding that 'he cried more easily than any man I have ever known'.

Most of us have heroes, I guess. Mine – along with millions of other fans – is the cyclist Lance Armstrong. Watching him pedalling his way through the fields of pain in the Tour de France, I am struck by the absence of any sign of emotional lability.

V677
Pretoria Central Prison
Private Bag 45
Pretoria

2/10/64

Darling, darling Ann

… Apart from the rooster I mentioned to you before, and the occasional dog, there's a resident cat. For quite a while I really thought there was an excellent cat-imitator about! I've now seen it several times and patted it once or twice – it's quite small, furry, & mixed mid-brown & dark in colour. Also, there are the cicadas – very reliable, sometimes surprisingly loud …

Birds are chirping outside, as they always do, just before & at daybreak. They are a great deal more reliable than that silly rooster!

Your very own John

Professor Pierre Pollak
Department of Neurology
Central University Hospital
Grenoble

Dear Professor Pollak

Michael Holman at the *Financial Times* has suggested I write to you. I am a foreign correspondent, currently based in Johannesburg, working for *The Guardian* newspaper in London and its sister publication, *The Observer*. I have advanced Parkinson's and would like to be considered for the same 'pacemaker' operation you have recently carried out on Michael. I am 53 years old.

Parkinson's was diagnosed by the late Professor Eric Marsden in London in 1992. I am under the care of Professor James Temlett in Johannesburg and Dr Andrew Lees in London. I also recently consulted Dr Roger Melville, a neurosurgeon in Cape Town, who has experience performing the operation, to get an early opinion as to my suitability for it. He advised me that my condition should benefit from the operation and recommended I have it performed by your team in Grenoble. He offered to carry out any such assessments as might help you decide whether I should travel to Grenoble for a preliminary examination. Professor Temlett is encouraging me to go ahead with the operation and Professor Lees has previously offered his cooperation should I decide to undergo the operation.

Yours sincerely,
David Beresford

V677
Pretoria Central Prison
Private Bag 45
Pretoria

7/10/64

My very darling Ann

… The rose petals were in good fragrant condition. They fairly *leapt* out at me as I opened the letter, & cascaded over my lap, more falling further …

All my love,
Your John

Darling John

Will tell you in three different colours that
I love you
I love you
I love you
And also show off the capabilities of my new pen …

Forlorn

- *Makana. Makana's Island? It's the old name for Robben Isand. He was a Xhosa chief in the Eastern Cape who fought against the English. He was beaten at the Battle of Grahamstown. They put him on Robben Island, with some of his men. But he made a promise that he would one day return, to lead his people to victory against the English.*
- *And?*
- *He escaped. They found a boat somewhere and they rowed for Bloubergstrand. But the boat overturned in the surf. Makana got to a rock and clung onto it for a while, shouting encouragement to the others over the roar of the waves before he was swept away. They were all drowned. But the Xhosas in the Eastern Cape wouldn't believe he was dead; because he'd promised to come back and lead them to victory. They kept all his possessions at his kraal, all his clothes laid out, waiting for him to come. Now there's a phrase in Xhosa, 'the coming of Makana.' It means a forlorn hope.*

The 'budgie' picture

Four photographers; two won a Pulitzer; two died and two wrote a book. There is something grimly playful about the two's, in that the couples are all-inclusive, but do not repeat. Greg and Joao wrote the book. Kevin and Greg won the Prize. Ken and Kevin – they're dead.

Greg Marinovich, Joao Silva, Kevin Carter and Ken Oosterbroek.

I didn't know them very well. Just in the way one knows photographers; a nod, or a wink, a 'Howzit, Kev' and a 'See ya, Greg' – the studiously casual that locks in somehow with the terrain of unexpected casualty. I was a scribe, a correspondent, a hack, a person who would explain all with the tones of detachment required of 'our man on the spot'.

At times one got a touch too close to the fabled spot and with a lurch of the stomach would look wildly around before seeing one of them 10 metres ahead, as reassuring a sight as it is to a shipwreck survivor seeing a gull carrying a fish with its promise of land.

They were reassurance as to how much more the envelope could be bent without the stamps falling off. They were the tough guys. They had to pin the tail on the donkey.

A game? A dance with death? A proving ground? In the end it is what you want it to be. Archbishop Emeritus of Cape Town Desmond M Tutu seems to think – judging from his foreword to the book – it is about liberation and the Third Force. To others, the theme would perhaps be more universal than that, making of it a classic of wartime reporting. And then it is more personal, intensely so – speaking from the personal to the personal and as such a prime exhibit for the argument that the only writing worth writing is introspective, the rest no more than finger exercises.

It was a story that could only have been told by a collaborative effort, but it demands a single voice. The voice is that of Marinovich, a young white South African of Croatian descent who has lost his God and his mother when he sets out on 17 August 1990 on a 25-minute drive to Soweto for what was to be 'the start of a new life for me'. The juncture is artificial, but then they always are in life. It is a point that Marinovich seems to understand by the selection of images, such as the following.

'Towards the very end the drugs she had been prescribed were not enough to keep her completely pain free and Mom knew she was too far gone for a cure. Every day, when the pain grew too great, she would ask me to run a hot, hot bath for her. Since she was too weak to bathe herself I would help her undress and lower her into the steaming water. She would gasp from the heat, but it would help the other, mortal pain. I found this experience very hard to handle: my mother was helpless and in immense pain, yet

I was embarrassed by her nakedness and it was difficult to accept that this fiercely independent woman could not even dress herself. I cannot recall what her face looked like at the time, but I clearly remember her plump belly in the water.'

A photograph is famously worth a thousand words. That took only 144, proving perhaps that words reach places that silver bromide cannot go. The silver bromide is there, including the Pulitzer pictures: Carter's of the vulture landing behind the crawling, starving, naked baby with no name in the Sudan and Marinovich's of Lindsaye Tshabalala's last petrol-soaked dance in a colourful costume of flame, a rhapsody in orange and red at F5.6.

Cameramen talk of the 'decisive moment' when the elements of a picture come together and are snatched, frozen by the great photographers. But decisive to what, one is tempted to ask at times? Decisive to the baby's life, or the cameraman's? Superficially Carter's picture was a symbol of world poverty. But its relevance to the life or death of the baby is a complete mystery, since he omitted to discover her fate. She may have lived happy ever after, for all we know.

But we do know that 'the budgie pic' – as it was to become known among professional colleagues – was decisive for Carter. It was a giant banana skin planted on his lifeline. From the moment he took his telephone call of congratulations from the *New York Times* – too doped with Mandrax and marijuana to understand what they were talking about – he began the last catastrophic slide to self-destruction with certainty, with the predictability almost of an actor captive to a script. He committed suicide, with a pipe up his car's exhaust.

In terms of human tragedy, Carter's story is far more deserving of a prize than the simplistic juxtaposition of a vulture and a baby, if not in the silver bromide category. For a start it moves beyond symbolism into the realm of storytelling with the presentation of a sublime paradox; that what may have been one of the great images of our time, in its appeal to our humanity, was snatched with such apparent inhumanity by a photographer who seemingly did not bother to see what happened to the baby, much less tried to help it.

But paradoxes do not exist, being merely an assertion, or a confession as to lack of understanding. And understanding of Carter is to be found there, in the accumulation of images that makes up the Bang-Bang Club.

The 'club' never existed, declare Marinovich and Silva at the outset. But it does and has long existed. It is not a professional organisation, or a drinking circle, but an association. Membership is open to those who survive the day to be left asking themselves not why Carter failed to pick up the baby, but why it was there. Not why Silva kept on taking pictures of his best friend's death, but how a round from a 'peace-keeper's' gun was fired at point blank range into Oosterbroek's chest.

'I was one of the circle of killers, shooting with wide-angle lens,' Marinovich writes of a mob murder at Soweto's Nancefield Hostel, which put him – a previously broke freelancer clutching 'obsolete cameras' – on the road to international reputation.

But the cameras are not just obsolete, they are irrelevant, as one discovers in the words he finds to conjure up the images of that long-ago murder: 'The Zulus and I took after him, a pack hunting its terrified prey ... the slithering, whispery sound of steel entering flesh, the solid thud of the heavy fighting sticks crushing the bone of his skull. Sounds I had never heard before, but they made sickening sense, as if this was exactly the noise a roughly sharpened, rusty iron rod should make when pushed deep into a human torso.'

There were no answers to be found there, in the circle of killers, even if one were able to stop the action and inquire of the participants. Marinovich did not join the club in Nancefield Hostel, but when he lowered his mother into the bath.

A camera, a page, a paintbrush, a musical score, the instrument one chooses does not matter; anything that comes to hand will do. Whether the images are from war or peace, from hostel or home, makes no difference. Membership is not to provide answers, or even to pose the questions. It is to fill the silence.

The disease

For most of the 20th century, Parkinson's disease had been treated, as a last resort, by burning out a malfunctioning section of the brain. This is the procedure, for instance, that the actor, Michael J Fox, underwent in the late '90s. But about 10 years before, a team of doctors in Grenoble, under the leadership of the neurologist Pierre Pollak, and the brain surgeon, Alim-Louis Benabid, had developed a new and less destructive technique known as DBS, or deep brain stimulation. In this procedure, an electric current is delivered to the trouble spot via a pacemaker buried under the collarbone. The operation is reversible and the results tend to be miraculous. Nobody is sure how or why it works, although there are theories.

The problem with DBS is that, in order to find the trouble spot, the patient needs to remain fully conscious. The Grenoble team is the best in the world at the technique, but being a research institution is also slow – 11 to 15 hours is the average duration of an operation. The length of time one's head is bolted down. Without benefit of anaesthetic. Or an aspirin.

The legend of Zuma

A favourite technique of identifying enemy agents in the liberation movement was to make members endlessly write their autobiographies. The theory was that an enemy agent trying to stick to their cover story, or 'legend', would sooner or later make a blunder that would be pounced on by their interrogator.

It seems that senior members of the ANC and members of the South African Communist Party (SACP) were not exempt from the rule, because on 2 May 1985 one Jacob Gedleyihlekisa Zuma sat down to write his biography. He seems to have been a conscientious man, or perhaps took the task seriously, because he managed to write 1 500 words – not bad for the son of a washerwoman who had not been to school. At the time he was a 'senior functionary' with NAT (Mbokodo) as well as a member of the National Executive Committee. A senior intelligence official testified to the NRC that 'powers' of the Mbokodo were 'pervasive'; NAT did not consider themselves accountable 'to the ANC generally or answerable to anybody specifically other than its head'. He was also a communist.

He had joined the SACP – or 'the family', as he euphemistically referred to it in his autobiography – at the age of 21, in 1963. His ANC and his government biographies do not mention his lifelong membership of the SACP, nor does his recently published biography by the Johannesburg journalist, Jeremy Gordin. But, by his own account, when he was incarcerated on Robben Island he confided the fact to Harry Gwala who was a fellow inmate at the time as well as a hard-line Stalinist. The ANC's Natal warlord told him that 'the whole question as to how the party was going to function was being considered'.

At the time a fierce ideological dispute was raging on the Island, between Gwala's followers and Nelson Mandela's supporters, making it necessary 'that some of us [communists] should not be exposed', Zuma quotes Gwala as saying to him.

Zuma completed his 10-year sentence in 1973, left South Africa in 1975, did four months training in the Soviet Union and on his return joined the Mbokodo (NAT).

NAT was a confused and confusing organisation, as was Zuma's role within it. It had been set up in 1969 under a former general secretary of the SACP, Moses Mabhida. It was answerable to the Revolutionary Council, which in turn fell under the Office of the President, Oliver Tambo.

'There was confusion over the role of NAT in the 1980s when it drifted away from intelligence-gathering and towards disciplinary activities as well as – in the case of Quatto (the ANC's main detention camp in Angola) – guard duties.'

In 1981 NAT was taken over by Mzwai Piliso. He was succeeded by Alfred Nzo on a temporary basis, and in 1987 Joe Nhanhla was appointed director of the Mbokodo with Zuma his deputy

In November 1989 came the death of Thami Zulu.

The Longest Day

Saw the chief neurologist, Pollak, and he indicated I was very suitable for the op. Looks like I'm on, in March/April next year. Gives me some time to ruminate. Tired. Nothing to what it will feel like on the day, I suppose. 'It will be the longest day of your life,' he said. Guess so.

Dear Tina

I would like to write to you. There is no need to reply, although replies will be very welcome even if they are only a sentence long, to reassure me this fax is working. I'm pretty slow at typing nowadays – using my left index finger most of the time – but I don't have much to do, other than to eat the delicious meals your daughter whips up for me and wait for a summons from the surgeons in Grenoble.

Ellen tells me you are in some pain and that the morphine patches are not helping much. Speaking as one with a low pain threshold (the dentist has to call in reinforcements to hold me down), it must be hell. Fortunately this weird illness I have got does not give me physical pain.

It's strange that I should have such an aversion to pain, because my father – who I did not know very well, but greatly admired – never had a painkiller in his life and never had an anaesthetic at the dentist despite many visits.

I can remember that he once made an appointment for me to be seen by his dentist. I was quite literally in a state of blind panic at the thought of even being examined by this man who, by his readiness to inflict pain on my father, was clearly a born torturer and no doubt a direct descendant of the notorious Marquis du Sade.

My father gave me quite clear directions as to how to get to his dentist's torture chamber: Room 510 in Such-and-such a building, at No. 15 So-and-so Street.

After the appointment and in response to an impatient call from his dentist, I was summoned into my father's presence. I was able to assure him that I had indeed presented myself at the appointed time on the fifth floor of No. 15 So-and-so Street, but that there was no trace of Room 510. There was a Room 509 and a Room 511, I explained, but the most meticulous examination of the wall in between had disclosed no trace of Room 510. It had gone, vanished, disappeared without trace, I assured him.

'What about the other side of the corridor?' my father asked.

I must say the dentist turned out to be a quite an amiable character as he inquired: 'With an anaesthetic, or without?'

I was an adult when my father died, but unfortunately I was still in those younger years when one thinks one understands everything. So I never did get around to asking him why he elected to be treated by his dentist without anaesthetic, or how he dealt with the pain. 'A Stoic,' I would have shrugged in those relatively pain-free years without even knowing who the Stoics were.

I often wonder, looking back now on my longer term of adulthood with more of an understanding as to the value of experience, why do we not get older people to leave records for their children and grandchildren. A sort of manual, or handbook which, when the youngsters run into the problems of adulthood, they can dig up from the bottom of some dusty drawer and rifle through its pages murmuring: 'I wonder if she ever faced a problem like this ...' As it is one finds oneself so unprepared, often only appreciating in retrospect that we have taken decisions without even recognising a decision was involved.

The only manual of that kind I have come across was the *Enchiridion*, which, as you probably know, was the handbook of the Stoics. I read it some time ago. If I remember correctly it offers the familiar Stoic advice – treat with indifference those things you cannot change, like the pain of a broken leg, and concentrate on the things you can change. I was a bit puzzled, however, by another piece of advice it gives – to hold one's wife and children at a distance, treating them like someone else's family, so that if one dies you will not grieve so deeply. There would seem to be a contradiction between those two bits of advice, which, I suspect, would have been recognised even by the boy looking for Room 510.

I wish you could be here with us, but Ellen tells me the doctors will not let you fly. Be assured that you are very much in our thoughts every day.

David

Death in the low country

A brave woman was cremated in Holland, in the small town of Groningen, mourned by many, unnoticed by most. She was the mother of my partner, Ellen. We didn't know each other particularly well, Tina Elmendorp and I; her English was not very good and my Dutch is nonexistent. Several years before, when she was visiting us in South Africa, I determined to sit her down and question her about her wartime experiences. I knew she had lived through the battle of Arnhem – of *A Bridge too Far* fame – and had been pregnant with Ellen at the time.

But I was startled when I asked whether she had ever feared for her life under German occupation and she replied thoughtfully that there was a period, when she was hiding a Dutch pilot who had escaped from Berlin, which had been frightening. When I mentioned it to Ellen, she was also startled. It transpired that Tina had never mentioned it to any members of her family.

It was, I suppose, something I should have born in mind when she announced she wanted euthanasia. I thought she would never go through with it.

It was her right, of course, under Dutch law. She was 92 years old; she has been battling bone marrow cancer – one of the most painful forms of the disease – for the last few years with the help of an oxygen tank and morphine. Her three daughters – settled in Germany, South Africa and the USA – were taking turns in nursing her.

I have long been opposed to euthanasia. My main objection is based on the same grounds as my opposition to the death penalty; that it dilutes the general taboo on the taking of human life. To my mind it is no coincidence that Franz Stangl, the commander of Treblinka, was effectively trained for the job on the Nazi euthanasia programme. But in this case my objections were more personal and I wrote to her explaining why her decision troubled me.

I had no objection to the idea of someone taking their own life. As John Donne put it, some 400 years ago: 'Whenever any affliction assails me, I have the keys of my prison in mine own hand, and no remedy presents itself so soon to my heart, as mine own sword.' Needless to say, I told her, after 10 years of Parkinson's the remedy had on occasion 'presented itself' to me as well.

My main concern where Tina was concerned was the daughters and the trauma for them of watching her go through with it. I nurse what I regard as a healthy scepticism towards the medical profession and was worried the doctors were not doing enough to deal with the pain. At the back of my mind was also the long-held suspicion that Socrates' noble end was something of a myth and that Seneca's botched job with the hemlock was a more likely scenario when it came to doing away with oneself.

Tina wrote back, saying that she had enjoyed a 'beautiful life' with her children and grandchildren. She had told her doctor and her daughters that she would 'try her best', but that the time would probably come when she could no longer get out of her chair and the pain was such she would no longer wish to live. That time had now arrived.

The mail is slow in these parts, so I only received the letter as I was writing this. But she made her decision clear by giving her family the precise time and date that she would drink the fatal mixture, rather than having the alternative of an injection. The doctor wanted it to be a Monday. He only carried out euthanasia about once in two years and always found it emotionally draining. Mondays were the easiest days to take off.

As required by Dutch law, a doctor specially trained to handle euthanasia cases who was a stranger to the family had visited her the week before to make sure there was nothing more that could be done to alleviate her condition.

The family had a Champagne party with her the night before and Tina made a speech. She was proud of the speech, noting in her diary that the Champagne had helped her speak well.

The doctor arrived on time the next day. Her children and grandchildren were beside the bed. The doctor asked her formally if she wanted to go ahead. Sometimes patients change their mind at this stage, but not Tina.

The youngest daughter handed her the cup. She drank it without hesitation, but as was her habit with tea and coffee, left some dregs. The doctor, knowing of cases where this was enough to make the dose less than fatal and forced a resort to a lethal injection – often with traumatic effect on the family – asked her to drink up. It took about 15 minutes to work, as the doctor had promised.

The funeral was scheduled for the Saturday. She had insisted that she would spend the intervening days in her own bedroom, in her own bed, rather than in a coffin or a funeral parlour. Undertakers came to the house and put a refrigerated slab under her body so that she could stay.

The week was like something out of a novel by Gabriel Garcia Márquez: the old matriarch lying, marble-like, upstairs and, downstairs, the family having dinners with lots of talking, laughing, crying, eating, drinking – just the way the old lady, who loved good company, would have wanted it.

The funeral was well attended. The eldest of the three daughters, Marianne, read out the lovely lines of desolation from WH Auden's love poem: 'Stop All the Clocks', slightly amended:

She was my North, my South, my East and West,
My working week and my Sunday rest,
My noon, my midnight, my talk, my song;
I thought that life would last for ever: I was wrong.

Ingrid, the youngest, described the qualities her mother had always shown. Her sense of curiosity, the attention she showed others, her persistence, her uncomplaining nature. 'She never moaned. I have tried it out for the week since she died and it is not easy.'

'I miss so much not being able to tell her how well it all went,' Ellen told the mourners. Euthanasia was a scary thought and everybody had been dreading it. 'But she made it easy for us. In spite of her pain and weakness, she managed to conduct her own death in such a way that we could find peace with it,' she said.

'It was clear that her decision had given her back her old pride and dignity: she was now in control – not the illness, not death, and not even us. She was once again the strong, wise mother of before. She took her decision and – just like when she would travel to see us – her suitcase was packed a week before. She had organised everything down to the last detail.'

When Tina swallowed the fatal cocktail and was waiting for those last 15 minutes of her life to pass she turned to the four grandchildren around the bed and asked: 'Aren't you bored? Don't you want to make it nicer, go and get some cakes or something?' She had been a teacher and lecturer all her working life.

Her last words were: 'Thank you, all.'

A conspiracy not to die

Probably the worst moment of his life came when he was about 15 years old and at boarding school. Two prefects came through to the dormitory and said the housemaster wanted to see him. He walked into the master's study to be told his brother was dead.

The next clear memory he was able to recall in later years was of reading a comic book in the housemaster's home across the road and of his wife peeking around the door and whispering to someone behind her: 'I think he's OK, he's reading.' He remembered being vaguely troubled by that comic book; feeling that it was somehow inappropriate to be reading one and hugely enjoying it on such an occasion. But, peering back across the decades at the boy that was me, I can understand the compulsion in the need to escape reality.

St John's Gospel says: 'The truth will set you free.' But the authority is undermined by the fact that it is carved in stone above the lobby at CIA headquarters in Virginia, which prompts immediate suspicion of duplicity. As any intelligent intelligence agent could testify, if they were stupid enough to do so, too much truth can just as easily blow the circuits as set one free.

Just as extreme physical pain will trip a safety fuse in the brain, allowing an escape into unconsciousness, so too the mind looks for ways to flee mental pain. Suicide is the ultimate escape from reality. 'Life is hard and then you die,' goes the saying and in the fearful anticipation of those twin certainties is born the longing to control the uncontrollable – an impulse in which much can be discovered by way of human behaviour. What is the attraction of wealth if not the potential it offers for the construction of an alternative reality in which the plumber will be too overcome by admiration for one's golden taps to sneer at one's ignorance as to the nature and the whereabouts of the stopcock?

For those who do not have access to the pretensions of money, escape tends to be into virtual realities created by others – notably those of popular culture in which the good guys not only always win, but are never known to suffer haemorrhoids. But how much more powerful is a custom-made, controllable reality in which the dreams are summons-able and the author is oneself.

The promise of such an escape route was there in the endlessly switchable, multiple channels of satellite and cable TV. The realisation of it is seemingly to be found in the addictive popularity of e-mail and the other forms of Internet chatter in which pseudo-identities offer endless means to the reinvention of personal reality.

Lights were out in the dormitory when he got back, so the comic book was no more help. In its place, in that long boarding school night, he created an alternative reality that his brother had gone to save the world on a mission so secret that nobody was allowed to know that he was still alive. So they pretended that he had died.

One day, he promised himself, he would see him across a street. He could never figure out if he should say hello to him when he saw him, or if that would put his life in danger. So he decided that he would just smile and his brother would smile back and they would walk on by. As if it was a conspiracy between them, a conspiracy not to die.

9/10/64

My darling, darling Ann

… Two amusing stories from the letter: one is about an eminent Scottish (Scots?) who believed (late 18th century) 'that we were born with tails and that it was a worldwide league of quick-witted midwives who had prevented this great truth from being known hitherto' …

Sorry, beetle, but I'll have to end this letter now, as I've had a brain test (with an EEG machine) & as part of the test they gave me sleeping pills which are really having effect now …

[Ann to John – no date]

I really am well, full of bounce. Even Meg according to her letter is having feelings most inappropriate to her way of life. I am reading (Ray Bradbury at the moment), listening to Joan Baez (especially 'Dona Donna'). I love the bit about the swallow and Brahms (a good indication of my strength of mind) and learning to drive – wait till I am zooming around the corners on the S13 tyres.

Feelings: I just long to be with you again although I know it may be some time. But you know you have all my love and that's all that really matters. Other things come and go but that never changes and never will. We are what we are because of the years we have been together. But I try to send you some more tangible love with every sweet and every … They come with all the love I cannot give myself.

Drama at the movies

I had a rough time at the cinema. I took a slight overdose of the L-dopa to counter the effects of a hurried chicken braai, but it was not enough and I got a bad case of the shakes in the middle of *Captain Corelli's Mandolin*. The people in the seats behind must have been a bit puzzled. But it was nothing on what was going on in my mind.

These are serious shakes, mind, at times approaching the severity of an epileptic attack. Everyone is watching the film, which is building to the usual Hollywood Third Act climax being assiduously milked by the hams on the screen. Being seated, I am not sure to what extent the shakes are accompanied by freezing.

If I try for the exit I may compound the disruption for those around me. What if I freeze while groping my way over people's legs, crutch in hand?

The incline of the auditorium is steep. I could lose balance and topple over into the row of seats in front of me. Talk about shouting 'Fire!' in a crowded cinema. Imagine the screams of a young woman with her boyfriend's tongue in her ear when a vibrating stranger falls into her lap from above … It's time to have the operation.

Professor Pierre Pollak
Department of Neurology
Central University Hospital
Grenoble

Dear Dr Pollak

You will recall that we met in October, when you found that I was suitable for bilateral subthalamic nucleus stimulation and said it would hopefully be possible to operate within the first half of this year. You were also kind enough to allow a television crew to film part of my examination and to interview you on camera in anticipation of a possible film about the operation.

To bring you up to date on the project, Britain's Channel 4 television station has formally commissioned an hour-long documentary on the operation. There is a possibility it will also be broadcast in the USA by *National Geographic*.

I appreciate the enormous pressure you must be under, but if it is possible to update me as to your likely operating schedule I would be very grateful. Needless to say I am, personally, most anxious to get an indication as to likely dates and any such information would help the film-makers with their own scheduling.

My apologies for troubling you with this.

Regards,
David Beresford

I've just had an e-mail from Grenoble offering 3 September as the 'big day'.

Killers at the movies

This day started with a trip to Springs, a small bustling town some 25 miles from Johannesburg, along the East Rand. The students wanted the law clerk to see the families of the dead in the Guguletu cinema incident a week before.

The events at Guguletu cinema, in KwaThema township in the early hours of a Tuesday morning, were overshadowed by the drama of the funeral later that day of the four hand-grenade victims, during which another two youths were allegedly shot by police in front of television cameras. But the police account of what happened at the cinema is on the record: 'Yesterday at 3 am a crowd of 400 people gathered in Nkosi Street, KwaThema, and threw various objects at the houses. The police arrived on the scene and some of the crowd fled into a nearby cinema. In an attempt to evade arrest, some climbed into the ceiling. One black female was injured when she fell through the ceiling and another after being hit by a rubber bullet. Three black males injured themselves in an attempt to flee. Thirty-six arrests were made, three of them female.'

In Springs, 27 blacks were waiting for us in a trade union office, ranging from a pastor in his dog-collar to bulky matrons in skirts fashioned out of blankets. The law clerk started methodically taking down their stories, most of which were similar: their sons or brothers had gone to the cinema for a prayer vigil for the hand-grenade victims – killed in premature explosions last month – and had later been found dead in the mortuary.

There was Leonard Marokoane, 19; Elias Vilakazi, 30; Abraham Twala, 18; Wellbeloved Mbatha, 16; David Maclontsela, 32; Vivi Mzizi, 17; Melba Mudontsela, 16; Aubrey Khubeka, 15; Archibald Ndaba, 14; and Thomas Nkambule, 19.

Wellbeloved Mbatha's father, Jeremiah – a well-built, middle-aged man in a sports jacket – wanted to get a couple of points off his chest. Whites at his works had said his son must have been up to something bad if he went to a meeting in the middle of the night. The whites did not understand that it was part of African tradition. 'A night vigil is one peaceful thing a black man does. It is part of our culture,' he said. 'It is the duty of the black people to come together for a vigil before a funeral.'

And he also wanted a message passed on to the Minister of Police, about the armoured personnel carriers used by security forces. 'That vehicle is called by the children "Death". When it comes, they just see "death". They don't throw stones at police, they are throwing them at death. To try and drive death away.' If this could be explained to the Minister, he said earnestly, perhaps he would remove 'death'.

Four students who said they were in the cinema – Shadraic Mhlanga, 18; Johannes Busakwe, 20; Millicent Kgwadi, 20; and Simon Marule, 19 – offered their account of what had happened. The students had planned an all-night prayer vigil in the cinema because there would be too many of them to gather in the homes of the four hand-grenade victims.

In the early hours of the morning police had started firing tear gas into the cinema – the doors of which had been locked since about 10 pm – and had then started breaking down the doors. Most of the youths had scrambled up two steel ladders at the sides of the screen to try to hide in the ceiling. But one boy among them had started crying and the police, hearing him, had opened fire with rubber bullets at the ceiling from the auditorium.

One or two girls had fallen through the ceiling. The rest of them clambered through a small door at the back and found themselves on the roof. They had waited there until police had left, and then escaped.

The cinema itself, in KwaThema, still bore the marks of the incident. The windows of the two ticket offices were starred from the impact of missiles, and side doors were splintered on their hinges. Inside the modern, if shabby, auditorium the ceiling, about 50 feet high, was studded with gaping holes and underneath one of them seats numbered 664 and 665 were buckled out of shape. Rips in the huge screen had been crudely patched together and there were bloodstains on the curtains. Behind the screen, in a corridor lined with offices and strewn with broken glass and old movie posters, the stench of tear gas was still overpowering a week after the event.

The projectionist said he had seen it all from the projection room. Police had come in with gas masks on, some of them with fixed bayonets. Yes, they had fired at the ceiling and two girls and one boy had fallen, one of them onto those buckled chairs. People had also taken refuge in the corridor at the back of the screen. Bloodstained items of women's underwear had been found afterwards, but he did not know what had happened there. No bodies had been found in the cinema and he only saw rubber bullets and tear gas being used – no conventional rounds had been fired.

The students said they were planning to bury in KwaThema all those who had died. No, they did not know how many they would be burying.

Then they insisted on dragging us over to Tsakane township to see Vusimusi Radebe's family. The story there was a familiar one. Vusi, aged 11, had gone out to play football. Later, his friends came running into the house to tell his aunt, Maria Khumalo, to come and look: Vusi had been shot by police. Khumalo said she went to the spot, a few blocks down the road, and found her nephew lying dead with a bullet wound in the back of his head. But the sun was sinking across the veld and it was time to go.

The Foreign Editor
The Guardian
119 Farringdon Rd
London

Dear Paul

… Had a long chat with Mike Holman, the Africa correspondent at the FT with Parkinson's. He has just had a pacemaker inserted in his brain in France. It seems to be a considerable success. It took 11 hours, fully conscious and bolted down – literally bolted down with titanium bolts in his head. Halfway through, they all took a lunch break. They left him bolted in, of course. But he says he could hear them around the luncheon table and 'they sounded so jolly I knew I was going to make it'. Great stuff! Of course Mike was diagnosed in '86 and I wasn't until '92, but he feels he should have had it done earlier. Tough one to call, but it sounds right. So I'm off to a local neurosurgeon to get a (very much) preliminary assessment next week. Still thinking of going off to see my Nobel laureate in Sweden next month in the hope he really does have a magic pill, rather than bolts to offer. Wish they'd hurry up with those bloody stem cells they're always blathering about.

Best wishes,
David

Darling, darling John

It was wonderful to get your letter (the one on yellow paper) especially as the last bit was only one day old. I am so glad you've seen the sun. I shall send you some special love wrapped up in sunshine every day ...

We now have a servant, Edith, who also 'dotes'. The other day I found her singing him to sleep with, not a Zulu lullaby, but 'My Friend Lollipop'.

I am not getting on very well with my driving at the moment. I don't seem to have enough nervous energy left for practising, but I am doing quite a lot of letter writing, keeping in touch with everybody ...

When you feel downhearted think of me and the millions of others who are behind you. Never doubt that for one moment.

This letter comes with all the love and pride that I have.

From your wife Ann

A solemn feast

It was on 26 March 1658 that Samuel Pepys, the diarist, underwent his operation for the removal of a kidney stone. Every year thereafter he celebrated the anniversary of 26 March with a dinner, 'this being', as he put it, 'my solemn feast for my cutting of the stone'. And so, in imitation of one of the most immortal of English writers, I hope to similarly celebrate 3 September.

The occasion, in my case, will not involve the cutting out of any stones. Instead there will a bit of drilling through my skull and some rummaging around in my brain. As ordeals go, mine (hopefully) will not match up to that of Pepys. Although the explorations by my surgeons will also be without benefit of anaesthetic and the procedure is scheduled to last at least 11 hours – as opposed to a matter of minutes during which, I presume, Pepys was under the knife – the operations are of course as different as the three and a half centuries separating them would suggest.

Pepys's operation took place some two years before he began the diary and he seems to have left no description. Perhaps one should be thankful for the omission; I, for one, would hesitate to read such an account out of respect for his powers of observation. But I do recall reading, or being told a story of how a latter-day Pepsyian scholar had dug up the surgeon's household accounts and discovered there a clue as to why the diarist had survived.

The accounts were said to show that the surgeon in question, Thomas Hollier, had happened to purchase a new knife a day or two before it was used on Pepys. The suggestion was that the apparent good fortune enjoyed by Pepys in being among a minority of survivors of Hollier's practice was due to the chance use of a comparatively clean blade.

I have been unable to establish the veracity or discover the source of that story. But the memory of it set me puzzling over the parameters of due prudence in the face of chance. To what odds will pain, or discomfort drive one; how far would one, or should one go by way of gambling with one's life in search of their relief? As far as patriotism?

Dicing with death in the name of patriotism is brought to mind by way of a remembered conversation with the commander of an American 'Bradley Fighting Vehicle'. It was at the end of the first day of the ground attack against the Iraqis in Kuwait during the Gulf War.

I had remarked that the war was akin to a turkey shoot in which the turkeys were predictably having trouble shooting back. He answered, thoughtfully, that they had been told during training those in his position – with head exposed above the turret of their armoured personnel carriers – had a only a 50 per cent chance of survival in battle conditions.

Would Pepys have accepted the bet if he had been told it was evens on his survival? Would the pain of the stone – said to have been the size of a (small, 17th-century) tennis ball – have been sufficient justification for him to share the odds seized by Bush's bushy-tailed boys? Would I have accepted the gamble if they had been the only odds available for a chance to put a (favourable) end to my shuffles and my shakes?

As it is, I have it seemingly easy. I am assured by the doctors planning to plant the brain pacemaker, designed to calm the malfunctioning area in my head, that there is only a two to three per cent chance of things 'going wrong'. Similar odds were given in reassurance by the rocket scientist, Wernher von Braun, to the US government and Alan Shepard as the astronaut prepared to become the first American in outer space.

My companion, Ellen, marked my birthday by producing a meal of Karoo lamb, which even a bon vivant like Pepys would have acknowledged to have been a feast. Two of my guests gave me books by Alain de Botton, showing their fine appreciation of the consolations of philosophy, particularly the potted, in times like mine.

But a more immediate lesson was offered by a third guest, a

civil rights lawyer and a silk, who recently survived a stroke. He described how, on his admission to hospital, his neurologist had cheerily advised him to keep his head as still as possible until they had assessed the damage on an I scan.

In the quiet and measured tone of irony with which he used to spear apartheid's officers in the witness box, he observed that the experience of knowing that a cough or a sneeze could 'switch off the lights' changed one's perspective.

He offered no amplification. But, watching him contentedly join in the feast laid before us, it struck me it does not matter when we celebrate. And the bookmaker has little relevance to the happenstances of time.

Dear Ellen

Just a short note I'll stick in an envelope to go with the will. I don't expect my 'literary estate' to amount to much and would like to make a nominal gesture to the kids by way of a present. I'd like the antique corner cabinet to go to Belinda. Tell her my mother said it was her most valuable personal possession and I suspect it is mine and it is in effect a bequest from both Faith and myself. Norm and Joris I leave to your discretion. You were always better at those sorts of decisions. And Maia so she doesn't feel left out? There are the antique card table, my binoculars, my old Boer War telescope, the Leica and the Johnson dictionaries. Heavens, not very much, is it?

I would have very much liked to give something to Sara and Daniel. The Walter Meyer for Sara? I've always loved it, not least because it was a present from you, so you can give it as a love present – a bit of South Africa – from both of us. I wish I had a nice chess set for Dan on which he and you could keep on playing. But tell them both I hope they will benefit a little in the end from my small bequest to you.

Give them all my love
And to you, too.
Your David

J'accuse

If this is 'J'accuse', then Thami Zulu must be its Dreyfus. His real name was Mzwake Ngwenya, but everyone knew him as Thami Zulu or 'TZ'. He lies in a cemetery in the tiny kingdom of Swaziland. He was buried there in November 1989.

It was a strange funeral. The mourners were limited almost entirely to members of the dead man's family. Which was what made it strange, because they were burying a hero.

If there had been any doubt that he was a hero, the doubt would have been laid to rest by a statement read out at the graveside. Signed by Joe Modise and Chris Hani, Commander and Chief of Staff respectively of the ANC's Umkhonto we Sizwe, it contained ringing tributes to the man who was being buried: '... [The] glorious army of our people salute you ... we remember your efficiency and competence ... we recall with sheer pride and emotion ... this giant and gallant fighter ...'

But for all the tributes, the statement had to be read out by the dead man's sister, because the few anti-apartheid activists present at the burying of the hero were too scared to do it themselves. And the story that lies behind that fear – a tale of paranoia, personal tragedy and that most cowardly form of murder, by poison – is one that haunts the South African liberation struggle.

The tragedy of Thami Zulu is that of the lonely death of a man who had all the courage of a warrior, but lacked the knowledge as to where the enemy lay.

He was born in Soweto, the huge sprawling township outside Johannesburg, the eldest child of two school principals. That was an advantageous beginning for a township boy in a country where the authorities made the stunting of young black minds a matter of policy. He took full advantage of his parentage, claiming first-class honours at school in Soweto and then in Swaziland, where the brightest of black South African children escaped the limitations of apartheid's system of Bantu education. He had wanted to go on to Johannesburg's white University of the Witwatersrand to study civil engineering, but was refused racial exemption. Instead he enrolled at the University of Botswana, but abandoned his studies in his first year to join the ANC.

His rise in South Africa's main liberation movement was sensational. He was sent for training in the Soviet Union where, by one account, he was so successful that an attempt was made to recruit him into the Soviet army. But he returned to become a commander of the Umkhonto we Sizwe training camps in southern Angola. It was there that his talents were spotted by the Chief of Staff, Chris Hani, and he was appointed to overall command of the Natal theatre of operations, basing himself initially in Swaziland and later in the Mozambique capital of Maputo.

Natal was a difficult battleground, fought over with particular viciousness by both the South African security services and the ANC. Thami's predecessor as regional Chief of Operations, Zwelakhe Nyanda, had been assassinated by South African agents. During his time Thami managed to step up the onslaught to the point where the coastal city of Durban was known as 'South Africa's bomb capital' and he was soon being talked of as a future successor to Hani.

But his career came to an abrupt end after two disastrous incidents in 1988 near the town of Piet Retief in the southeastern Transvaal, in which 19 combatants were massacred in two separate ambushes after crossing the Swaziland border.

The killings of the 16 cadres had a traumatic impact on the ANC. Thami's deputy, Cyril Raymond – alias 'Ralph' and 'Fear' – and his wife, 'Jessica', were summoned to Lusaka. Cyril subsequently died in detention, having refused to sign a confession to being a South African agent. He is said to have drowned in his own vomit.

Cyril's wife – then a probationary member of the Central Committee of the South African Communist Party – was imprisoned as a suspected spy. Then Thami himself was called in by headquarters, placed under house arrest and eventually formally detained.

Thami's detention, which came as a shock to the military, was without the sanction of either Modise or Hani. The two commanders made furious demands inside the ANC National Executive to know the basis of Thami's detention and to have access to him. Both were refused. Hani did manage to see him briefly at an early stage, in the company of Thami's father who had flown to Lusaka from Johannesburg to find out what had happened. Thami insisted he had no idea on what basis he had been held.

The former Natal commander was finally released in Lusaka – after 14 months in detention, including eight weeks in solitary confinement – on 11 November 1989. Five days later he was dead, at the age of 35.

Brain surgery and claustrophobia

Strolling through the corridors of the University Hospital in Grenoble, in the company of a neurologist, Professor Krack, I hesitated as we were about to walk into a lift. 'Aha,' said the neurologist. 'Claustrophobia! We'll have to do something about that for the MRI machine.'

He was referring to the giant scanner into which patients are slid, to the great discomfort of claustrophobes among their number. He was quite correct, needless to say. I had, in fact, survived two trips into an MRI machine. But I did have a mildish form of claustrophobia, which made me a bit more unhappy than other lost souls who might inadvertently clamber into a steel coffin masquerading as a lift.

At the same time, I was reluctant to acknowledge the point. As a man who likes to be known as ... well, if not exactly a war correspondent, then a foreign correspondent with a few 'small wars' under his belt, it seemed to me to be a bit unseemly to be susceptible to panic caused by enclosure in a not particularly small space like a lift. For, in truth, you'd be surprised at the number of stairs I've clambered just to avoid those closing lift doors.

I returned to South Africa, after my 'getting to know you' visit to Grenoble, determined to do something about the claustrophobia. What I had to do seemed fairly simple – accustom myself to enclosed spaces, and *voilà*. So I stuck my head into a gap created by a particularly heavy coffee table we had at home. Soon I felt I had that little phobia mastered and moved on to what I saw as a related problem: in the form of what I thought of as 'the bolts'.

In the early days of my wait for the Grenoble ordeal, it used to give me some satisfaction to inform the ill-informed that my brain operation would be conducted without benefit of anaesthetic, with my head bolted down, and that the procedure would last a minimum of 11 hours. The looks of horror and squeals of concern prompted by this announcement would give me great satisfaction.

After a while, however, as the clock ticked away towards my appointment with the brain surgeons, my bravado began to give way to concern. I found myself questioning my 'guru', the *Financial Times'* Africa editor and doyen of the rat pack on the dark continent, Mike Holman. 'Holman of Africa,' as he is respectfully known, had lived with Parkinson's for an extraordinary 17 years, and had had the (hugely successful) operation himself. 'Uuugh, Mike,' I would find myself saying on the telephone to him, with much clearing of the throat. 'Uuuugh, these bolts.'

'Yes, what about them?

'Well, where exactly are they attached?

'To your head,' he would say.

'Ahhh, yes. I see, of course …'

Finally, one day, I got my courage up and, with the no–nonsense tones of a foreign correspondent who has seen it all before, I cornered him. 'Uugh, Mike.'

'Yes, David?'

'You know those bolts?'

'Mmm …'

'Well, you've got them bolted, on one side, to your head?'

'That's right.'

'Uuuuugh, what about the other side?'

'What's that?'

'Uuuugh, well, what will I be bolted to? I mean, presumably these titanium bolts are bolted to something?'

'Oh, to various things,' he said. But I had gone too far down the path now to be put off. 'You mean I will, in the end, be bolted down?'

'In a manner of speaking. Ultimately, yes. They're incredibly light, you know.'

'Huhhh?'

'The bolts, they're made of titanium. They cost about $200 each. It's very important your head doesn't move.'

'Ohhh yes, I can understand that. Ha, ha, ha, ha …' I said, carefully replacing the receiver.

Either way, I must confess I was scared witless. Bolted down. Cautiously, I tried the words out. 'Bolted down'. 'BOLTED down'. 'Bolted DOWN'. No, I realised, there was no other way of putting it. Bolted down was bolted down and that was that. You were either bolted down, or not. For 11 bloody hours. At least.

I have always suspected that my phobia was wider than fear of enclosed spaces and that the real problem was fear of restraint. I won't go into it in detail here, but I knew from my reaction to the sight of men in shackles and handcuffs that I had a horror of forced restraint. It was so embedded in me that, on one occasion many years ago, I was entertaining a young woman in a posh restaurant with a show of worldliness when I said, grabbing her hand: 'Aha, a Claddagh ring – that's from Ireland,' and absent-mindedly slipped it off her finger and on to mine, only to find it was stuck.

I will pull the curtains down on the rest of the scene; worldly correspondent squawking, head waiter and sidekicks hurrying over with blocks of butter, hot and cold water and so forth and so on …

Well, if it was more than claustrophobia, the solution remained the same, I reassured myself. Training, familiarisation. I was going to a gym by this stage, on the urging of a friend who saw a need for me to prepare for the coming ordeal. Or at least to be distracted from it. I had the proprietor of the gym tie my head down with straps for a few minutes and managed to convince myself it would all be easy in surgery.

So it was that on the day before what I thought of as Brain Day – the day I was to have various French surgeons of great distinction poking around inside my brain – that I found myself being trundled to the basement of Grenoble University Hospital for an I scan with what I suspect may have been a happy grin on my face. Not only had I assured myself back home that my claustrophobia had been beaten and that being bolted down didn't matter a fig, but I had had another quiet chat with the neurologist.

He had explained that it was essential that my head be kept absolutely still during the scan; to make absolutely sure that there would be not a trace of a shake. There was no shame involved. I just had to have a full dose of L-dopa and two of liquid Valium before I went into the I machine. So, who was I to quarrel?

It was with considerable confidence, therefore, that I headed for the lair of the I machine, in the Grenoble Hospital basement, only to find a young man awaiting me who spoke very good French until he heard mine. 'Ah, well that makes it easy,' he said with an unmistakably American accent.

This was Brad.

In the belly of the beast

Let me be clear from the outset. I have no prejudice against Americans. As I have had occasion to observe before, the world is – at least in my belief – fairly fortunate in its choice (if choice is involved) of modern imperialists. They strike me as not too bad as imperialists go. But one prerequisite for ruling the world is, of course, self-confidence. Brad, bless his soul, had oodles of it – oodling out of every pore.

I had, of course, heard of Brad before. A surgeon from Florida, I had been told, had attached himself to the Grenoble team to learn the technique of the Parkinson's operation. But somehow, until I met him, I had not expected him to be so young, so busily efficient. And so bubbling over with bloody confidence.

Brad had confidence in aces, spades and any other trumps a card table might care to designate. In seconds he had me out of bed. 'Here, we'll just use this,' he cried out, bundling me into an office chair on castors. He scooted me into the MRI room.

'I'll just screw this on,' he announced, busily screwing the helmet that was the stereoscopic frame on to my head.

'Aaaaah,' I said, trying to raise myself from my throne with one finger waving in the air. 'Aaahhhhh,' I repeated, Ozymandias trying to reimpose his authority on the landscape. 'Claustrophobia!' I squawked.

Brad would have none of it. Slam, bang and I was on my back. Click, clack and the grill that was the MRI helmet was shut. 'It'll all be over in a moment,' said Brad cheerily, as the motors began to whine and the I carefully lifted me, ready to slide me into its steel womb. 'Here, you can press that if you have a problem,' placing the emergency button into my by-now limp hand. I heard the patter of feet as he hurried to the control room.

In my defence, I was prepared to have a go at it. But I knew that without the L–dopa I did not have a chance of maintaining at least the minimal stillness required by the massive magnetic camera. Sure enough, no sooner was I in place than my right arm began its pathetic waving. Bang, bang, bang, it tapped against the steel wall … bangity bang. An incredulous silence came from the control room.

Another patter of feet and an anonymous hand grabbed mine, gave it a reassuring squeeze and pattered off again with an air of confidence, a job well done. Bangity bang. There was another incredulous silence. The anonymous hand came pattering back, squeezed and departed.

Bangity bang, went my hand, hopelessly. A loud speaker clicked on and a voice made a declaration in French. It could have been an announcement of an outbreak of fire as far as I was concerned. I clutched the emergency button, briefly contemplated my hard work under the coffee table at home and then – with the abrupt thought, 'Ah, fuck it!' – abandoned the hopeless struggle and, with a short prayer that it was not a dummy, pressed the emergency button.

I was bundled out with impressive alacrity, and, ensconced once more on my makeshift throne, scooted into an anteroom. 'Just get me Dr Krack,' I said wearily. Half an hour later, with Krack's comforting hand on my shoulder and a cocktail of L–dopa and liquid Valium sloshing around in my blood, I made it through the I in a chemical haze of happiness.

And so it was that, after reassurances that the only difference the next day would be that my head would slide into the helmet, rather than vice versa, I anxiously awaited what Pierre Pollak, the chief neurologist, had assured me would be the longest day in my life.

Countdown

Outside, birds call in the treetops. Inside, a woman wails next door, at times with impatience, at other times with hopelessness. 'Mama, mama,' she cries day and night. One must be charitable towards the mother for her desertion. The daughter is in her nineties, seemingly lost to time in the thickets of a senile mind.

The window on the second floor of the university hospital frames the Massif du Vercors in the lower Alps. In one week the surgeon will be drilling into my skull and beginning the long slow trek into my brain. Into my mind? I ask myself, gazing out of the hospital window in the old French town of Grenoble.

The neurological wards are distinguishable from others, apart from the cries for mother, by the fact that the windows are all locked shut. 'In case of suicide,' the staff explain kindly.

I try to explain that I'm from Africa and likely to be reduced to a suicidal frame of mind by a lack of fresh air, but it does not help.

Eventually my roommate, who looks like the French actor Michel Piccoli, but has been introduced as a Marseilles fisherman, helps me force the locks with a nail file. We stand triumphantly in the fresh air. A cleaner wanders in. At the sight of the violated window, she pirouettes in her canvas shoes towards the door and carefully closes it behind her before running, squealing down the passage.

We glance at each other. Nobody comes. We begin to gabble in mutual incomprehension, my French having proved less endurable than the memory of the clubs of boredom and canes of reprimand with which they had attempted to bludgeon the language into me, in the bushveld some 40 years before.

I think I have understood enough to establish that my roommate is a successful fisherman, owning either a large boat boasting two propellers, or two boats of a more moderate size with a largish propeller each. I've made several sallies on the subject of fish-stocks, whaling and the iniquitous malpractice of Spanish trawlers in the south Atlantic when my Ellen, who is Dutch and multilingual, arrives with our son who is a linguistics scholar.

My newfound fisherman friend is transformed on the moment into a Marseilles magistrate with a boat run for fun and in the enjoyment of fresh air.

The window changes when I'm handed over to the neurosurgery department in a neighbouring block. It is still locked shut, but frames the mountains of Belledonne in which the resistance fighter, Jean Moulin, and Klaus Barbie, the Gestapo chief of Lyon – who eventually captured and tortured him – used to hunt one another.

This time my roommate is a truck driver of 34, who underwent surgery three years ago for a tumour on the brain, which proved untreatable. The next two operations were emergencies, when he developed brain infections. All three operations took place on 25 August. 'I don't believe in coincidences,' says the mother.

My French is too limited to ask what she does believe in. From her smile of greeting, quite a lot. The son's air is one of preoccupation, but the smile when it does come promises to haunt me.

I have to face three operations: one, an hour and a half under general anaesthetic, to insert the bolts in my skull; then the 12-plus hours with drill and electronic probes, bolted down without anaesthetic, in search of the malfunctioning part of the brain; finally there will be the connecting up of the planted electrodes and the implantation of the pacemaker.

'It will be the longest day of your life,' Pollak had predicted. The longest day? I play with the notion in my mind. What would it have been before – the Gulf War? I smile to myself: captured three times in 48 hours by the Allies – the world's first virtual reality war. They should have played it in a penny arcade.

Waiting for Mandela? Perhaps. Sometimes I wonder if that wasn't when something went pop in my brain – facing a 20-minute deadline to paint a word-picture of the culmination to the long walk to freedom by the great man. A walk I had not seen, but which the rest of the world had.

Or was it that rugby tackle, which left me unconscious for an hour? Or the pieces of the Scud missile I had picked up in the Gulf. Or was it the members of South African Military Intelligence who had me under surveillance, trying out the latest devil's brew whipped up by their chemical weapons chief, Wouter Basson?

In a window on the fifth floor of the university hospital in Grenoble, I can be seen hunched over my keyboard, waiting for the signal that it is time to go home.

Ready, steady …

They came at 8.30 am. He had been awake since 6.15 am. He had had his shower, emptying the bottle of antiseptic soap and anxiously washing his bellybutton, like the sign said on the wall. Infection was the killer. At 7.20 am the nurses had bundled him into his bed, wrapped in sheets and blanket. Routine, he thought. What did he expect, a farewell party? Cheering crowds?

The neurologist cursed and threw something into the rubbish bin.

'What's gone wrong?' I asked wearily.

The Angel's face popped up from below the level of the operating table. 'Nothing is wrong,' she said happily. 'Why did you think something was wrong?'

We smiled at each other, me and the Angel. Stupid of me to have forgotten her name under the surgeon's knife. Angel would just have to do.

Actually, I was under the surgeon's drill. *Drrrrrrr … drrrrrrr … drrrrr.* It sounded like an old-fashioned hand drill, I thought idly. Not the dentist's drill I had been promised. Don't move your head. You can't move your head. Oh my God, I can't move my head. Don't think of not being able to move your head. Don't think of it, don't think of it …

Recollections in tranquillity

On consideration, the longest day in my life was a double marathon I ran as a teenager in South Africa as the result of a foolish debt. I did finally stagger across the finishing line with some 14 minutes to spare, sit down in a beer tent and have myself a couple. When I tried to get up my leg muscles were in spasm and I had to suffer the humiliation of being carried away by course officials in a sitting position, which was to last three days. The pain was indescribable; suffice to say, never again.

The Grenoble operation was not quite as bad, although – the main coping mechanism being denial – much of the memory of it has no doubt been lost. Being bolted down in the helmet was rather like being pinned down to the table like an ant by a massive thumb. The question as to whether it was the thumb pinning me down, or me being pinned down by the thumb seemed to be an issue of massive irrelevance in the circumstances. The point was that I was pinned down, for something like 13 hours.

If several aspects of the operation are lost to memory, some may have been invented by a fevered brain. Did the neurologist curse in the middle of the proceedings as he threw what I was convinced was an essential working part into a nearby rubbish bin?

But I do clearly remember lying there in a state of misery, trying to imagine what had gone so dramatically wrong.

When it was all over and I was unbolted by Brad and wheeled away, I found myself weeping. Brad, bless his soul, could not figure that one out. 'But it is all over,' he kept repeating. 'You've done it!'

I couldn't find the words to explain to Brad that the operation was nothing, just like the drama of the MRI machine was nothing. I was weeping at what had driven me to them: 10 years of living in another country known as Parkinson's disease.

Bewitched

Some years ago Martha Gelhorn passed through South Africa on her way to Mozambique. A dinner was given in her honour. Asked what she planned to do in Mozambique, the writer and former war correspondent – then in her seventies and almost blind – said she hoped to do some diving around the coral reefs there.

Then she added darkly that she also hoped to see a Shangaan sangoma, or witch doctor to put a curse on the Harley Street surgeon who had nearly blinded her with a bungled eye operation.

Subsequently Ellen and I had a drink with her in her London flat and I asked how it had gone with the witch doctor. She said off-handedly that he had thrown the bones, but had told her not to waste her time on the doctor. He was already dying of a terminal disease.

I once consulted a witch doctor. It was in the northern Transvaal and it did not go too well. About 15 metres away from me, across an open space from the sangoma's hut, there was an old woman tethered to a stake. She seemed to take a great interest in me, gibbering and gesticulating. I asked the witch doctor, busy over his bones, who she was. He said it was his mother. I was disconcerted by this. The rubric, 'Physician, heal thyself' may have fallen into discredit in modern times, but I could not help but feel that he could have done a bit more healing where his mum was concerned. Shortly afterwards he announced that the bones were not working. He seemed to blame me for having insufficient faith.

All medicine, I suspect, demands an act of faith; none more so than for those who enter the plague houses that are modern hospitals. Once, in Belfast, I had to rush my daughter to the Royal Victoria Hospital with a minor hand injury, only too see her land up in an isolation ward, being treated for an infection that they only managed to stop by the amputation of the end of one of her fingers. Here in South Africa my neurologist, like Gelhorn, underwent an eye operation and nearly died as a result of an infection in his own hospital. 'It nearly reached my brain,' he told me later with the tone of a man who knew better than most what that implied.

All of which is by way of self-justification for the length of time it has taken to report back after my recent brain operation in Grenoble for Parkinson's. In matters of health, it seems to me, it is as well not to tempt fate. It was nearly three months after the operation before I nervously took stock. Was it successful?

The expectation with this operation is that the patient will improve by about 84 per cent and I would say that the figure is fair enough in my case. The shakes that notoriously characterise Parkinson's have largely gone – surfacing only if the stress level gets too high. My mind, as such, seems unaffected. In fact almost the only traces of the operation are a piece of wire, which could be mistaken for a vein, or sinew, neatly threaded under the scalp from the top of the skull and running down behind my ear to the pacemaker. The pacemaker in turn looks like an old-fashioned fob watch that has lodged itself inexplicably under the skin, below the collarbone.

I have been able, nearly, to give up the main anti-Parkinson's drug – the miraculous and yet dreaded 'Popeye drug', Levadopa. Instead I take a small dose of a dopamine agonist – a less-powerful drug that mimics L-dopa – to deal primarily with a condition known as 'restless legs'.

It is a peculiar syndrome, restless legs. The English language does not appear to have a word to adequately describe it. 'Burning … itchy … hot … ticklish …' None of them fits. It appears to hit people whether or not they have Parkinson's and is marked by an overwhelming urge to stand and, if possible, to walk about and move one's legs. It can be hell in a cinema, or as a passenger in a car, or stuffed into an aeroplane passenger seat.

The story is told of one woman in New York who had it so badly that she and her husband installed an exercise bike in the back of a van. When they wanted to travel, he drove and she pedalled.

Before the operation, or 'before Grenoble', as I tend to refer to it, I had a mild case of restless legs, which seemed to respond to stretching exercises. Since Grenoble, the condition has become much worse. The syndrome is fast becoming recognised in the medical profession. Classified increasingly as a 'movement disorder', it has been found that most cases respond to Parkinson's drugs, again whether or not they have Parkinson's.

And then there is the psychological side: What is it like to be a 21st-century cyborg, with wires coming out of my skull? When I think of it – which is not often – the thought of a wire running deep into my brain is vaguely unsettling, but nothing more. But there are other thoughts.

It is perhaps something of a cliché that when one comes

through a life-threatening experience, one does feel a need for change, a reluctance to return to the old ruts of habit, a longing for a new understanding of something that lies just beyond reach of the mind.

One begins to question what was previously unquestionable. Before Grenoble, I spent much of my time revisiting, as a journalist, stories I had done in the past – trying to figure out what precisely drove me, puzzling over the industry's priorities, our pursuit with such passion of murder, massacre and genocide, of misery and death. Why does the world press photo exhibition so often resemble a slaughterhouse? What drove me, retching, to the rocket-blasted walls of the church at Ntarama in Rwanda, to peer at its hideous congregation of corpses?

Life tends to be thought of as movement and, perhaps understandably, a person who has Parkinson's develops something of a fixation about freedom of movement. The sense of movement to be found in driving my rusty old Mercedes sports car, or soaring through the air with a vet-turned-pilot in a micro-light, dive bombing the crocodiles and hippos in the Kruger Park's Olifants River. It all seemed a sublime escape from the shuffles and the shakes symptomatic of Parkinson's.

But now that I have the opportunity again to do those things, I realise that they represented only temporary escape, as opposed to the liberation I was looking for. Perhaps I was not looking for relief from immobility, but from fear; fear of Parkinson's and all it entails – fear of paralysis, fear of unemployment, fear of loneliness, fear of death.

V677
Pretoria Central Prison
Private Bag 45
Pretoria

17/10//64

My own darling Ann

... Today we've been married exactly five and a half years ...

My love, I keep feeling a sense of great necessity to tell you emphatically how I love you. Please let this fact permeate you, sink into your essential fibre, be part of your core. You must know this, as you know that $1 + 1 = 2$ ...

Your own John

Double, double toil and trouble

During the 1990s, the conflict in Venda centred primarily on witchcraft and medicine murders, which had become increasingly widespread during the 1980s. During the 1990s, protests against witchcraft were closely linked to the rejection of the homeland government, which was believed to be responsible for or complicit in this practice. Protests against the homeland government lead to a military coup in April 1990 in which Chief Minister Ravele was ousted. Between January and March 1990, about 20 people were reported to have died during anti-witchcraft unrest. People accused of being involved in medicine killings or being witches and wizards were hacked or burnt to death. After a rally in Venda capital, Thohoyandou, celebrating the release of Nelson Mandela in February 1990, more than 50 houses were burnt down and hundreds of people had to flee their homes. Many of the victims were elderly. The link between anti-homeland government protests and anti-witchcraft protests in Venda is reflected in the amnesty applications of a number of youths involved in the murder of alleged witches and wizards. The amnesty applicants specifically state that they believe their actions contributed to the downfall of the former Venda government, that medicine murders were associated with the homeland government, and that the practice of witchcraft by witches and wizards had to be routed out as it reflected backwardness and superstition. By eliminating such 'backward' practices, they believed that they were helping to ensure that Venda became a modern and democratic society. The Commission received some statements from people who were attacked on suspicion of being witches and consequently suffered gross human rights violations.

(VOL. 3 P731 TRC FINAL REPORT)

Beating depression

'These are for you,' I said, walking into my brain surgeon's Cape Town rooms with a bunch of flowers and presenting them to him. 'You've made my speech worse and I suspect you've screwed up my balance. But what you've given me has a price greater than rubies.'

I am blessed with the attendance of a number of brain doctors around the world for the Parkinson's disease I suffer. After Grenoble, I got any post-operative treatment I needed from a local surgeon in Cape Town. A few days before presenting him with the flowers, I had been in to see him complaining about the deterioration in my speech. He fiddled around with a magnetic switching device used to adjust the pacemaker and off I went, after promising to report back and tell him if there was any improvement.

That evening I happened to be speaking on the telephone to my youngest son in Holland when something he said started me laughing. To my embarrassment the laughing would not stop. Eventually I had to say a hurried goodbye and cut the call.

It was not until the following day that I began to realise something fairly fundamental in me had changed. And not only in me, it seems, but for mankind.

Some months before I had made a post-operative visit to my neuro-team (as I like to think of them) in Grenoble I raised the issue of depression. Was I depressed? And if so, was it a result of Parkinson's disease, or of the operation and the pacemaker? The neurologist proceeded to cross-examine me, asking – among other things – whether I had thoughts of suicide. 'Heavens, yes,' I replied, 'often. But I have no intention of committing it.'

I should perhaps explain here that I saw suicide (or so I told myself) as a philosophical issue. My mother-in-law, with cancer and in her nineties, recently opted for euthanasia and carried it out with extraordinary courage and single-minded determination.

My father had been trapped, by a series of strokes, in that awful place from which one can no longer communicate with the world. Suffering a degenerative disease myself, I'd be almost remiss if I never thought about it. But depressed! Me?

'Yes,' said the French neurosurgeon. It was not serious, but could become so and he prescribed an antidepressant. Back in South Africa I dutifully took the drugs, but when they had failed to have any significant effect after several months I took myself off them.

Which is where things were when I arrived in the rooms of my Cape Town brain doctor, demanding that he do something about my speech.

The day after my fit of laughter on the telephone to my son, life was transformed. An overcast day was no longer cause for despondency, but a glorious change in the weather. I used to wake at 9 am in the morning, sometimes at 11 o'clock (in Africa, of all places, the continent of the early riser), now I was waking at 5 am and – after nervously taking mental stock – couldn't (or wouldn't) go back to sleep. There was so much to do and such fun to be had. Who wants to sleep when there is life to be lived! The value of rubies? They are as bits of coloured glass and worthless when measured against the things that really matter.

I hurtled down the lower slopes of Table Mountain on my bicycle into the city centre, frightening the children and local dogs by my attempts to yodel as I went. In the lovely old building that is the South African National Library, with its banks of computers, I dived (metaphorically, of course) into the Net. 'Deep brain stimulation' and 'depression', I asked Google.

And there was the answer.

'They're using deep brain stimulation to treat depression,' I told my Cape Town brain doctor with wonderment.

'I don't know anything about that,' he replied candidly.

'The Canadians seem to be leading the way,' I said. 'You must have done it by accident.'

I sent a hurried e-mail to Grenoble, telling them what had happened. Back came the reply in the form of a lengthy message with attachments from learned journals. How did I miss it, I groaned to myself? And I have family and friends who think I am obsessive in my fascination with Parkinson's!

It is an astonishing story contained in those journals, which can perhaps best be told by starting with a paper that must have Nobel prize-winning potential. It was published by the journal, *Neuron*, by Mayberg HS and others. In the paper, Dr Helen Mayberg and colleagues from Toronto University reported the discovery that a small area in the frontal cortex is implicated in depression. Application of electrical stimulation to the area had 'striking and sustained remission' in four out of six patients suffering treatment-resistant depression.

The implications are extraordinary. As they observe, 'treatment-resistant depression is a severely disabling disorder with no proven treatment options once multiple medications, psychotherapy and electroconvulsive therapy have failed.' Not only does it offer a means of treatment for tens of thousands, but – in the words of one senior neurologist – 'this paper really is the beginning of the return of psychosurgery'. Which is enough to have me, and no doubt many others, offering up a short prayer to the international neuro-community: 'Please, guys, don't screw it up this time.' Because last time the screw-up was spectacular, thanks to Freeman and Moniz.

Walter Freeman and Egas Moniz are two names that are likely to be forever associated with a pioneering form of psychosurgery. The story of lobotomy is well known. But, briefly, Moniz won the Nobel prize in 1949 for the medical breakthrough on which lobotomy was based. Unfortunately the prize had the effect of giving an imprimatur to Freeman's performance of the operation. Freeman in effect ran amok, using an ice pick with gay abandon to separate the prefrontal lobes of his patients. It was said his surgical technique was so upsetting to observers that seasoned physicians were known to collapse in his operating theatre with nausea. Thousands suffered his attention, the most famous being the beautiful actress and political activist, Frances Farmer, who was lobotomised on the grounds she was too much of a rebel against authority.

Another paper I received from France threw some light on my mirth during that telephone conversation with my son. It was published by the journal *Movement Disorders* and written by my Grenoble neuro-team, 'Paul Krack et al.' The authors included the two leaders of the unit at the University of Grenoble, the surgeon Alim-Louis Benabid and the neurologist, Pierre Pollak, who have become world famous through their development of what I call my 'pacemaker operation' – technically known as deep brain stimulation (DBS) of the subthalamic nucleus (STN) – which is fast becoming the standard treatment for advanced Parkinson's.

The paper's title is self-explanatory: 'Mirthful Laughter Induced by Subthalamic Nucleus Stimulation.' If emphasis were allowed, it would be on the word 'mirthful'. As the paper points out, pathological laughter is known to be associated with neurological disease, including epilepsy. The difference was that 'the laughter attacks reported in this paper were associated with humour, appreciation and mirth.'

The paper describes the cases of two patients on whom they had experimented by raising the stimulation levels to a point where laughter and associated dyskinesias (uncontrolled movements) were induced. One of the patients seems to have been particularly witty. 'The laughter was highly infectious and several neurologists who were present in the room also fell into a hilaric state. For example, when looking at the nose of Professor Benabid, the patient thought of the nose of Cyrano de Bergerac (as he told us later) and started another burst of laughing, pointing at Professor Benabid's face. When Dr Krack could not restrain himself anymore and fell into a burst of laughter, the patient shouted "*il craque*" (he has a burst) and this pun led to a generalised burst of laughter of all the people present including the patient.'

In both cases, extreme stimulation resulted in improvements in mood, motivation, libido, and a general enjoyment of the pleasures of life.

Will my improvement follow their course and my newfound happiness be sustained? Every morning when I wake up I repeat that nervous stocktake to find out. My big worry is, of course, the fear of mood swings. The thought of being as unhappy as I am now happy is a frightening one. Laugh as one may, the jury of researchers is still out. Although most pointers are positive, there have been cases where the operation seems to cause depression, rather than alleviate it.

Witchcraft and a wedding

In the bushveld, in the far north of South Africa, a small village celebrated a marriage. The dusty road that runs through it had been meticulously swept into leaf-like patterns for the occasion. Two puppies dozed contentedly in the late afternoon sun.

The men, fingering freshly sharpened knives, gathered around a cattle kraal made of interlocking tree trunks, anxiously eyeing and even more anxiously being eyed by a bullock that was to be the centrepiece of the feast. Young mothers in berets and headscarves chattered convivially round a nearby table, cutting pumpkins. On mats the old folk in their Sunday best murmured memories. It was an idyllic picture of rural contentment, spoilt only by the knowledge that they were there because they would otherwise have been burnt alive.

The model village, at Helena Trust Farm near the town of Pietersburg, was a particularly ugly dumping ground. Its 73 residents, from one-year-old Moloto Michael to 90-year-old Ngoepe William, were refugees from an ancient and yet very contemporary blight on the face of South Africa – witch-hunting.

Almost weekly the South African media – in reports, the

briefness of which points to the routine – noted atrocities committed in the name of black magic:

'A woman and two children burnt to death at Mashamba village on Thursday morning … Three women were stoned to death near Tzaneen after having been accused of being witches … Three men were killed separately in Lebowa and their bodies mutilated in suspected ritual murders.' The precise statistics are not known, but the deaths number in the hundreds each year.

The plight of the 'witches' reflected the prevalence in South African society of a belief in the existence of an otherwise harmonic cosmos in which any misfortune – from a failed examination to a bolt of lightning or a case of Aids – is attributable to the supposedly malign influence of some innocent member of the immediate community.

Again, figures are unreliable, but an indication of the grip witchcraft has on South Africa was provided by one academic authority that estimated that there were 10 000 practitioners of 'traditional medicine' – witch doctors and herbalists – in the greater Johannesburg area alone, consulted by 85 per cent of the black population and supported by a national network of 40 000 traders in magical herbs. The African Traditional Healers Association claimed membership of 179 000. But the centre of 'witchcraft' was in the Northern Province, one of the nine administrative regions, abutting Botswana, Zimbabwe and Mozambique – from Devil's Kloof (home of the great Rain Queen, Rider Haggard's 'She') to Moria, focus of cult worship for the millions of the Zionist Christian Church.

A commission of inquiry was set up by the Northern Province government to look into the phenomena. The authorities staged a 'summit' of churchmen, witch doctors and community leaders in the provincial capital of Pietersburg to try to thrash out a joint approach to the problem. The 1996 Ralushai Commission's report was the stuff of which nightmares are made, but offered one of the first comprehensive studies of the witchcraft phenomenon in South Africa.

It recorded the wide belief that witchcraft tends to be passed through the mother's milk and tells of a test that women put their infants through to check for malign infection. 'The baby is thrown against the wall, and if he clings to the wall, such a baby will grow up a witch ...'

Men as well as women are open to suspicion of witchcraft, it explained, and beliefs are the same as European medieval traditions – of succubi raping the sleeping; naked crones whisking through the air on broomsticks (among other, more indigenous vehicles); and familiars ranging from the customary cat to leopards and the 'professor of witches', the baboon.

A myriad of misfortunes, as well as petty jealousies, were sufficient to precipitate a witch-hunt, but the most common trigger was lightning.

Typical of the cases recounted by the Commission was an incident in the village of Dibeng, for which a group of residents are awaiting trial on murder charges after a 70-year-old woman was struck down in a storm. The villagers reacted to the tragedy by summoning eight witch doctors living in the area to identify the 'guilty' party. Forming a circle round the spot where the lightning struck, they summoned the diviners into the middle one by one to throw their 'bones'.

A duly appointed 'secretary' solemnly recorded the proceedings: 'The results of the divining were as follows: Three said that their bones see nothing. Four said their bones see a Lemba woman from the Venda tribe. One, Kgosiyaka Mohlake, said that her bones show a man who was among the eight of the diviners present and she pointed out Johannes Mpai.' The 'writing was on the wall for Mpai', notes the Commission, 'as the crowd immediately decided to kill him. The crowd then stoned him and set him alight.'

Even more chilling was the Commission's account of 'ritual murders' in which people are killed and their body parts used to make *muti* (magic medicine): a skull or genitals buried in the foundations of a building to guarantee business success; human hands to attract clients; human fats to raise temperatures in iron smelters; human eyes to encourage far-sightedness; and women's breasts for fertility.

'Parts of the body are taken while the victim is still alive, since this assures the potency of the medicine. It is said that the magical power which is addressed is awakened by the screams of the victim,' observed the Commission.

A curious aspect of the report of the nine-member Ralushai Commission – made up of, among others, a retired magistrate, a local CID chief, a solicitor and a former ANC representative in Washington – illustrated the hold that the belief in witchcraft had on all levels of society in South Africa.

At one stage the commissioners note, with seeming approval, that several witnesses, 'especially scholars who have read William Shakespeare's *Macbeth*, strongly argued that Shakespeare would not have referred to witches if they did not exist during those days'.

The report recorded at another point that the province's ANC Police Minister, Seth Nthai, who set up the Commission, told the summit that the law had no business regulating citizens' religious beliefs. But warning that religion and superstition offered no grounds for interference in the lives and property of other citizens, Nthai, a barrister, scornfully recalled how he had challenged the commissioners to bring him a 'zombie'.

His scepticism was supported by the government's Commissioner of Traditional Affairs, Benny Boshielo, who reduced the conference to gales of laughter with his anecdotes about an uncle working as a witch doctor who mistook the burbles of a malfunctioning electric water-heater for the murmurs of evil spirits.

Boshielo also recounted how, when he was a student at a local university, news reached the campus that three 'witches' had been burnt alive at his home village. A group of students got together and agreed to return home to intervene and stop the madness. But one of them protested that he believed in witches and refused to accompany them on their mission.

The group returned to tell the recalcitrant student that the three dead witches were his mother, an uncle and a cousin, and that he himself could not return home because it was automatically assumed by the villagers that he was devilish spawn.

The story momentarily stunned the summit. Then one of the delegates rose to his feet to ask, plaintively: 'But what do we do with people who confess they are witches?'

Ow!

In 1994 South Africa finally won liberation and I decided it was time the new country had a court jester.

Dear Walter,

I have been distracted over the past week by the imminent publication of my autobiography. I had quite forgotten that I was writing it and no doubt you have been unaware of it as well.

You will remember how I used to keep a diary on the island, recording the number of press-ups I had done each day and other routine observations with which one whiles away time in prison – as to the frequency of one's bowel movements and the number of lumps one has discovered in the morning's porridge? Well, when I was released from Victor Verster word somehow spread as to the existence of the diary, causing great excitement in the publishing world.

My old friend Fatima Meer decided that we should sell it and an auction was arranged in London. After some fierce bidding it eventually went to an American company labouring under the name of Little Brown, for the sum of $1,8 million. I duly handed the precious document to them, but it transpired that it was insufficient for their needs. In fact, they became quite aggressive about the number of dollars they had had to pay for each lump in my porridge, not to mention other sightings.

After some terse transatlantic exchanges, a deal was thrashed out by which they hired a New York journalist for some $300 000 to write my autobiography on my behalf. It seemed a rather strange arrangement to me, but it appears it is a firm tradition in the US for other people to write other people's autobiographies, those important enough to write their own customarily being illiterate.

The choice of the author also seemed strange: a young man whose name constantly escapes me, but who is apparently the world authority on takkies, which are known in the US as sneakers. I was assured, however, that these items of foot apparel are central to American culture and that he was ideally qualified for the job.

Lumps in the porridge seemingly being insufficient to inspire this young man's creative drive, he took to following me around clutching a tape recorder. He appeared to share Joe Modise's affection for footware and obviously used his $300 000 to indulge his perverse passion by donning a new pair of takkies each day, which squeaked horribly as he pursued me. Irritated beyond measure by the noise, I tended to answer him a little brusquely and at times no doubt thoughtlessly. The result is this appalling autobiography, which I suspect will haunt me for the rest of my days.

It is not that the book is untrue; it is more that it is a gloss on my life. 'Air-brushed' is, I believe, the word used in America.

Take the account it gives of my circumcision. In bare outline it is reasonable enough: a group of my youthful contemporaries and I were made to sit naked in a clearing – watched by parents, aunts, uncles, chiefs, kings and anyone else who could afford the entrance fee – while we awaited the ministrations of the *ingcibi*, the circumcision expert.

But the book then has this elderly man skilfully performing the operation with an assegai, each one of us responding bravely to the painful cut with a cry of '*Ndiyindoda*' (I am a man). Now this is all very romantic, but quite untrue.

The *ingcibi* was elderly, but he wielded an axe. We all had to stare straight in front, but I remember the initial thud of the instrument followed by the cries of the first boy: 'Help! Police!! Fire brigade!!!' This was followed by a succession of further thumps and then the rasping of a stone on metal as the axeman belatedly sharpened the blade.

The second boy cried out – but not '*Ndiyindoda*', he cried '*aaaaiinnaaaahh*'. A silence fell on the clearing, broken by the old man mumbling: 'It was too long, anyway.' I blacked out for a couple of minutes, so I do not know what happened to the next two, although I did hear that in later years they were in demand among male voice choirs for soprano parts.

You know, Walter, I have often been asked over the years how I discovered the courage and the stoicism to face a possible death sentence so impassively at Rivonia and endure all those years of incarceration without a whimper. The answer is a simple one: after circumcision life has seemed very easy.

I came around from my momentary blackout to find myself staring straight into the squint and frantic eyes of the *ingcibi*. With one hand he was heaving on my foreskin. From the difficulty he was having with the other, in raising the blood-spattered axe above his head, he was clearly suffering from an advanced case of Parkinson's disease.

The axe fell. I looked down. The ancestral spirits were with me and my dearly departed part wasn't.

'I remember walking differently on that day, straighter, taller, firmer,' records my autobiography. I thought I was doubled over for a week. But then who am I to quarrel with my memoirs?

Yours fondly,
Nelson

The second coming

Office of the President

Dear Walter,

For a moment, I must admit, I was a little carried away. But, in the circumstances you can hardly blame me. I was aching for a change in diet from Tante Kriel's 'Koeksusters à la Droëwors'. So when an invitation dropped on my desk to attend dinner with the leadership of the African Methodist Episcopalian Church on Saturday night I gladly accepted.

I was anticipating a quiet evening in the company of a few grey-beards. Instead, I walked into a gigantic hall packed with more than 1 000 people dancing and writhing on the floor, waving chains, ringing slave bells and shouting hallelujahs. It transpired that these were the descendants – spiritual, if not genetic – of a group of 19th-century American slaves who, upon their manumission, had dedicated themselves to the cause of self-realisation with religious fervour. This, it transpired, was the cause in which I have been labouring for much of my life – judging, at least from the worshipful attention I received at the hands of the assembly. It was not just Bishop John Adams' reference to my 'toughness of mind, greatness of spirit, everlasting patience and complete unselfishness', or Bishop Frederick C James' passing references to my 'dignity beyond dimension, courage beyond contention'. But then they started to refer to me as 'the soaring symbol, the shining son, the ANC angel, the magnificent manifestation ...' I blush to go on.

You can imagine this, coming on top of fillet medallions topped with onion soubise and complemented by a sweet pepper and Drambuie sauce with chocolate Bavarians, was a fairly rich diet. When I finally staggered out of the gathering with the words of Bishop Adams ringing in my ears – 'your humility is such it does not allow you to understand how priceless you are' – I was in a pretty thoughtful state of mind.

By the time I made it back to Mahlamba Ndlopfu, the question loomed larger and larger: Was it possible …? Could I be …? I absent-mindedly said goodbye to my security detail and was trudging up the staircase to my room when the thought suddenly struck me: there was, after all, a simple test!

I hurried back downstairs and tippy-toed across the lawn. It was a moonless night and pitch dark. After colliding with several of the garden gnomes Marike de Klerk had declared national monuments before surrendering her precious Libertas to me, I finally made it to the small, shallow fishpond. Groping my way carefully, I stepped over the edge. And I walked, Walter! Without so much as getting my shoes wet!!

You can imagine I went to bed in a fairly disturbed state. I mean, apart from the burden of responsibility, it posed certain questions of a personal nature: what effect would it have on my tax status, for instance? And would Winnie still be entitled to half my estate?

The next morning I was awakened by an anxious-looking Parks who said the polygraph man had arrived. A morning session with the lie-detector machine has now become obligatory for all security force commanders, cabinet ministers and above to enable Mufamadi to keep track of all the fibs being told on a daily basis.

I hurried down to the Truth Room, which has been set aside for this purpose and was duly strapped in by the operator who, as is customary in these sessions, opened by inquiring who I was. I told him. He gave a nervous laugh, slapped me on the back, looked at the machine and his mouth dropped open. A series of hurried questions followed, relating to my father's occupation and the circumstances of my birth, before the polygraph operator abandoned his machine and rushed babbling down the corridor.

Word spreads quickly. By the time I got back to my bedroom a crowd had overwhelmed the guards at the gate and was gathering on the lawn. I walked out on to my balcony to chants of 'Show us!

Show us!' Raising my arms to command silence I had just begun to declaim, 'I am what I am ...' when to my horror I spotted the fishpond behind them. It was empty! I had forgotten that Kader drained it as part of his drought relief programme.

What can I do, Walter? The people are expecting miracles.

Yours

Farewell, Dear Walter

Comrade Walter Sisulu,
C/O The Pearly Gates,
The Entrance to Heaven

URGENT
Dear Walter,

I have just received the news of your departure. I immediately sat down to write this letter, confident in the knowledge that, dead or alive, it would reach you. Admittedly, with our postal services, it may take a little while. But I have marked it urgent and I am sure it will get there in the end – which is to say some time before the Last Trump is sounded.

And, after all, when one considers that even Robben Island did allow us to send the occasional letter, I have every confidence that the authorities in the parts where you find yourself will want to be seen to be doing a lot better.

I have to tell you there has been a lot of weeping and wailing around here at the news of your going, Walter. You are going to be greatly missed. But then I hardly need to tell you of your popularity. People seemed surprised that I was not joining in the general sobbing and somewhat bewildered when I tried to explain that you had merely gone ahead to do some organising for the ANC.

Basically, it appears that people just cannot understand the strength of a friendship like ours. I mean a friendship that can survive your introduction of me to Winnie is not going to have any trouble in coming to terms with death.

I must say, I am looking forward to hearing from you, not only to confirm that you are getting on OK (have you started another estate agency?) but in the hope that from your privileged vantage point you will be able to help solve some of the great metaphysical questions of our time.

For instance, when He decided to make man in His own image,

does that mean He looks like FW or Thabo?

Why did He unleash PW Botha on the world? Not to mention Hendrik Verwoerd, JG Strijdom and John Vorster?

Are all 11 languages given official recognition Up There? If not, what is He going to do about it?

Does He pay IUEF contributions for the angels and are the working hours fair and the levels of pay adequate?

Do they have a written constitution, a Bill of Rights, a universal franchise and is His reign limited to two terms, like the presidency here? (If not, I guess you and I will have a lot of work to do.)

On the vexed question of Aids and the HIV virus, does He think Thabo is as stupid as I do?

What did Winnie do with the money?

Do you have any insight, from where you are, as to when Robert Mugabe plans to come out of the cupboard and what he will be wearing for the occasion?

Do They have the pencil test (well, you never know!)?

Where is Tutu? Upstairs or downstairs?

And so forth and so on.

Old friend I guess that – as in life – nothing is certain in death and there is a possibility that this letter will never reach you and that I will not be getting a reply. If that is the case then I guess that this is the end of a correspondence, which I have greatly enjoyed.

When I look back, over that long road to freedom that we trod together, I realise that our story is anyway a never-ending one. It is a story that will not end with the death of you, or me, but will be handed on from generation to generation. The story of how two young men, one an estate agent and the other a lawyer, destroyed one nation and replaced it with another, much fairer one. A story which, were it not true, would need to be invented, because in so many ways it is so bloody funny.

Hambe kahle, Walter. You can go with pride.

Your friend,
Nelson

Tea for two and two for tea …

They made the most unlikely gathering for a tea party. The guest of honour, Nelson Mandela, and his hostess, Betsie Verwoerd, the 94-year-old widow of apartheid's architect. The *burgemeesters* of this Afrikaner bastion also gathered in their Sunday best to greet their president as he stepped from his air force Puma helicopter.

Betsie Verwoerd was waiting for him on the steps of the community hall close by, with twinkling eyes, gleaming dentures and silver hair in a no-nonsense bun. Her son-in-law, Professor Carel Boshoff, the guru of the Afrikaner Volkstaat (homeland) cause, hovered in the background. With long hair swept back, a neatly trimmed beard, cravat, blue suit and brown waistcoat, he had dressed for the role of a Boer leader, although the effect was more of an East End snooker-hall owner fussing over a visit by the VAT man.

After the obligatory cup of tea in a side room they emerged to meet the press. Mandela adroitly parried questions about Orania's whites-only admissions policy. 'I did not have to ask for permission to come,' he said in mock innocence. Then Betsie Verwoerd unfolded a two-page handwritten speech but became distressed as she tried to read without her spectacles.

Mandela, peering over her shoulder, began softly prompting her in Afrikaans, a half-smile on his lips, as he shepherded her through the text: '… I ask the president to consider the Volkstaat with sympathy and also to decide the fate of the Afrikaners with wisdom.' The ordeal over, she beamed her gratitude at Mandela.

There followed a hurried tour of the town's sights, including the likeness of one of the world's most notorious racists. 'You've made him so small,' President Mandela blurted out in surprise at the Lilliputian dimensions of Hendrik Verwoerd. The visit was soon over.

As the helicopter rotors began to roar, I asked Prof Boshoff whether blacks were now welcome in Orania. He smiled. 'There are so many other towns for other people to live in,' he said.

The Attorney-General

He looked more like an aged sparrow than the ruthless prosecutor that history remembers. As Percy Yutar came face to face with the man he turned into a living martyr in that epic courtroom battle 30 years ago, one could only marvel at how time heals.

'Hello, Doctor, how are you? You still look young and fresh,' Nelson Mandela beamed, as the bird-like figure in homburg hat and black overcoat nervously mounted the stairs of the presidential mansion.

'That's kind of you to say it. I'm very grateful to you,' the former Attorney-General murmured, clutching the hand of the figure towering over him. He had the slightly desperate air to be expected of an 84-year-old confronting a head of state he last saw in the dock as Accused Number One on a capital charge.

President Mandela invited Dr Yutar to lunch as part of his efforts to promote by example the cause of national reconciliation. After teas with the widows of Hendrik Verwoerd, JG Strijdom and John Vorster, and convivial meetings with PW Botha, it was the turn of the man whose advocacy nearly carried Mandela to the gallows.

Dr Yutar was one of the most controversial figures in South African legal circles. Joel Joffe, a member of the Defence team in the Rivonia Trial, said of him: 'All the counsel and all the accused developed a loathing and a hatred for this little man such as none of us had ever had for any of the prosecutors we had crossed swords with as counsel, or accused.'

But there have been glimpses of some complexity in the little man. He fell victim to anti-Semitism as he tried to work his way up civil service ranks in the 1930s. Years later, he wrote: 'I remember coming home to my lodgings in Pretoria, closing my door and crying myself to sleep. These miseries, instead of acting as a deterrent, hardened my determination (to) become the first Jewish attorney-general.'

Dr Yutar was clearly on trial – by ordeal, if not due process – as Mandela ushered him in to face an avid press. His dependence, for his defence, on the man whom he once denounced as a hardened criminal was only too apparent. What were the president's feelings about the man who nearly had him hanged? I asked Mandela. 'Well, that is now in the past,' Mandela said. 'His part was a small one ...'

Dr Yutar turned gratefully to his protector. 'It shows the great humility of this saintly man,' he said. 'All I can say, with all the sincerity at my command, may the Almighty bless him with good health and years.'

As if encouraged by his own apostasy, Dr Yutar went on piously: 'I just did my duty ... When I was assigned this prosecution I was urged to charge the accused with high treason. I exercised my discretion and charged them only with sabotage. Because at the back of my mind I felt: they do not deserve the death penalty ...

'In July of 1983, I approached four cabinet ministers in turn and separately pleaded with them: "Please let these people go! They have served 19 years and are about to enter the 20th year."'

The ministers were in favour of releasing the prisoners. 'But,' Dr Yutar said, his voice plunging sorrowfully, 'they phoned me one day to tell me my wishes could not be granted, and they gave me the reasons why. I shall convey them to the state president in due course.'

With that, a wryly smiling Mandela led the little man through to lunch. The jury was out, it signalled, never to come back.

V677
Pretoria Central Prison
Private Bag 45
Pretoria

26/10/64

Ann darling,

You see, as you were saying I'm being my old pessimistic self. As David pointed out, there are still possibilities & we fight on.
Stiff upper lip, both for you & for me.

All my love,
Your John
PS. NB Try to prevent Mom & Dad from really cracking.

Burial of the little general

'In another country you may have been a choirboy,' said the Rev Dr Peter Storey. 'South Africa made you a little general.' They were as appropriate an epitaph as any said over the small coffin of Stompie Moeketsi Seipei.

The townships of South Africa have seen many a funeral of youths whose lives have been cut short by political violence, but few can have been as tragic as that of Stompie, the 14-year-old at the centre of the Winnie Mandela scandal.

For a start, nobody seemed certain it was Stompie that they were burying. And then he was not able to attend his own funeral service – at least until the last minute – because his corpse was in such a state of putrefaction that the undertakers had advised against bringing it into the church hall.

Nevertheless, they turned out in their hundreds, the people of Tumahole, to say their farewells to the boy who may or may not have been a political prodigy or a police informer, the target of a child-molester or a murder victim – a boy whose death, whatever he was, shocked a nation.

The mourners poured into an angularly modern Catholic church at the entrance to the township, dancing on the pews to shouts of 'Viva the ANC!' while cameramen jostled for a view of Stompie's mother weeping by an empty bier. Absent from the mourners, but present in most minds, was the woman who had particular reason to regret the death of Stompie: Winnie Mandela – whose bodyguard is suspected of killing Stompie, and who herself started the confusion over the corpse by claiming that 'Stompo', as the locals call him, was still alive.

Despite graffiti to be seen on the funeral route – 'Mandela is a killer' – there was a seemingly tacit understanding among the mourners that the scandal behind the corpse would not be mentioned. 'We don't point fingers at people who haven't yet been found guilty,' a local civic leader, Lister Skosane, told the congregation.

Skosane announced that he wanted to deal with the allegation that Stompie was an informer. 'It was alleged that he went to Johannesburg to suck information out of Comrades there,' he said. The suspicions had arisen from questions as to where the boy had obtained a camera and a tape-recorder. 'We investigated the whole thing,' he said. 'We found Stompo got the items from someone in Priscilla Jana's office [a prominent Johannesburg solicitor]. Today everyone must know Stompo was not an informer.'

There was also the question of the identity of the body. The chairman of the Tumahole Civic Association, Adam Mosepedi, told the congregation he had seen the body. 'I don't want to tell lies,' he said. He had not believed it was Stompie. But then the family had been called in and they had identified it. 'So let's leave it in God's hands,' he said. 'He knows Stompo.' With that tacit agreement that they were indeed burying a hero of the resistance, they sang a song of mourning for the dead guerrillas of the African National Congress, and danced in the traditional celebration of the passing of a martyr to the cause.

There was a moment of drama when the Rev Paul Verryn stepped forward to speak – the Methodist minister from whose church house Stompie and three others were abducted by Winnie Mandela's bodyguards and whom she has accused of sexually molesting them. 'I come to express to the people of Tumahole my own sadness and loss at his death,' he said.

Then Stompie's small white coffin was brought in by pall-bearers singing their continued support for the jailed ANC leader: 'Mandela, show us the way to freedom in the land of apartheid.'

The good Samaritan

The same night I saw a light at night and my cell was opened. I did not see who was opening my cell. I did not look at the person. She said to me, 'Ivy, it is me. I am Sergeant Crouse. I have fetched your medicine.' She rubbed me. She made me take my medicine. I told her that I could not even hold anything but I can try. I told her I was going to try by all means. She said, 'It is fine, do not worry yourself. I will help you.' So she made me take the medicine and then she massaged me. Then after that I could at least try and sleep.

(VOL. 4 P314 TRC FINAL REPORT)

Life of a schoolgirl rebel

Gertrude Mzizi's home was easy to find, on the main road into Thokoza township, east of Johannesburg. The front gate was gouged and twisted and the yellow brick front wall was pockmarked, all by the impact of AK47 bullets. The house itself was riddled with bullet holes, including one that had spoilt the mock leather cover of her sofa. The lamp above the side door was missing – it was sliced off by another bullet and landed like Newton's apple on Gertrude's head as she was crawling for safety towards her backyard, past the engine that was all that remained of her old Renault 5 after five hand grenades were tossed inside it.

Gertrude was going for the hole in the back fence when she heard gunfire coming from that side as well, so she decided to take her chances with the gunman out front and crawled back. She was halfway across the road when she heard a soldier shout in Afrikaans, 'Shoot that woman there!' so she decided that after all home was where the heart should be and was running for the door when the birdshot hit her from behind. She displayed a well-turned leg and pointed to a smear of blood where she had just pulled out another of the 37 lead pellets that were buried in her body.

Gertrude was what might be described as a living target. It was uncomfortable referring to her as Mzizi, even if she was a mother of four. There was still the air of the schoolgirl rebel about her as she chortled the stories of how she built an underground still for the boys in her class and disconnected the school's electricity supply to get a bit of additional shut-eye. That was at the Moshoeshoe

II High School in Lesotho. How she avoided getting expelled is difficult to fathom, although no doubt it had something to do with the fact that she was a cousin of the paramount chief Moshoeshoe II.

Not that she looked much like royalty, stomping around her three-bedroom house in red ankle stockings, a blue towel wrapped around her head, shouting down the telephone at a caller from the peace secretariat headquarters that she was damned if she was going to go across the road for them again to look for more people kidnapped by the Zulu hostel-dwellers, because as far as she was concerned it was all a plot to discredit her with the Zulus and why didn't they call on the police and have them put together the biggest damned contingent of helicopters and armoured cars and go in there themselves.

She clearly relished the image and repeated it: 'The only advice I am giving to you is to call the largest ever-seen police contingent with helicopters to go into the hostels … I am not available.' And with that she slammed the telephone down.

It was a hard world, in the East Rand townships, when they became the epicentre of the South African political conflict. And Gertrude was necessarily a tough woman to have survived there for a decade as a leader of the local Inkatha Freedom Party's (IFP) Women's Brigade. She was also a bit short of sleep, having been up before dawn trying to persuade the *indunas* (headmen) at the Zulu hostel across the way not to allow their men to go on the rampage after someone had fired an RPG7 rocket at them the night before, demolishing one of their toilets.

It has to be said that toughness is not enough to explain her survival; luck clearly played a part. When she talked about having lost count of the number of times they have tried to kill her, it was no figure of speech.

But some attacks stood out in her memory.

Such as the occasion in August 1990 when she was walking home from the butcher's shop down the road, carrying her nine-month-old baby. 'There was a group of about 150 [members of the ANC] Youth League. They told me to put the baby down on the ground. Then they poured a 20-litre [can of] petrol over my head and they hung a tyre around my neck.

'The only thing I remember is them shouting at one another for matches: "Go to that house and get matches, we want to burn this dog." And I heard the police Casspir approaching the corner. That is all I remember, because I woke up in hospital the following morning.' The Casspir had beaten the matches to the draw; all she was suffering was shock.

It was a tough life and she was under no illusions. 'I know I won't die of natural causes'. Ten years later, in post-apartheid South Africa, Gertrude was still alive and an IFP MP in Gauteng.

Under loquats

Piet the mongrel is dead and buried at the bottom of the garden, I am told, under the loquats tree. Most pets tend to have been special, post-mortem; it is perhaps the selective nature of memory. But, although some might say the quality is not discoverable among animals, I think he could be described as a courageous dog.

He was not big – he resembled a half-size Alsatian – but he showed a complete indifference as to the size of any dog squaring up for a fight. And he would stagger away from even the most savage mauling with his tail wagging – his regimental colours, in a sense, held aloft to demonstrate all was not lost. Knowing it, I guess that's where I let him down in the end.

He had a rough time of it, towards the end. He had been reduced to a three-legged dog by some mysterious accident when he went missing for three days and an operation had failed to help. He was supremely indifferent to the handicap. And then he got cancer and he was as indifferent as he could be to that.

The vet gave us painkillers and the advice: 'It'll take about a month. When he can't bear it any more bring him in and I'll give him an injection.' That was about six months ago.

When I left, before Christmas, I hesitated over whether to allow him – force him? – to drag himself into the 21st century. I suppose it was an evasion of responsibility not to have him dead and buried before I went. But large in my mind was a rebellion against the expectation.

George Orwell captured it best of all, in that wonderful essay of his describing how, while a policeman in Burma, he had been called out by frantic villagers to shoot an elephant that had run amok. He caught up with the beast to find it peacefully grazing and no threat to anyone, having apparently passed through the period of 'must' familiar to elephants.

Nevertheless, as Orwell recounts, he felt compelled to shoot the harmless animal by the sheer pressure of expectation among the villagers.

The expectation that one should put down an animal in pain is strong in South Africa, which is, in many respects, a no–nonsense frontier society where 'a man's gotta do what a man's gotta do'. One of the things he is expected to do is blow away the family pet from time to time. Fresh out of an era in which misbegotten paternalistic duties – born of a sense that 'the master knows what's good for you' – has created a pain-filled wreck of a society, my rebellion against such expectations in this country is perhaps a reflex.

There is a superficial contradiction in the no–nonsense approach to animal euthanasia in that its strongest proponents tend to be of the same school who insist that in the wild 'nature must be allowed to take its course'. As a result, television audiences are treated from time to time to the sight of such as a wildebeest literally being eaten alive as it runs despairingly from a pack of African wild dogs. It will be a wonder if the up-coming generation does not insist on knee-capping Rover before he is finally put out of his misery, considering that such footage is customarily broadcast during children's viewing hours as educational.

But the contradiction is superficial, the obvious answer to this apparent paradox lying in a distinction between life in the wild and that around the hearth. If an animal is brought into domesticity, it is brought under an umbrella of domestic, cultural and human values. The corollary is that when an owner decides to put down a pet he or she is offering something of a statement of those values, which is also part of the reason why we hesitated over-long before having the dog put out of his misery.

The gap between the value one puts on a dog's life and a human life is a huge one. Yet situations can bridge the gap. Once I read an account by the Australian art critic, Robert Hughes, of how he had been trapped in a car accident and had begged a would-be rescuer to kill him if a fire started.

'Put him out of his pain.' The phrase resonated in the excited debate that attended a Johannesburg car accident not so long ago in which a passerby stopped at the scene, pulled his gun and blazed away at the driver caught in an inferno. One could almost sense the *frisson* of pride – 'a man's gotta do what a man's gotta do' – as the country debated whether the passerby should be charged. The pride turned to embarrassment when the pathologist reported the gunman had missed.

That takes one again to the question of euthanasia, a subject that always takes me to one of the most remarkable and revealing books I have read on the human condition, *Into That Darkness* by Gitta Sereny. It is a study of the life of Franz Stangl from his days as worker in a euthanasia centre to his command of Treblinka extermination camp.

One particularly haunting episode from that book is the story of the Jewish *kapo* (trusty) called Blau and the Lazarette. The Lazarette was a small building camouflaged as a Red Cross clinic in which impromptu executions were carried out. Inside, a low earthen wall ran the length of the building, a continuously burning pit on the other side. Victims undressed, sat on the wall, were shot in the neck and pushed into the fire.

One day Blau approached Stengl and asked a favour: his 80-year-father had just arrived on a transport. Instead of being gassed could he be dealt with by way of the Lazarette and could he give his father a last meal? Stengl agreed.

Later Blau approached him again, Stengl recounts. 'He had tears in his eyes. He stood to attention and said: "Herr Hauptsturmfuhrer, I want to thank you. I gave my father a meal. And I've just taken him to the Lazarette – it's all over. Thank you very much." I said, "Well, Blau, there's no need to thank me, but of course if you want to thank me, you may."'

But I digress; they were human beings and I was writing about a dog.

In our absence, three friends were worthy companions for Piet the mongrel's last minutes: a film producer, a university lecturer and a newspaper editor.

Of course the dog was not interested in their social standing, but he does seem to have been appreciative enough of their presence to summon up a few final wags.

If there had been occasion for an oration under the loquat tree I would have wanted to say of him: 'Whether it was the business of living, or of dying, he did it with indifference to what he could not control and for the rest, as far as he was able, he did it with style. What more can one achieve in a dog's life?

V677
Pretoria Central Prison
Private Bag 45
Pretoria

29/10/64

My darling girl,

… Here's a paragraph from Moritz' latest letter. I know you'll like it.

'Ann continues to be absolutely wonderful, as you will know from seeing her every day at the Palace of Justice cells. Underneath those gentle outward appearances, women seem to have a core of tempered steel when faced with real adversity. I have so often noticed this paradoxical fact of life, and Ann embodies it more strikingly than anyone else I have known. The two of you together make a whole, a single entity, that none of us who know you will ever forget. You are an example to all of us; do not forget this.'…

The police dog unit

I received a call from my newspaper in London, expressing curiosity as to the circumstances in which the upholders of law and order in my part of the world used human beings as dog meat.

Dutifully I solicited a copy of the video from *Special Assignment* at the SABC and, after popping a capsule of St John's Wort in the vague hope it would prove a prophylactic against future nightmares, popped the cassette in the machine and, for the first time, watched training techniques of the East Rand dog unit, I tried my best to convey, in the article which I subsequently wrote for *The Guardian*, the full horror of those 47 minutes in the day of a South African dog unit and the terror of those 47 minutes ripped out of the lives of three black aliens who fell victim to it. There was the awful sense of the routine that attended the proceedings.

There were the shouted orders: 'Let the fucking dog go!' ... 'Look at the camera' ... 'Kaffir, show where the dog bit you; nice, nice ...!' How the cameraman lingers over the bite wounds of the three with an almost lascivious attention. And the final act of savagery as two of the bulky policemen took turns in using the three battered and bleeding men as punch bags. 'That's a beauty,' applauded one as a colleague sent a cowering black man sprawling with a straight right. 'Let me have a go as well,' he said, flattening the second with an uppercut and belting the third to his knees with a hook before finishing him off with two brutal kicks to the head.

The inadequacy of verbal description was made apparent to me. I was reminded again of the old editorial rubric: 'A photograph is worth a thousand words.' And it was a striking aspect of the film that, although nobody died in the incident and far worse atrocities were reported in detail by the Truth and Reconciliation Commission, none of them had as much of an impact on the public consciousness as the antics of the dog unit. Which invites an extension of the earlier rubric, with the observation that a few minutes of video convey more than an archbishop's seven-volume accounting of 'the truth', at least where South African security force atrocity is concerned.

But why?

Flicking back through the memory banks I come up against an image that, in retrospect, probably traumatised me as a boy when I came across it in a public library. It was a photograph of a man in a concentration camp carrying a bucket, which, the caption said, was full of human testicles.

The shock effect of this picture was, when I think back to it, the familiarity of the bucket. The bucket was an ordinary bucket. I had carried just such a bucket on many occasions. I knew how a bucket's handle felt in my hand – the way it swung when it was empty and the way I staggered when it was full. I knew the uses of a bucket – in conjunction with a mop for cleaning the floors; my mother putting soiled underwear and socks in it with boiling water; builders carrying cement; my uncle on his farm carrying milk; myself tottering with a load of hot water determined to make up the midwinter deficiencies of the bathroom geyser.

They were all part of the subconscious memories to which the brain resonates when confronted with the utilitarian, almost comforting image of a bucket. It is like the familiar chords of familiar song being played on a record that is torn apart by the caption – 'human testicles' – the needle sent ripping through the vinyl tracks on the turntable to an accompanying shriek across the loudspeakers.

Fast-forwarding through memory I find myself peering again through the shattered walls of that church at Ntarama in Rwanda, at the assembled corpses of the prayerful dead. Again the mind resonates with familiar images – the pressure of praying knees on the floor, the warm and polished wood of the pews, the smell of the song book, the mellow chords of the organ, the cadences of the Lesson, the fondly reproving look of a mother, the proud bass of a father, the mildly reproachful tones of the preacher – scattered by the shriek of the needle sent tearing into the mind by the smell and sight of rotting flesh slipping off skulls and skeletons.

And so it is with the dog unit. The blue fatigues of law and order, clothing the reassuring figures of authority. That shredded shirt there, it's like the one I bought at the flea market, amid the comforting hubbub of Saturday morning stalls! Even the Alsatians; one guards my sleeping daughter at night, while another belonging to a cousin slobbers a wet tongue of welcome across my face, reducing me to splutters and my grandson to giggles.

Once again the needle rips as the familiar men in blue curse the familiar dogs on, sending their teeth tearing through the familiar shirts, into the familiar flesh of humanity, into friends and family, into my sleeping daughter, into my giggling grandson and into the collective memory until the shriek across the loudspeakers becomes just another track in our record of normality.

Poison

Furious controversy ensued in the ranks of the ANC over the death of Thami Zulu. The leadership was forced to set up an internal commission of enquiry under the chairmanship of Albie Sachs, the law academic who had nearly been killed himself by a car bomb the previous year.

The Commission found there was no evidence Thami was a South African agent. The cause of death was variously reported to have been Aids, pneumonia, or tuberculosis.

The story of his death is an extraordinary, if still confused one. It appears Thami was seriously ill when he was freed on that Saturday morning. He went to stay with a friend who was a doctor, who himself was taken suddenly ill – it is believed with a burst ulcer – and rushed to hospital. When he came around after the operation he sent a message to MK, to check on Thami. Hani and Modise themselves went to the house, but found the gate locked. The two commanders scaled the wall and found Thami inside, too weak to get out of bed.

On the Tuesday Hani returned to the house to find Thami still in a bad state. He did not want medical help and appeared to be worried that the Security Department was going to 'finish me off' if he got into their hands. On the Wednesday night Hani called in a doctor to attend to him and left two members of MK to keep watch at his bedside. Thami was suffering severe attacks of vomiting and diarrhoea. On Thursday he started gasping and was rushed to hospital where he died.

The Lusaka post-mortem report concludes that Thami died as a result of tuberculosis. It is known that Thami had TB – he had been treated for it in Swaziland – and from the post-mortem it appears that this had spread like wildfire during his detention. It is not known whether he had Aids, but it is possible in view of the virulent spread of the TB, which could have been due to the collapse of his immune system.

Whether or not Aids was a compounding factor, the post-mortem finding of death by TB – signed by a 'Dr Zhurovich' – is extraordinary. A copy of a report of an analysis made of Thami's blood and stomach after his death states that 'Diazon, an organo-phosphorous pesticide was detected in both specimen.' The pesticide is a particularly toxic poison. The fact it was found in the blood means that it killed him, rather than the TB.

It is known that the South African security forces used such poisons – only a few months before Thami's death the South African church leader and anti-apartheid activist, Dr Frank Chikane, had fallen ill with organo-phosphate poisoning. These two factors, coupled with the absence of any apparent grounds for Thami's detention, led to suspicions that a South African agent had infiltrated the Security Department to a high level and was using the position to target key figures in the army.

When I first looked into the Thami Zulu story I took the analyst's report and the post-mortem findings to South Africa's leading forensic pathologist, the late Dr Jonathan Gluckman, perhaps best remembered as a star witness in the Steve Biko inquest.

Dr Gluckman said that on the basis of the medical reports – while the tuberculosis was so widespread that it would eventually have proved fatal – the immediate cause of death was, without question, poisoning. The presence of the poison in the dead man's stomach and blood signified that he had drunk it. The toxicity of the poison was such as to suggest that it was taken within 24 hours of his death at the most.

To describe the death of Thami Zulu as a cause célèbre within the ANC is almost to understate it. Investigating the story one discovers that it is the focus of a bitter, if unspoken antagonism on the part of the army towards the Mbokodo, the department of intelligence and security.

'Die baas'

In the final analysis, perhaps, one can only judge oneself and I guess I will just have to remember that voice and make of it what I will. 'Hello,' she would say tentatively, answering the telephone in her room, 'Who's speaking?' 'Die baas!' (The boss!) I would growl sternly and wait for the giggles.

It was a running joke between us, because I was becoming increasingly incapacitated with Parkinson's and dependent on her for physical support. Whether or not she fully appreciated that irony, I don't know. She was a simple 'domestic worker', Susan, and, as some say in these parts, one never knows what's going on in 'their' minds. Which prompts the thought: 'Not surprising, considering the difficulty I have in understanding what's going on in my own.'

We buried her on Saturday. Ourselves and about 400 mourners who gathered in Soweto with us to say the last farewells.

We first said hello to her eight years ago when she arrived on our doorstep trudging along, looking mournful, but determined. She got the job, because she seemed young and presentable and was first in the queue, I guess. She had a small daughter, which was nice, because the schools in Johannesburg's traditionally 'white' northern suburbs had been thrown open to all races. Our zoning meant the child would be attending one of the country's better schools.

'Domestic service' is a difficult issue in South Africa. The system is deeply suspect politically, exploitative and (at best) paternalistic. But there does not seem to be much pressure to reform it, basically because the process would be too painful to the two sides (the masters of apartheid tried to destroy the system for ideological reasons, without much success). The relationships between employers and employees vary considerably in terms of their nature and their complexity. The interdependence is fundamentally unhealthy, but in ways almost as inescapable as is the heavily polluted air of the 'Big Sulphur' that is Johannesburg.

Anyway, Susan seemed to be happy with her job and home. She doted on Ellen. She seemed to have an enviably extended family and network of friends. Her tiny cottage was always bustling with visitors, music and the noise of the latest needle match in soccer, being fought out to a chorus of cries and moans – which Ellen greatly enjoyed, being Dutch with a Latin temperament. They headed off to Cape Town two years ago, Ellen with her kids from Holland to show Susan what the sea looked like. She was awestruck.

For me, personally, Susan was part of the background who was coming in to the foreground. It was when I found that I was having trouble carrying a cup of tea from the kitchen that she began helping me, first to carry it, then to make it … which was when the 'baas' joke was born.

Susan always seemed to have nagging health problems: nothing very serious – 'flu, earache, shingles, pneumonia, allergies, unspecified pains here and there. It was difficult to discover the problem, because as soon as she contracted something she would start mumbling, the one symptom common to all her afflictions being the collapse of vocal facilities. We sent her to the hospital, took her to specialists – one for the ear problem, which left her partially deaf, and another to check for rheumatoid arthritis – and to our family doctor. The problems were treated symptomatically and seemed to disappear as quickly as they came. On occasion it would be irritating. 'Susan's sick again!' Sometimes she would disappear, ignoring Ellen's pleas to let us know where she was.

It was a Thursday, I think, when we found a note in the morning informing us that she had gone to the Johannesburg General hospital. She returned with a diagnosis from a private clinic in Soweto: an ulcer. A few days later a Soweto doctor announced it was a bladder infection and she needed rest.

We decided it must be HIV/Aids. We had discussed the possibility before, of course. Ellen had first speculated on it about three years before, had worriedly given her a lecture and pamphlets on the issue and had hesitantly suggested a test.

We both knew something about the subject. I had written about it in general terms. Ellen had recently written an article for *The Observer*, in relation to a 'virgin-testing centre' she had been photographing in KwaZulu-Natal.

We tried to take in the implications of Susan having Aids. The government is refusing to distribute ARV drugs. Leaving aside the side effects and difficulty of administration, it is an expensive, life-long treatment. 'Well, we know from the movies what we have to do,' Ellen smiled ruefully. But those were decisions we could take once we confirmed it, we agreed. The priority was the diagnosis.

Again we both knew it was illegal to force an employee to have an Aids test. But surely we could persuade? I tried first, battling to control my waving limbs and sound 'masterful'. Susan seemed suitably impressed, at least by my agitation if not by my masterly qualities, and she agreed – she would be going to Soweto on Saturday and would have a test.

On the Monday we heard Susan had been admitted to Soweto's Baragwanath Hospital. On the Tuesday Ellen visited her with flowers and fruit. Susan seemed OK. Tentatively Ellen asked what the doctors had said was wrong. 'Kidneys ... something wrong with the bones …' mumbled Susan. The Aids test was not mentioned. Ellen was struck that half the patients in the beds seemed to be made up of thin, young women. Susan walked with her out of the ward.

On the Thursday Ellen found a polite message on the telephone answering machine from one of Susan's brothers. 'Susan has passed away. Thank you.'

V677
Pretoria Central Prison
Private Bag 45
Pretoria

31/10/64

… Most of this Thurber is fairly serious. What control he has over language – I wish I were less pedestrian at expressing myself. Not only has he limpid clarity – but the words dance as he wills. I can, with considerable effort, push them into motion, but for him they prance effortlessly.

'We could go to jail'

Incredulous, we raced out to Bara and found Susan's corpse wrapped in plastic and a blanket on a neatly curtained-off bed.

We tried to find out what had killed her. Two seemingly senior nurses, asked if it could be Aids, replied: 'Even if we knew we could not say, because then we could go to jail.' We saw the doctor who had tended to her and he said her red cells were down, he had planned to give her a transfusion, but had been delayed and had not reached her before getting a call to say she had collapsed. They were unable to resuscitate her.

'Aids?' I prompted. He shrugged, said he would have to see the results of 'tests' that had not come in and carefully wrote down our telephone numbers with a promise to call when he knew. The call never came and we were unable to contact him again despite repeated phone calls and another visit to Bara. We did manage to ascertain, from the undertakers, the official cause of death on her death certificate. It was 'natural causes'.

'To say one has Aids is an insult to the family,' said an old man and in this society the advice of the aged is often best respected. Ellen raged a bit, which is her way, but in the end accepted it. She saw hostility in the eyes of some of the family, though, and – never being short of courage – drove back to Soweto to confront them. How she managed to do it without using the word, Aids, heaven knows, but as I said earlier, peaceful relations were seemingly restored.

I made a gesture towards the appeasement of my conscience, writing a short speech – 'oration', if one likes – in which I referred to the terrors of being ill without diagnosis and offered the strangulated wisdom that 'there is nothing to fear, but fear itself'. Ellen read it to the congregation, along with her own and other family messages of condolence, from the pulpit in a packed church across the road from Susan's Soweto home.

Sitting in a pew towards the back I could hear my clichés clatter off the stony walls of incomprehension followed by a murmur of satisfaction as Ellen, her voice aching in its clarity, read the last words: 'When I was told that she had died I felt the sadness, the grief I would only expect to feel if a close friend of mine had died. And when I thought about it I realised how important she had become in my life. She had, in fact, become a friend. I wish I could speak to her just one more time, to tell her that. To tell her that she was a friend and I will remember her as that.'

In the low murmur of satisfaction that greeted these words and Ellen's use of the traditional farewell, '*Hamba kahle* (Go well), Susan', I came to the appreciation that this was not the time or place for explanation and diagnosis. The family just wanted to bury her quietly and with dignity.

Besides, what did I know? 'You don't know it was Aids, do you!' a friend in the medical profession had demanded in an attempt to comfort me a couple of days before. 'I can offer all sorts of alternative explanations.' Which was no doubt true.

A lot of burying is going on in Soweto at the weekends, nowadays. There was something of a traffic jam as we tried to follow Susan's coffin, hearses and cars filled with mourners jockeying for position in rival processions. But we found the burial site eventually and I managed to make it into the fringes of the crowd and lean against a tombstone.

I could not hear the preacher from where I stood. But listening to the distant buzz of recitation as they went about the business of burying Susan in the warmth of the midwinter's sun I found myself groping in my memory for another preacher's words.

The last time I had been in Avalon Cemetery, as far as I could remember, was to see Queen Elizabeth II belatedly honour the dead on the *Mendi* – the South African troop carrier that sank after a collision in the middle of the English channel during World War I. On a memorial stone she unveiled somewhere in a corner of the sprawling cemetery are inscribed the words of the preacher who summoned the support troops to a military parade on the deck of the ship as it went down: 'Be quiet and calm, my countrymen, for what is taking place now is exactly what you came to do. Brothers, we are drilling the drill of death. I, a Xhosa, say to all my brothers – Zulus, Swazis, Pondos, Basuthos – we die of Africa. Raise your cries, brothers, because although they made us leave our weapons at home our voices are left with our bodies.'

Susan of course did not enjoy the comfort of such a gloriously rousing end. In retrospect, amidst the awful silence attendant on her lonely death, one can imagine the fear this young woman suffered, twisting and turning from doctor to hospital in terrified search for an explanation, fleeing from the unspeakable terror that seemed to be stalking her, seeing treachery at the end even by us, the ones she had been most counting on for protection who were now demanding she open the door and let the monster in.

It is in the collective silence of denial that we, her survivors, are surely left to face an inescapable betrayal.

Flowers at Auschwitz

Pieter-Dirk Uys called it his wailing wall. Certainly it was enough to reduce an outsider to wails of incomprehension. The wall, inside the comfortable Johannesburg home of the mimic, actor, playwright and comic, was covered by messages – letters of congratulation from, among others, South Africa's chief censor as well as the present leader of the Opposition, the right-wing extremist Andries Treurnicht. Others included Archbishop Desmond Tutu and the woman whom black nationalists liked to describe as the 'mother of the nation'. She had scrawled on a less-than-flattering photograph of herself: 'The day you are me I hope you'll look like this. I admire you. Love, Winnie Mandela.'

'Racism is not funny,' declared a framed pamphlet distributed by members of the Anti-Apartheid Movement who picketed him when he brought his show to London. South Africa did not agree. To them, not only was racism funny, but – it would appear from the rapturous reception he got from domestic audiences – so is the threat of the country's collapse.

'What is the difference between PW Botha and the Emperor Nero?' Uys demands of an audience in Johannesburg's Market Theatre. 'Hell, at least Nero could play the violin,' he deadpans, to roars of laughter.

Admittedly the laughter was not always there. Playing local audiences with an almost insolent confidence, he was capable of silencing the mirth with stunning abruptness. Sometimes he did it with savagely cutting effect, as when he had a policeman discussing torture techniques: 'You stroke him with a live wire gently, avoiding the sweat pools of his terror so that you don't blow the fuses and put the whole place in darkness.' At other times he just clubbed them: 'You must remember that we white South Africans are world famous. Not just for gold, or Zola Budd … we are world famous, because out there everybody has seen us on television, killing black children.'

He ascribed his ability to get away with such lines, without alienating his audience, to his understanding of them. 'I am like a mosquito,' he said, 'I plug into their veins.' Quoting the theatrical aphorism of a cracked mirror being held up to an audience, he added: 'But now black South Africa is looking over my shoulder and also saying: so what's happening here …?'

And the black audience are always there, nowadays, in South Africa's racially desegregated theatres. Inevitably they are grouped around the edges of the auditorium; the townships have no 'computickets' – no advance-booking facilities – so they tend to be the door trade, the latecomers relegated to the less-popular seats. As Uys performs he can just see the white faces, turning uncertainly to see black reactions; and a circle of white teeth as black faces 'laugh at what we do to them'.

'When PW Botha told us all to adapt or die in 1981 he wasn't joking, hey. Since then we've adapted a little and died a lot.'

But if blacks enjoy them, his shows are intended for whites. 'I write for Pretoria,' says Uys. Or, rather, Pretoria writes for him. It is a point he has made repeatedly, and demonstrated in performance – on occasion reducing his audiences to paroxysms of mirth simply by reading out, deadpan, government statistics on the numbers of South Africans who have been granted 'reclassification' from one group to another.

He made the point even more effectively by producing a book – published by Penguin – made up entirely of quotations by PW Botha. It proved uproariously funny, with quotes like: 'Where in the whole wide world today can you find a more just society than in South Africa?'

The dedication page at the front of the book carried a line by Uys himself, which made his admirers wince with the thought that this time, surely, the satirist had gone too far for his own safety. 'The name of Dimitri Tsafendas comes to mind, without whom we might still be deep into the reign of Emperor Hendrik the First.' But once again Uys seemed to have got away with it – the book is to be seen in most popular bookshops.

'Dancing in front of the firing squad', Uys assumed almost heroic proportions as he taunted South African listeners and the State. But there was a dichotomy about it; heroism presupposes danger and, despite his tango on white corns, he was the first to acknowledge that there is no threat of the firing squad.

'The only time theatre has changed politics is when they shot Lincoln,' he cracks. 'I don't think theatre has ever changed a political reality and in this country the government could not give two bloody hoots what happens in the theatre'.

It is the immunity enjoyed by a court jester and that, perhaps, was Uys's role in South Africa. But his success in the role lay in his recognition of the principal that it is tragedy that feeds comedy. 'Tony Hancock was tragedy. Lennie Bruce was tragedy. All the great funny men – the clowns – it is all tragedy. South Africa is made for comedy.'

Once, after a London performance, he was approached by a

member of the audience who said: 'You remind me of a Nazi with a good heart who shows me a photograph saying: "We planted daffodils at Auschwitz."' It is a remark that has troubled Uys ever since – the charge that he is putting a gloss on the reality of South Africa.

V677
Pretoria Central Prison
Private Bag 45
Pretoria

9/12/64

... Very heavy rain tonight. The smell of wet earth is coming in –
very pleasant. Odd raindrops are blowing in, too ...

Looking for Walter

Houghton is a suburb just north of Johannesburg, an area of grand old houses and leafy avenues. It is famous in South Africa not only for its wealth, but also because through apartheid's darkest years it defiantly returned the country's only liberal MP to Parliament. The cynics would say the people did so because they were insulated by their high walls from a prospect of the 'black tide'. And there may have been some truth in that. Certainly, when the black townships of the Transvaal erupted into that awful orgy of factional violence that claimed at least 800 lives, the only ripples to lap against Houghton's suburban walls were the sensational headlines and dramatic pictures on the pages of the daily newspapers which, three weeks later, were still full of the effects of the carnage, with reports of mortuaries crammed with bodies. So it was with concern that a South African barrister, Robert 'Bob' Nugent, returned from work to his Houghton home only to be met by his maid with the announcement: 'There is trouble. Walter has disappeared.'

Walter Nkosi was the brother of the housemaid, Maria. He was a Zulu migrant worker living in a single-men's hostel in Alexandra, one of Johannesburg's townships. He was well known to the Nugent household, occasionally to be seen sauntering up the driveway to see his sister.

Maria lived in the servants' quarters round the back, and other members of the Nkosi family were often there. Another sister, Esther, was with her that Friday. Together they anxiously explained what had happened: Walter had gone missing from the hostel and the factory where he worked. Nobody had seen him since Wednesday.

Bob suggested that they go to Alexandra to see if anyone knew anything. The following morning Esther headed off for Alex, but returned in the evening even more disconsolate: Walter's friends knew nothing of his whereabouts. So the wearisome rounds began. Bob tried the factory and police stations. Esther went from township to township, scouring the hospitals, examining unidentified, comatose black patients. After about 10 days the hunt was becoming hopeless.

'It was obvious what had happened to Walter,' Bob recalls. 'He was dead. It was time to try the mortuaries.' Esther, the older sister, was horrified by what she saw in the main mortuary at Hillbrow: the bodies had been piled on top of each other 'like sacks of mealies'. The attendants told her to look through them, but she just did not have the stomach or strength for the task. They told her to come back with an assistant. Another brother in the Nkosi family, Moses, a coal miner, was summoned to help, and he, Esther, and a friend duly rummaged through the bodies. But there was no Walter.

On they went to other mortuaries: Diepkloof in Soweto, and then Thembisa on the East Rand. One night Bob came home to find Maria cooking the supper, Esther sitting next to her, both looking distraught. 'We have found Walter,' Esther announced. 'Walter is dead. We have found him at Boksburg government mortuary. He has a big gash in his head from an axe or a panga.'

It was extraordinary: they had gone to Boksburg, about 25 kilometres east of Johannesburg, on a tip-off that bodies from Alexandra sometimes ended up there. It had been a long journey: a taxi from Houghton to Johannesburg; a taxi to Germiston; a third one to Boksburg; and then a long walk to the mortuary on the outskirts. As they arrived at the little brick building, a van drew up. Two bodies from Boksburg hospital were unloaded in front of them, and one of them was Walter.

What made it more extraordinary was that the body bore papers showing him to be somebody completely different: a Xhosa, not Nkosi. If the family had arrived a few minutes later, Walter's body could have been lost forever, buried in a stranger's name. Phone calls were made to the rest of the family in Natal, and a van was booked to collect the body.

Bob took the next day off work and went to Boksburg with Esther and Moses. A sergeant, one of two white policemen in the mortuary office, looked at Moses and Esther and said: 'Oh yes, they were here yesterday. But I've got the papers for the body from Boksburg hospital, and they say he is a Xhosa.' Moses, a young man, was becoming impatient: 'It's Walter. We've seen him, and we've got to take him now.' Bob told him to calm down: 'Look, go and look at the body again and make absolutely sure.' Moses stormed off to look, came back, and said: 'Yes, it's Walter.'

Moses had Walter's identity document with him, and Bob said to the sergeant: 'We've got a photograph of him here. Why don't you go and see if it's the same man.' The sergeant ordered one of his lackeys to lay out the body for him, and disappeared with the identity document. When he returned, he said: 'You're right, that's who it is. It's the same man.' So they took Xhosa's papers, scored out the name, and entered the name of Nkosi.

The sergeant, 'a very helpful fellow', explained that they now had to go to the government offices in Boksburg to get a death certificate from the Department of the Interior, and a removal certificate allowing them to send the body to Natal. Then they had to buy a coffin. At the Department of the Interior they found the births-marriages-and-deaths office, and Bob asked the woman behind the counter how he could get a death certificate. 'A black one or a white one?' she asked. 'A black one.' He was sent to another room where there was a long queue. It was getting late. The mortuary closed at 3 pm, and they still had to get a coffin. So Bob went back to the other office, and said: 'Tell me, do you issue death certificates here?' 'Yes, for white people,' came the reply. 'Is this Boksburg apartheid?' he demanded.

The officials were indignant: they just had two different registers. But eventually they decided to intervene, and soon Bob had the certificates: Walter Nkosi was officially dead, and the family had permission to bury his body in Natal. On they went to the undertakers where they were ushered into a room stacked with coffins. A salesman pointed out a popular model. 'You get a shroud thrown in as well,' he said. Esther protested that it was too expensive. Bob insisted that he was paying for it. It was agreed the coffin would fit Walter very nicely, and Bob wrote a cheque. They asked that the coffin be sent to the mortuary.

Then the three drove back to Houghton to report to Maria and wait for the rest of the family to arrive from Natal. In the early afternoon a van drew up with five or six family elders on board: distinguished, grey-haired uncles in dark suits, looking solemn. They asked Bob if he would go with them. The sisters and Moses climbed into Bob's BMW, and off the convoy went to Boksburg.

'It was a mournful trip,' Bob recalls. 'Gladys was sobbing in the back. Maria, next to me, said it was better that we knew he was dead.' At the mortuary they were told the coffin with the body was round the back. Under the sweltering sun the men folk moved forward into the concrete courtyard, the women standing back respectfully. Bob asked the sergeant if they could unscrew the flap and take one last look, just to make sure. It was done, and the men folk crowded around.

A lengthy discussion ensued. The men moved to the bottom end of the coffin and started unscrewing a couple of screws there. One of them levered the top up and peered at the feet. The policeman said: 'Hey, don't do that, you'll break it.' But he continued to peer in, and then turned to the others, held up crossed fingers, and said something. There seemed to be a problem with the toes. More discussion and a shaking of heads.

Bob went forward and asked what was the matter. It was not Walter, they said. Bob asked Moses: 'Is that the man you saw yesterday?' Yes, said Moses. 'Is it Walter?' Yes. But the old men continued to shake their heads. All the screws were undone and the whole top lifted off. By then everyone was gathered around: the men, the women, the policemen, debating whether it was Walter. After about 15 minutes, judgement was reached. By majority decision – Moses was still shaking his head – it was not Walter.

And there was no way they were going to bury him …

The body was taken out of the coffin, which was loaded into the van, and they all drove off. Xhosa was abandoned on a slab in the sun, and the sergeant was left clutching Walter's death certificate. The van headed for Natal, and Maria and Esther drove to Houghton with Bob.

There was not much to say. Esther was shaking her head. Gladys was no longer crying. Back in Houghton, life resumed. Esther declared that she was not going to hunt for Walter any longer; she insisted that the man in the coffin was not the man she had identified in the mortuary the day before.

Concerned that this belief would have disturbing consequences, the Nugents telephoned Boksburg hospital. They found a nurse who had attended to the man before he had died. She was able to describe how he had been admitted unconscious, with a gash on the head. He had been visited by members of his family who had identified him as Xhosa. So it was beyond question: the body was not Walter. When this conversation was relayed to Esther, she said, yes, she accepted it. But it was apparent that she did not really believe it, and that the tale of the theft of Walter's body was going to become a family myth. Until one day when Bob was finishing breakfast and the telephone rang. He picked it up. 'Boss, hello. It's Walter. Can I speak to Esther?

Testing for HIV

I've had an HIV test. I decided to go, with some hazy notion of 'setting an example'. An example for whom, I am not sure, because I told nobody. It just seemed the right thing to do in present circumstances of national denial. Besides, it meant that if President Mbeki did emerge from hiding to hold a press conference I could put the crucial question, safe in the knowledge that he could not throw it back at me with an attendant charge of hypocrisy.

I assumed it would just be routine. My world-weary doctor

who's 'seen it all' administers a blood test every couple of months for liver damage, which can be a side effect of a drug I take for Parkinson's. He would, no doubt, crack a reassuring joke and the whole thing would be quickly and comfortably over.

Of course I arrive to find he is moving house and his stand-in is a pretty young woman. She sits bolt upright when I say, as offhandedly as possible: 'Oh, throw in an HIV test as well'.

'Will you be able to handle it if it is positive?' she asks earnestly.

I try to look the heroic war correspondent, muttering something dismissive while waving one shaky hand in the air with what I hoped was a nonchalant gesture.

'I'm sure you'll be negative,' she adds hurriedly, busying herself with bottles and syringes. 'You are after all wh … wh … er … wealthy … well comparatively,' she observes, catching sight of my battered shoes. 'So you know you are from a low-risk community.'

In an attempt to assert myself, I announced in a meaningful way: 'My maid died recently from Aids.' I sat back half-expecting some recognition of the article I wrote on Susan.

Instead in the pregnant pause that followed my announcement, it dawned on me she thought I was confessing to an extramarital affair with my maid …

I survived that encounter to find things only get worse. The next day, a Friday, a receptionist telephones with the glad news that the blood test is OK! I am battling to contain my relief and reply with the casualness demanded of a man on first-name terms with Death, when the voice adds in a furtive tone that of course the 'other' test would take a bit longer.

The weekend is a flaming hell of 'what if's' … What if mosquitoes really do carry it? … Remember what they said at school about toilet seats? … By Monday I am convinced they've sent it to the Mayo Clinic for confirmation. Tuesday and I picture my doctors (now two) arguing over the telegram. 'Give him another day of happy ignorance,' pleads the world-weary one. 'We've got to get him off the streets, now!' hisses the pretty one.

Wednesday and I am eyeing the phone with a growing sense of paranoia when I am interrupted by the editor who drops off the manuscript of a book entitled *Debating AZT: Mbeki and the Aids controversy*.

'It's by Anthony Brink, the guy who started Mbeki up on the dissidents' cause,' says the editor. 'He attacks me and the paper,' he adds with a knowing grin, 'But you don't even make it into the footnotes.'

The editor understands me: if there is one thing likely to infuriate me it is being ignored. Already enraged I retreat to my study with the ravings of this drivelling conspiracy-theorist, loony, crackpot, fruitcake ...

Now I'm a professional at spotting weirdoes. One of my formative lessons as a young journalist was delivered by a young woman (let's call her Mary) who walked into my office with a miraculous story of how she had been separated from her twin brother when they were orphaned as babies and been reunited in a chance encounter at a record bar not an hour before. There were tears in her eyes as she told her sweet story.

There were tears in my eyes as I wrote it and tears again in my eyes after I took a call from the local mental asylum asking if I knew where they could find Mary.

'Yes,' confirmed the bored voice, she'd escaped. 'No,' it said with a giggle at my discomfiture, Mary had been an only child and the brother a focus of her condition.

The lesson I learned as a newspaperman was to beware of the so-called 'mad' because they are far greater at acting than the greatest professional actor. Their performances, I realised, are born not merely of Stanislavsky's teaching, but of the actuality of an alternative reality.

While not wishing to get bogged down in theological debate with the holy men and women of the TRC and the HRC as to the truth of truth and the reality of reality, I would venture that there are commonsense yardsticks as to what is probable.

If, for example, as in Brink's case, a Pietermaritzburg lawyer is claiming to have uncovered a worldwide scientific conspiracy to destroy the collective health of a large proportion of mankind, one is best advised to marvel at the resources of the local library's science section, tip one's hat and hurriedly move on.

Wishing to distract myself, however, in the wait for the call from my doctor I read on in search of more evidence as to the nuttiness of the said fruitcake. I tut-tutted at his characterisation, as a 'racist', of a distinguished *New York Times* journalist. I sneered at the less-than-scholarly language Brink uses in introducing a letter from the leader of the Opposition to the president, which I had previously read and admired for its reasonableness. And I guffawed at the testimonials Brink offered.

As I read on, however, Brink's position began to make a strange kind of sense. The incompetence of the medical fraternity and the greed of the drugs companies were well known, I mused to myself. The international conspiracy was improbable, but what would the odds have been against Red Rum winning the Grand National three times? How many stories has one not heard of labs mixing up test material? How could I be certain that, if my test did show positive, it was not some ghastly mistake, or conspiracy by the pharmaceutical industry to stitch me up for a lifetime's supply of AZT?

Reading Brink's account of how AZT was originally packaged as poison, I seized my telephone and dialled my doctor. He answered. Barely managing to keep a civil tone I inquired as to the outcome of my test. 'Oh, hold on, I did see something …,' he muttered.

I listened to papers being shuffled, mentally debating how best to react: announce my intention of proceeding immediately to litigation, or inquire sarcastically as to which sangoma had done the analysis?

'Yes, I've got it here. It's negative, you're fine.'

I was humming a happy little tune to myself as I collected together Brink's manuscript and tossed it into my rubbish bin.

TRC balls–up

An undertaker in Louis Trichardt, Transvaal, told a Commission investigator that his father, who had owned the business before him, had been visited by the police in 1987/1988 and asked to come to a farm in the mountains where they 'were going to shoot blacks'. His father was to collect the bodies, accompanied by his son.

The undertaker pointed out approximately 70 graves in that area. Of the 20 bodies exhumed by the Commission, all were found to be ANC members from exile who were tortured before they were killed. Some of the bodies were headless; some without arms or legs; some had burn marks from a cutting torch.

It was found that members of the Nylstroom, Pietersburg, Messina, Louis Trichardt and Tzaneen security police in the Transvaal joined with local farmers to form a group that 'specialised' in capturing, torturing and then killing ANC members who infiltrated the country.

(VOL. 2 P544 TRC FINAL REPORT)

In 1998, during the course of an exhumation of three persons at Boshoek Farm, an additional 12 remains were found in the same area. These remains were also exhumed and held at a local undertaker's morgue. At the time it was believed that these remains belonged to former combatants and the site from which they had been removed constituted an illegal and secret burial ground.

However, once the above discrepancies in the exhumation programme became apparent, the Commission decided that before further decisions could be made regarding the reburial of the unidentified skeletons, proper forensic examination should be made ... Examination of the skeletons revealed that more than half the bodies were of elderly people. Nine of the skeletons had plastic hospital bracelets round their wrists, suggesting that this burial site was used possibly by a nearby hospital.

(TRC REPORT TO THE MINISTER OF JUSTICE – EXHUMATIONS BY THE TRCM SEPTEMBER 1999)

Africa time

Joseph Menold had to be hurried away from his own funeral service, thanks to apartheid. He was dead inside his big wooden coffin, but he was still in danger of breaking the law. Menold, aged 33, was one of 18 people who were buried in Duncan Village, a black township less than a mile from the centre of the South African port of East London.

He had to leave early, because his was the only corpse classified as 'coloured' under South Africa's race laws. Apartheid extends its grip even beyond death: under the Group Areas Act, his body had to be buried in a coloured cemetery.

Apart from the Group Areas Act, the coloured and black cemeteries are separated only by a wire fence, a small hillock, and a few hundred yards of bush. But for some local, bureaucratic reason, the coloured graveyard closes earlier in the afternoon than its black counterpart. The organisers of the mass funeral had to rush his coffin away from the service as discreetly as possible so as to get him underground before 4.30 pm.

18/12/64

My darling sweetest Ann,

I know you'll have a fine Xmas, beetle. Thank heavens for the 6 Harris! Haven't they made a vast difference? And because they've made this difference to you (especially) & to our little David, they've in turn made a great difference to me. I do hope they realise how immensely glad & grateful I feel – it's hard to convey this at visits.

Which reminds me – any one of these days I should receive another letter from Peter. His letters really are interesting – he has a knack of knowing what will absorb me. By the way, what do you think he'll be when he grows up?

I'm glad your quest for Xmas presents seems to be going well. And I hope that you'll like my Xmas present to you. I've not yet seen it myself, but it sounds just right for you. Ad & I considered an umbrella/sunshade, but when she suggested a ring, & described more or less what she had in mind it seemed just right to me. A week today I'll have seen it, no doubt!

It's getting rather late now, dearest Ann. So for this letter it's good-bye.

Good night, love,
from your John

Saving a shoe

He was covering an anti-apartheid demonstration in a Pretoria side street. The riot police were wielding whips and truncheons, beating demonstrators into the waiting vans. One protestor lost a gleaming new track shoe. The policeman, ignoring his shouts and frantic gesticulations, righteously dragged his battered captive away.

Standing in the watching crowd he shared the prisoner's indignation. On an impulse he brushed past inquiring faces and found himself in the middle of the suddenly clear road.

He walked deliberately for the shoe and felt a sense of exultation, as if he was on a stage, the audience focused on him. He can anticipate every line of the script – every movement, every exquisitely understated gesture with dazzling clarity; a warrior rendered invisible to bullets by a theatrical potion.

Too soon he reached the shoe, the fit still upon him. He stooped, plucked and with a few more strides slid it home through the open window of the packed police van. He turned and saw the police roaring off and the crowd melting away as if ignorant of his lonely triumph. It dawned on him: the country burns and he has saved a shoe.

House of hunger

- *A guy called Dambudzo. Dambudzo Marechera,* The House of Hunger. *He was a writer I interviewed once, in Harare.*
- *Let's sit here.*
- *A friend of mine made a film about Dambudzo's return to Zimbabwe after the settlement. We were looking at some early rushes – an interview with Dambudzo before he set off on his journey home. He was filmed sitting on the floor of a London flat, which he was squatting. He was a diminutive figure with a gamine face, dreadlocks and a colourful, sort-of caftan shirt. He was describing how he had*

been picked up on vagrancy charges and put into Wormwood Scrubs prison. He had to fill in a form giving his personal details. One of the questions was for the name of his next of kin. Dambudzo had no family in the UK. So he asked a warder what he should put down. The warder said wearily, 'Whoever you want informed if you die.' Dambudzo asked if his publishers would do. The warder said 'that's fine'. And at that point of the interview Dambudzo looked straight at the camera and said with an impish grin: 'Imagine being buried by Heinemann's!' I promised myself that the next time I was in Harare I would find him and interview him myself. Is this where Jan Smuts used to walk?

– *I suppose so. It drives all one's tensions away. The cars, they look like tiny toy cars. He was a real troublemaker – Dambudzo, I mean, not Smuts – but totally engaging. He had gone to Oxford on a scholarship. They threw him out after he had tried to burn his college down. The university offered to let him stay on if he would undergo psychiatric treatment. But I think Dambudzo knew it was the world that was mad, not him. After that he drifted around London. At one stage he set up home in Hyde Park, in a tent. The police asked him what he was doing there. He still had his student's card from Oxford and he persuaded them he was doing research on the flora and fauna in Hyde Park, so they let him stay a while. He wrote a famous book,* The House of Hunger, *about Rhodesia. It won* The Guardian *Fiction Prize. At the prize-giving banquet he threw crockery at the guests.*

– *At the guests!*

– *Yes. Thought they were poseurs, I suppose. He was always getting into trouble. Same when he went home to Zimbabwe. He was detained once by the Central Intelligence Organisation, because he had made a fuss about censorship in Zimbabwe at a national writers' conference. He got beaten up a couple of times as well.*

– *By who?*

– *Patriots. Zimbabwe patriots. Liberated Zimbabwe was meant to be heaven on earth and anyone who disagreed was a traitor. Or at least deserved beating up.*

– *And you saw him?*

– *In the mid-1980s, I think it was. I was on some assignment in Zim. I remember knocking on his door, in a block of flats in central Harare. It was about 10 o'clock in the morning. There was a silence and then I heard his bleary voice mumbling at me to try the back door; he's lost the front door key and the handle was wired up to a window frame. He was a skinny little guy. He made coffee for me, stewing it in a pot, standing there at the stove in his underpants. There were a couple of bottles of booze next to his bed. Later I took him to a beer garden. He was even more entertaining than I expected. I can remember one story in particular: He was writing his second book, but he had nowhere to live – he couldn't afford anything. So he used to sleep on park benches at night. During the day he would sit on a bench with this old, battered typewriter – in Cecil Square, right in the middle of Harare – and pound away at it. He used to go to parties in the evening, to get free food and drinks.*

One night he was at a party and got talking to this young white girl. He told her he was sleeping in Cecil Square that night and she said he couldn't do that. There was a spare room at her house and he could come and stay. But she warned him that they'd have to sneak into the house. It was late at night and her father, who was a former member of Ian Smith's Police Anti-Terrorist Unit, was strict. She said if her father caught them there could be trouble. They sneaked up to the house and she quietly opened the front door. And there he was, the father, waiting. He ignored her, he just looked at Dambudzo. The girl tried to argue with him, saying, 'He walked me home, daddy – he can't walk back now, so he's going to stay with us for the night.' The old man sort of grumpily let Dambudzo in.

It turned out the guy couldn't sleep. He was a sort-of Ancient Mariner. Apparently he had been shot in the head during the bush war and he had some injury to the brain that stopped him from sleeping. Dambudzo said the guy disappeared into the kitchen and came back with a flagon of wine. He said: 'I don't drink, but I think you do. Have some wine! Sit down!' And then he started telling

261

Dambudzo about his experiences in the police anti-terrorist unit.
He kept calling Dambudzo a terrorist, throughout the conversation
– 'you terrorists, this and that' – and saying: 'You terrorists, you
didn't play fair. You were sending children against us. We didn't
want to fight children, we wanted to fight men.'

Dambudzo said he didn't know what he was talking about and
the guy told him this story. He said there was this contact, a gunfight
in the bush. After a while all the guerrillas ran off, except one guy,
who turned out to be the their commander. He kept on shooting at the
police until he ran out of ammunition. And then he started throwing
grenades, until he ran out of grenades. And when the police came up
to him he didn't put up his hands. He simply stared at this guy – the
girl's father. He was about 13 years old. And the old man said: 'Do
you know what I did to him? I didn't order him to surrender, or take
him prisoner. I just shot him in the head.' Dambudzo said that while
he was telling him this, his host had produced a revolver. And he
said: 'Do you know I could shoot you now? What were you doing
with my daughter?' Dambudzo just said he had walked her home.
Nothing more. And they carried on talking, all through the night.
– *What happened to him?*
– *Dambudzo? He died of Aids. I saw him again, it must have been*
years later. I was back in Zim and went to a nightclub, La Boheme.
And he was there. He was furious with me, because for some reason
The Guardian *hadn't published my interview. His publishers had*
been looking for it, in England, and it never appeared. He started
shouting at me, in the nightclub: 'You're a CIA agent. You were just
spying on me.' His girlfriend dragged him away. And that was the
last I saw of my genius.

Ben Langa

The Thami Zulu case was not the only puzzling one of that period.
There was also the strange case of Benjamin Langa.

Ben Langa was a member of a distinguished family. The seven

siblings – five boys and two girls – included South Africa's chief justice until 2009, Pius Langa, and the famous playright, Mandla Langa. It was not the sort of family whose members get murdered easily. Certainly not as the result of a misunderstanding. Everyone knew the Langas; they were a well-liked family in Natal. Which is why the killing of Ben on 20 May 1984 came as such a shock to family and friends.

It was an easy killing, too easy. A friend of Ben's called out to him from outside his flat in the town of Pietermaritzburg. Ben opened the door for him. Two gunmen carrying pistols walked in and shot him dead. The gunmen, Sipho Qulu and Lucky Payi, were subsequently executed in Pretoria for the murder. The friend whose familiar voice cost Ben his life applied for and received amnesty from the TRC after giving a lengthy account of what had happened.

His name was Joel George Martins and, by his account, Qulu was an old acquaintance and fellow student activist in the early 1980s. He had gone into exile, joined the ANC and had returned, a trained guerrilla, in 1984, turning up at a flat where Martins was staying. Qulu told him they had orders from a senior commander in Swaziland called 'Ralph' to kill Ben for having 'basically sold out Comrades'. Martins said he had accepted the justification, because he believed the order came from the ANC.

Subsequently he had himself left South Africa and gone to Lesotho and Angola, via Tanzania. In Lesotho he had been told by a local ANC commander that he (the commander) had been told 'in no uncertain terms that that was not a bona fide ANC mission'.

The only other occasion on which he had discussed the killing was in Lusaka, 'much later'. The person he had discussed it with was 'Comrade Jacob Zuma' and it had been a 'brief' conversation.

At about this stage, according to the record of the amnesty hearing in June 2000, the chairperson of the panel demanded – with apparent impatience – of Eric van den Berg, counsel for

Martins: 'Isn't it clear from the documents and isn't it common cause that Fear, alias Ralph alias Cyril Raymond, was a Security Police agent, that he posed as a commander in Swaziland, that he instructed Qulu and Payi to come to South Africa and to kill Langa and that he was subsequently questioned by the ANC in Angola and that he died in Angola?'

'Those facts, Chairperson, are set out in bits and pieces of the bundle which is before you. The only issue which arises and that is dependent on the attitude of Terrence Tyrone is that in the criminal record Payi and Qulu say that in fact it was Tyrone who gave them the instruction but I know that he has been given notice, I know that he is present, but I don't know what his attitude is.'

Chairperson: 'Yes, I believe the – I don't want to – but as far as I believe he was present when they were conveyed into South Africa but he didn't give the instruction his attitude is.'

In other words, the man I identified earlier – as the deputy to Thami Zulu, who had drowned in his own vomit while in ANC detention and after refusing to sign a confession to being a police agent – was the man whom the amnesty panel was now fingering as being responsible for the murder of Ben Langa.

But there was seemingly a conflict of evidence at the capital trial of Payi and Qulu, the two assassins testifying that a 'Terrence Tyrone' and not Fear had given the instruction to kill Ben Langa.

Tyrone was in attendance at the amnesty hearing, but unfortunately it seems his 'attitude' was that he would not testify. In 1996 Tyrone was accused by Inkatha, in evidence to the TRC, of being behind a plot to assassinate Chief Buthelezi in 1987. Tyrone was described as being 'in charge of all Umkhonto we Sizwe operations in Natal'.

But Fear's 'culpability' has certainly won credence, thanks to the ANC leadership. The then president of the ANC, Oliver Tambo, personally apologised to the Langa family for Ben's killing. Then President Mbeki submitted a statement to the amnesty committee, which found its way into the Final Report.

It said: 'In a few cases, deliberate information resulted in attacks and assassination in which dedicated cadres lost their lives. In one of the most painful examples of this nature, a State agent with an MK name of Fear ordered two cadres to execute Ben Langa on the grounds that Langa was an agent of the regime. These cadres, Clement Payi and Lucky Qulu, carried out their orders. This action resulted in serious disruption of underground and mass democratic structures in the area and intense distress to the Langa family, which was the obvious intention of Fear's handlers. Once the facts were known to the leadership of the ANC, President Tambo personally met with the family to explain and apologise for this action. Qulu and Payi were arrested and executed. A triple murder had been achieved by the apartheid regime without firing a single shot.'

On what basis Mbeki was able to identify Fear as a police agent and a murderer is not known.

Tyrone is not the only one who failed to testify at this amnesty hearing. The lawyer who appeared for the Langa family, George Bizos SC, told the hearing:

'Now, Chairperson, we intended to have a statement from the Deputy Leader of the African National Congress, Jacob Zuma. I spoke to him both face to face and on the telephone. He was partly responsible for the investigation that led to the statement that is made in the submissions by the ANC. We thought that we had time to prepare a statement and get him to sign. Unfortunately, Chairperson, he went off to Geneva and we did not have an opportunity of getting a statement.'

Death has taken a heavy toll on the men involved in the Mbokodo. Oliver Tambo, the president of the African National Congress and the one man to whom the Mbokodo considered themselves answerable, is dead. Andrew Masondo, who returned to South Africa after the Apartheid War to become a practising sangoma, has since died. Mzwandile Piliso, who headed the Mbokodo from 1981 is also dead. Nhanhla, the man who succeeded Piliso, has died as well. Chris Hani was assassinated and Joe Modise, as Minister of Defence reputed to have been one of the most corrupt men to have held high government office in South Africa (he is said to have once sent a guerrilla unit to Johannesburg to buy him a pair of his favourite shoes), is also dead.

One particularly prominent figure in the upper echelons of the Mbokodo is still very alive, however, and is the president of South Africa.

The mysterious Zuma

The role of Jacob Zuma in these events and his activities during this period are something of a mystery. His biographer, Jeremy Gordin, in his published account of Zuma's life, notes that the on-line encyclopaedia, Wikipedia, devotes only a paragraph to the 15 years since his release from Robben Island. He observes, pointedly, that: 'Part of the reason for Zuma's non-appearance is that he never attracted any particular attention …'

Seeming to confirm that he himself had tried to find out more about this odd period in Zuma's career, but had been brushed off, Gordin says: 'He still will not talk in detail about the operational events of those days. In his view, these are the "property of the ANC, not his".' Which sounds about as thin as the case was against Vusi Mayekiso – the alleged super-spy whose dastardly deeds included the theft of cigarettes.

The little that is known about Zuma's 'missing years' is no more than a confusion of dates to be found in government biographies and listings of commanders submitted to the TRC. Released from prison in 1973, he left South Africa and, after undergoing four months' military training in the Soviet Union, was based in Mozambique from 1976 to the end of 1986. In early 1987 he moved to headquarters in Lusaka.

He was a member of the National Executive Committee from 1980 to 1994. From 1985 to 1994 he was a member of NAT and became deputy director of the Mbokodo in 1988.

Between 1976 and1980 he helped the Commiunist party chief, Joe Slovo, run operations on the 'eastern front' – Mozambique, Swaziland and Natal. He was the deputy chief representative in Mozambique until 1984. He was then appointed chief representative until 1987. According to Gordin, 'his main task was running its Swaziland/Natal operatons.' Colleagues say he was in fact in charge of logistics.

From the above, it appears that Zuma would have been well positioned to be informed and – being informed – carries a responsibility for the camps scandal and the scandal surrounding the mysterious death of Thami Zulu and the tragedy of Benjamin Langa.

V667
Pretoria Central Prison
Private Bag 45
Pretoria

24/12/64

… Just starting this letter has given me a feeling of closeness to you, & a sharing of the load. I'm sorry I was sombre today & hence caused you unhappiness, but to expose my sadness to you …

D'you remember what I quoted to you today, about how in times of the greatest stress we have ultimately to rely on Reason & Courage? I find that the former has been unified & strengthened in me – this is good, hey, love? But the second is a less faithful companion, I fear. Its greatest single aid – of dominant importance – is your understanding & love. Truly truly, darling, having the knowledge of your support has made the decisive difference to me. May it continue to do so, for the weeks (in all likelihood months) which lie ahead will put on increasing pressure …

Radio silence

A respectful hush fell in the 10-ton armoured personnel carrier as a police radio controller announced he had a message from South Africa's Minister of Law and Order, Louis le Grange. He wanted to congratulate his men on the good work they were doing; they were to keep it up and he would handle all the questions at the top.

Looking out of the window of the Casspir, at the battlefield of Crossroads, it was difficult to understand what the minister was talking about. The huge vehicle was surrounded by hundreds of blacks seemingly unaware that carrying a dangerous weapon is a criminal offence. Waving their pangas, spears, knives, axes and clubs, the vigilantes – their characteristic *witdoeke*, or white scarves, wrapped around arms and weapons – surged backwards and forwards, trying to whip themselves and each other into a killing frenzy, to attack the crowd of 'Comrades' facing them a few hundred yards down the road.

Police and troops watched curiously from their mobile forts … then roared off in search of the source of nearby gunfire, leaving the two mobs to get on with the killing, if they could get up the courage. In all directions mute testimony was offered to a conspicuous failure of Le Grange's men.

It was a surreal landscape of corrugated-iron sheets sticking out of the ground at crazy angles, interspersed by twisted beds, lopsided poles, and smoking debris – the homes of the KTC squatters, flattened in a terrifying, 48-hour rampage by the *witdoeke*.

The police and troops ran across open ground and leaned out of the open-top Casspirs and Buffels, with an easy insouciance that belied the danger behind the crack and thump of nearby guns. The danger was brought home when an elderly officer pointed out a man on a distant hill: 'He's got a gun,' he said.

We gazed and then dived for the floor as a shot clanged off the armour plating. As we clambered back to our feet and grinned ruefully at each other, a reporter, Bert van Hees, looked down and, mildly astonished, watched the blood pouring from his forearm. The shock of the impact had numbed the nerves that should have told him he had been hit.

Police tore at his shirt and bound a rough tourniquet as we roared out of the camp. Outside the police station in the nearby township of Guguletu there was an ambulance, but the medical attendants had little time for an arm wound. They were desperately bandaging and setting up a drip for a critically injured television cameraman, George D'Arth, who had been found badly hacked.

Our Casspir roared off back into Crossroads. The radio, crackling in Afrikaans, reported that a 'white' sniper had been spotted and that another gunman was firing at Casspirs from some sand dunes. We arrived at the dunes and three officers leapt off, the colonel in charge shouting after them as they loped off into the sand to watch out for 'Barnard'.

Warrant Officer Barrie Barnard is the subject of an unpleasant legend on the Cape Flats. A figure who features prominently in stories of police atrocities, he was apparently hiding in the dunes, waiting in ambush for the sniper.

The setting was wrong, but it all smacked of *Starsky and Hutch*. The policemen – some even clad in the sneakers and black bomber jackets favoured by the American television duo – playing out a cops-and-robbers fantasy while civil war raged around them.

The station commander at Guguletu is a long-distance runner and there is a picture of him racing on his office wall. The photograph carries the legend: 'Blessed is a man who perseveres under trial, for he will receive the crown of life.' It was difficult to understand what they were talking about.

Crossroads tea party

President PW Botha could not pronounce his name. But apart from that, it was a 'great day' in the life of Jonathan Ngxobongwana or, as he put it, 'the sort of day we have never thought we would have.'

Certainly it was a day he could not have anticipated back in 1980, when Ngxobongwana was languishing in jail accused of fraud, or again in 1985 when he was inside on attempted murder charges. Now he was eating lobster and smoked salmon and listening to the country's head of state hailing him as a man whose example could bring future peace and prosperity.

It was the apotheosis of a vigilante boss – of the leader of a bunch of thugs who, in the words of one, was responsible for 'one of the most brutal and well-organised forced removals in South Africa's history'.

The occasion of Ngxobongwana's political sanctification was the latest of Botha's well-organised forays into what might be described as his social hinterland – the black community – which he visits occasionally, not to seek the votes they do not have, but seemingly to play out a fantasy that has it that he is greatly admired by the country's disenfranchised majority.

His target this time was Crossroads, the Cape Town shantytown that became famous in the late 1970s for its resistance to forced removals, and then blew up in 1986 in an orgy of violence – as vigilantes and left-wing 'Comrades' fought for control. Hundreds were left dead.

After those horrific days, Crossroads and the nearby KTC squatter camp became the target of 'upgrading', a euphemism for a huge and largely secretive exercise devised by military strategists. Upgrading is aimed at dampening any revolutionary sparks by the improvement of social conditions in potentially volatile areas.

It was to celebrate the apparent success of this strategy that the familiar figure of President Botha, in his homburg hat, came bowling into Crossroads' new manpower training and work centre in his presidential and armour-plated Mercedes. His entourage included his wife, Elize, sporting a corsage of orchids, bulky bodyguards, assorted politicians, cabinet ministers and a media pack of nearly one hundred.

Whatever fantasies Botha may have nursed as to his popular support among blacks were gratified by a crowd of several hundred – mainly women and children – who gave him an enthusiastic welcome, waving miniature flags at him through a high security fence and past a phalanx of bodyguards who watched the demonstration with evident distrust.

The spontaneity of the reception was open to doubt. The area was then totally controlled by Ngxobongwana's authoritarian followers but the enthusiasm of the hosts for the guests and vice versa was beyond doubt as the president and the former vigilante leader took turns to sing praises.

'This centre is an example of the road you have set ahead for us in South Africa,' enthused Ngxobongwana.

'Although the road is in many places still under construction, and there are many dangerous curves, we already see the completed bridges behind us. Let us go ahead together as a team and I am sure you will not be disappointed,' he added.

'It is a pleasure to share your joy,' rejoined Botha. 'What we see here today is a monument of what can be achieved by a positive approach.' To which a choir responded by singing in Xhosa: 'PW Botha, we will follow you; we thank you; let's get together; we are all one family.'

The ceremony's culmination was Botha's presentation of a new 'Crossroads flag' to Ngxobongwana – an emblem made up of a white cross set in black background with a red motif in the centre. The colours, as an official explained ambiguously, represented South Africa's white and black communities 'and their blood'.

Tributes paid, the Bothas started off on a conducted tour of the work centre – a complex of elongated buildings made up of small workshops. As Botha waved his farewell to the people of Crossroads, reports were coming in from Natal of bulldozers protected by armed police flattening yet another shantytown, leaving 3 000 homeless.

It was a great day for Jonathan Ngxobongwana. But in other parts of the country it was just another day.

Pretoria Central Prison
Private Bag 45
Pretoria

4/1/65

... Beetle – I don't want to dwell on this, but it is very important & I do suspect that we dodge it more than we should: I'm referring to the chances of the worst happening, & what our present & future attitudes should be in the light of it. I think we're right in keeping up our daily spirits, in wishing for & hoping for & working for a change of the sentence, but I also think we shouldn't fail to make certain psychological preparations to accept the worst. This isn't a suggestion that we brood over it, but I think we also shouldn't fail to keep it in mind so that if necessary we'll have a basis for the required fortitude ...

Your John

V677
Pretoria Central Prison
Private Bag 45
Pretoria

7/1/65

My sweet darling Ann,

More than once I've thought of saying tender things to you during visits, but I don't think it's a good idea for I should certainly be upset in your dear presence. But lovekin, you know that every time I see you, every time I think of you I am emanating the great love that is in me for you. And there's no need for me to attempt some sort of description of that love, for you are altogether aware of its quality, its comprehensiveness & its intensity. Do be reminded of it, sweetest buz, every time you see me – I mean specifically reminded of it, not just generally aware …

Your John loves you so much, Beetle

The king who snored

– *My grandmother used to love telling a story about the English king, when he came out to visit South Africa, I think in 1947.*

– *King George VI, the year I was born.*

– *Yes. Anyway, he toured all over South Africa by train, because that's the way you travelled in those days. He was due to visit this one particular town; I don't remember where it was – Beaufort West, or Somerset West, or Colesberg, or something. And the town was very happy he was coming and they prepared like mad for him. They gave the railway station a new coat of paint and they hung up flags and banners and the local brass band practised like mad and they found all the best singers in the town and made a choir. The train was due in quite late in the evening, but when the time came they were all there; the band banging and tooting away and the choir harmonising and all the women dressed in their finery and the men in their frock coats and top hats and the town councillors in their robes and mayor in his gold chain, all talking excitedly as they waited for the train bringing the king. Just before the train was due to arrive a man from the British embassy came rushing onto the platform and he called for quiet. Then he told them that the train was coming and that the king was on board, but that he was very tired and he had fallen asleep. So they all had to be very quiet, to avoid waking the king. So that's what happened. The train came into the station …*

– *Oh no!*

– *… and they all stood there silently under the fluttering flags, the brass band, the choir, the ladies in all their finery, until the train and the snoring king disappeared into the distance.*

– *That's not fair, he wasn't snoring.*

– *Oh, yes, he was. All kings are fat and snore. Especially English kings. I wish my grandma was still alive. Her parents' home was burned down by the* rooineks.

– *In the Boer War?*

– *Yes. They burned all the Boer farmhouses down, of men fighting in*

the commandoes, and took the wives and children to concentration
camps. My grandma survived. And her brother. But her mother
died. She was a lovely person, my grandma. She smelt of lavender.
– *All grandmas smell of lavender. If they don't smell of lavender they*
are imposters.
– *Yes, but they don't all carry big guns. I slept in her bed one night,*
when she was ill in hospital, and I felt a hard lump under the pillow.
When I looked there was this huge gun lying there – you know, like
cowboys use.
– *A six-shooter?*
– *Yes. A pistol. She was in her eighties then and I bet she could still*
have used it. When she was still on the farm, after my grandfather
died, when she hired a new labourer she used to take him outside
and give him a shooting exhibition, just so that there was no
misunderstanding. She said her best shot was when she saw a snake
right up high in a tree, on the top branch, swaying in the wind, and
she shot its head straight off. Just like that.

Puddle of brains

It was difficult to find hope for South Africa at the scene of the
Bisho massacre, particularly when a puddle of human brains was
still coagulating a few yards away and the men who put it there
were up on the hill, squinting down through the sights of their
assault rifles. It was 1992 and the ANC were negotiating with the
government to dismantle the grotesque 'independent' homelands.
The scenes played out, while bizarre, were almost a celebration of
this country's extraordinary ability to overcome trauma and crisis.

Along a narrow road lined by a few stately gum trees, the focus
of attention was an imaginary line delineating the imaginary border
to an imaginary country. The only evidence of its existence was
a small green-and-white board on a pole stating simply, 'Ciskei
border'. A few feet beyond – seemingly insensitive to the symbolism
of their position – half a dozen armoured personnel carriers of

the South African police were drawn up in a barricade. The road was crowded with hundreds of ANC supporters, tired survivors of Monday's massacre and an all-night vigil. Up a pathway the killers of the Ciskei Defence Force lay stretched out behind their automatic rifles on bi-pods. Behind them, in the toy town that is Bisho, were the 'government buildings', a redbrick complex that could easily be mistaken for a large primary school. But there were machine-gun nests perched on top of the gatehouse.

Curiously, the army had forgotten to guard the gate itself and it was possible to drive in unchallenged. Past an unmanned security X-ray and up a flight of stairs to a door guarded by a soldier toting a submachine gun. The Council of State was in session, white South African advisers slipping in and out with distracted expressions on their faces. An official volunteered to take a message in to the 'Brigadier', emerging to announce that Oupa Gqozo, Ciskei's military leader, still had not decided whether he would be talking to the press about 'the delicate matter'.

Down the hill, down by the puddle of brains and the imaginary border, the performance of pilgrimage and theatre was getting under way. First on the scene were, appropriately, the country's religious leaders led by the Nobel laureate Archbishop Desmond Tutu. Surrounded by empurpled colleagues and scrambling cameramen, he bobbed confidently through a gap in the police barricade, kneeling in the dust as the Grahamstown bishop, David Russell, appealed to God to make leaders 'heed and recognise their responsibilities and not play games with your people, Lord'.

Then the archbishop returned to the people, mounting a makeshift pulpit – a stepladder borrowed from a television crew. In a pinstripe suit – his bald spot glowing blackly amidst white curls under the midday sun – he made an incongruous figure. But the incongruity was soon lost in a political sermon that, while lacking the measured cadences of a Luther King, stood the comparison in terms of passion and nobility. He developed his theme of freedom – as God's gift, rather than man's – to a climactic scene in which his congregation roared joyfully: 'We will be free. All of us. Black and white. Together.' And then he was gone up the hill with his fellow clerics on a mission to try to persuade the brigadier it was time for freedom.

By the imaginary line journalists hovered around Ronnie Kasrils, peppering him with questions about his role in Monday's tragedy. A short, stocky figure with a comfortable belly and his own bald spot glowing pinkly among black curls under the hot sun, Kasrils, a communist and former ANC intelligence chief, led the charge on to the Ciskei guns, escaping by a miracle. Obviously suffering under a private burden of self-examination, he doggedly defended the ANC's actions. He explained the genesis of the march, originating with local ANC branches demanding action to end the violence racking the Ciskei ... the endorsement of the plan without dissent by the 68-member National Executive of the ANC ... the collective decision on the ground that the ANC secretary-general, Cyril Ramaphosa, would try to talk his way past the barricades while Kasrils would make the flanking charge ... and then the charge itself, the disbelief that it could happen in front of the world's press – when a young colleague fell with a huge wound in his side, crying out: 'I think it was a live round!' 'One cannot regret what one does in good faith and in the best judgement of the collective leadership,' Kasrils pleaded. 'Casualties take place all the time ... We can't regret trying to go forward.' But there was a wistful look on his face as he walked off, tossing back the words: 'The trouble is I always was the best runner at school. There were others [leaders] with me, but they just could not keep up.'

A fresh stampede of photographers signalled another pilgrim coming down the country road. Striding with that familiar stately air, immaculate in black suit, it was almost a rerun of that memorable moment when he walked through those gates at Victor Verster Prison. The barricade of armoured vehicles was hurriedly opened. The police officers, all white, formed flanking lines – effectively a guard of honour. Advancing to a position between a broken line of razor wire Nelson Mandela, Ramaphosa, Kasrils and other ANC officials knelt and sang a lament reserved for dead guerrillas before turning back to the crowd. A police squad car driven by a white major led the way. An ANC official asked the major if they could use the car's loudhailer.

A woman took the microphone and led them in the singing of the ANC's national anthem, 'Lord Bless Africa'.

Unheard, a few yards away, by a puddle of brains.

Scoop?

'Investigative journalism' is a misnomer. Most 'exposés' are nothing more than competent journalism, often based on inside knowledge from a whistleblower. Certainly it is true of Watergate, that most celebrated of newspaper scoops where the whistleblower – Deep Throat – finally identified himself after more than 30 years.

Although I have never brought down a president, I can claim a number of major exposés, all of them dubbed 'scandals': from Infogate in the late 1970s, to Winnie Mandela's disgrace, Inkathagate in the early 90s and the unravelling of apartheid's hit squads. But they had little to do with 'investigative' journalism, and more to do with chance.

But it was with some fascination that I discovered I had on one occasion seemingly changed the course of South African history. This time it was not the result of chance, but of a complete balls-up.

It was to do with that 'puddle of brains' and the Bisho massacre. But the story starts a long time later as I was climbing on a plane from Cape Town to Johannesburg. I had just settled into my seat when I spotted Roelf Meyer, the former Minister of Constitutional Development and chief government negotiator, a couple of rows ahead of me. I knew him only slightly, as one does a government minister, and I waved a hello when I caught his eye. It was to my surprise, therefore, that he leaned across the intervening passengers and said: 'Whenever I see you I remember that piece you wrote that changed the course of history.' By this time the aircraft was powering up and he had to take his seat.

I was of course fascinated, knowing nothing about my changing the course of South African history. I intended quizzing him in the terminal building, but missed him. It was months later that I finally e-mailed him to solve the mystery.

My coverage of the Bisho massacre was something of a disaster. I missed it. The march was clearly going to be an important one. The constitutional talks had broken down and the ANC leadership had been sold the idea of 'rolling mass action' and the 'Leipzig option'. The idea was to force the Nationalist government into some kind of capitulation by a demonstration of the ANC's popular support. Bisho was the first big test of the strategy.

But I must have had some sort of a brainstorm, because instead of going to Bisho I went to attend some event in Pretoria, the details of which I cannot even remember. But what I can remember is the sinking feeling I had when I arrived there and was told what had happened at Bisho. I was frantic – talk about being wrong-footed (as a journalist, I mean)! I could not get on an early flight and only arrived the next day, by which time all the action was over. I did, however, find a puddle of brains next to a path and it was from there that I wrote my piece.

It so happened that a junior minister, Org Marais, was flying back to South Africa for a cabinet meeting. He picked up a copy of *The Guardian* at Heathrow and gave it to Meyer. It was enough to swing the debate in cabinet in favour of a resumption of negotiations.

'To my mind, the signing of the Record of Understanding was the turning point in the negotiating process,' recalled Meyer. 'In that document the ANC and the government agreed on the way forward for a constitutional settlement with the objective to bring about a democracy safeguarding individual rights for all South Africans on an equal basis. In later assessments it became clear that that was the real changing of the paradigm at least as far as the NP government's position was concerned. My recollection is therefore that your article played no insignificant role in helping us to that point.'

Don't let anyone underestimate the power of the Fourth Estate.

21/1/65

… Tomorrow I'll probably see our little David. That'll be fine. He's such an excellent little chap. Even though seeing him is upsetting it's also inspiring. Do film him quite a lot, beetle. Remember that he's changing very quickly & if you don't film him for a while there's a slice missing, as it were!

M'lud

The final legal battle for the lives of the Sharpeville Six began in 1988 when Sydney Kentridge SC, QC, rose to his feet in a wood-panelled courtroom in South Africa's judicial capital and delivered the familiar incantation: 'M'Lord, I appear for all the applicants with my learned friends …'

The No. 1 courtroom at the Appellate Division of the Supreme Court was packed with diplomats, press, and relatives of the five men and one woman who, some 250 miles away at Pretoria's Central Prison, were starting the 999th day of their ordeal on death row.

Up on the bench, five of the country's top judges listened with bland faces: PJ Rabie, the silver-haired Acting Chief Justice, looking like a benign grandfather; on his right MM Corbett and GG Hoexter, the two liberal judges of appeal; on his left CP Joubert, the 'legal antiquarian', and the 'youngster', HJO van Heerden.

Slowly, Kentridge began building the now familiar foundations to his case. A state witness, Joseph Manete, claimed to have been forced by police to perjure himself at the original trial. The Defence now wanted evidence of this introduced: by reopening the trial, or by a 'special entry' into the trial record. Both approaches posed difficulties. There was no precedent in South African law for the reopening of a trial and a special entry could only be made if there had been a 'material irregularity' in the proceedings. But first, said Kentridge, Manete's evidence should be placed against the background of the murder for which the Six had been condemned to hang – the brutal slaying of the Sharpeville local, Jacob Dlamini, in 1984. 'To put it shortly, a mob attacked his home.' They petrol-bombed the house, felled him with stones when he fled, and beat him on the ground. 'When he was lying there dying, but probably still alive, members of the mob poured petrol on him and set him alight. And he died.'

It was, said Kentridge, impossible to disagree with the trial judge's description of it as 'a gruesome murder of medieval barbarity'. And then there were the condemned. Oupa Moses Diniso had been found in possession of Dlamini's pistol two months after the murder. The trial court inferred that he was among those who had wrestled the councillor to the ground. 'He was not identified otherwise.' There was Reid Makoena, who had thrown a single stone, which had hit Dlamini in the back. Theresa Ramachamola was convicted on the evidence of a single witness who claimed she had shouted, 'Let us kill him!' and slapped the face of a woman who had protested when they started burning him. It appeared at this moment that Kentridge had brought home to the Appeal Court judges – all new to the case – the inappropriateness of the death penalty.

And so he moved on to the technical arguments over the power of the judiciary to reopen the case. There was no authority for the reopening of a trial once judgement had been delivered, Kentridge conceded. But there had to be an 'inherent jurisdiction' of the courts to take such a step 'whenever justice cries out for it to do so'. The Defence had found an instance where such jurisdiction had been exercised, Kentridge announced, pulling the case of *Lesley Sikweyiya v The State* like a rabbit out of the bottomless hat of legal precedent. He sketched the case: Sikweyiya had been sentenced to death in 1979 and had been refused an appeal. His subsequent petition to the Chief Justice for leave to appeal had also been refused. But 11 days after the refusal the petition was suddenly granted; an appeal hearing had been held and the condemned man declared innocent. There was no judgement explaining the reversal, said Kentridge. 'One's knowledge of it [the decision] tends to be anecdotal.'

It was a piquant case with which to confront Rabie, involving a memorable action by his predecessor, Chief Justice Rumpff. Although Kentridge carefully avoided detail, the story is well known at the South African Bar: the condemned man's father had gone to Rumpff's home in Bloemfontein to make a personal appeal for his son's life. The Chief Justice had been so impressed by his story that he had the refusal of the petition withdrawn and leave to appeal granted. 'One must regard it [Rumpff's action] as a deliberate illegality, or a case of inherent jurisdiction,' said Kentridge.

The judges began firing questions at Kentridge and he swung imperturbably to field them. 'Where did it [the concept] come from?' demanded Rabie. 'My Lord, it comes from the heart of the court,' rejoined Kentridge.

He moved on to the second leg of his argument – admission of Manete's new evidence by 'special entry' in the trial record. The trial judge, Justice Human, had refused it, dismissing the application as 'frivolous and absurd'. But Human had not heard Manete's evidence; only after he had done that would it be proper for him to find it frivolous. Kentridge was cut short by Rabie with a gesture at the clock: 'Well, my Lord, that is my submission. I'm sorry if I've rather overrun my time.' The court would give its judgement at a later date.

The odds were against the appeal succeeding, but this three-and-a-half-hour performance by South Africa's greatest lawyer, during which he never once faltered for want of a word, an answer or an argument, has shortened them. The appeal was indeed rejected but the changing times, and the pressure of international opinion right up to the UN Security Council, were on the side of the Six. By the end of 1992 they were all released.

V677
Pretoria Central Prison
Private Bag 45
Pretoria

24/1/65

My dear, sweet Ann,

... Today is Sunday, & you, mom & Dad & Jane were here this morning. I fear I was rather sharp; in particular I think of my getting somewhat worked up over the car, & then a little later being abrupt with Mom. Please phone Mom, give her my love, & say I'm sorry. And darling buz – I'm <u>so</u> sorry that I upset you. I get worked up, & though I do try jolly hard to keep things altogether under control I sometimes can't help some of the pressure from escaping ...

Your John

28/1/65

Dearest darling John,

During the last few days you have seemed so much better. I am so glad. You can be quite sure that everything possible is being done. Everybody is working hard. The last few nights have been very trying for me as Davey has been waking up six or seven times in the night. I have tried to have afternoon rests but these are never quite the same, certainly not for me. At last one thing that I have done during the last two or three days is write a lot of letters – 11. For me this is a record and I feel very virtuous about it, until I think of all the letters I have still to write.

[Ann to John – no date]

David is a popular boy this morning because he only woke once during the night. Now he is in the kitchen causing chaos at the breakfast table as his admirers are compelled to leave the table to pay their homage and have to be hustled back to their porridge. Last night I got two letters from you … both wonderful letters. Full of love and comfort. The special thing about letters is that they really do go from me to you to me and from me to you. Here is a special kiss and another kiss from me to you.

Your Ann

Mourning and jiving

For the most part, it was the sort of funeral he would have appreciated. It was not just the numbers, although it would be flattering enough for any politician to have 85 000 mourners attendant on his coffin and thousands more outside, banging on the gates. It was more the spirit of the occasion that made it a fitting farewell to a man who was distinguished, above all, by being much loved.

A small moment he would have enjoyed – as a military man who stood on discipline, but loved dancing – came at about midnight. Chris Hani's body had just been marched out of the giant soccer stadium by ANC soldiers, goose-stepping Russian-style in their olive-green uniforms.

The crowd left behind settled down for the all-night vigil: or rather, this being South Africa and Soweto, they exploded into a frenzy of dancing as a township band swung into one of those magical rhythms that is a mix of African jazz and rebel song. The dance was the toyi-toyi, the exuberant 'soldiers dance' of Umkhonto we Sizwe, the 'Spear of the Nation'.

It was as if the entire stadium had come alive, the huge concrete tiers heaving like a drum skin. The force of the unity of movement was literally terrifying, sending marshals – acutely aware that the toyi-toyi had derailed two trains earlier in the week – scurrying with warnings that it could bring down the main stand and its hanging galleries.

Down on the soccer field danced a few score mourners who had escape the cordons. Among them was a young woman in the traditional dress of the Xhosa people – blue headdress, blanket skirt and beads – and a shiny pair of white track shoes giving a dab of modernity. Tucked into her waistband glinted a pistol, which she drew every few minutes and fired into the night sky, percussion-style.

Nobody noticed, in the thunderous noise, until an ANC

security official strode over and tapped her on the shoulder. She turned and smiled shyly up at the figure of authority looking down on her. What he said is not known. But from his demeanour and gestures towards the main stand she was being told to accompany him to other figures and places of authority.

She demurred, coyly, but gave way as he slipped a custodial hand around her waist. And as they walked off, this pistol-packing Xhosa girl and her captor, their stride broke – without a word between them – into the toyi-toyi. Together they danced their way into the crowds.

The celebratory mood was the curiosity of the occasion. Perhaps the explanation was that given by one speaker, who told the crowd: 'We are celebrating as well as mourning, because this silly man has opened the door to freedom.' But, then again, perhaps it was because this is South Africa.

There was no lack of mourning. Through the Sunday afternoon they waited in three-hour-long queues along the back corridors of the stadium. Swept noisily down stairwells and through tunnels, they burst into the autumnal sunshine to make the pilgrimage across the turf and under the three gaily-coloured marquees to pay their respects.

Old men with grizzled white beards, raggedy youths, township mamas and be-suited dudes, some paused to give the Black Power salute, others bowed, others just hesitated – throwing curious looks at the waxen face of their hero, one cheek disfigured despite the undertakers' efforts to camouflage the passage of the assassin's bullet.

There was more, transparent grief as the afternoon shadows lengthened and colleagues in the leadership arrived. They were led by Oliver Tambo, then national chairman of the ANC, relying on a stick in the wake of the stroke that robbed him of the presidency. He walked hesitantly, but with a fierce air of independence that had his bodyguard constantly reaching to catch him in case of a fall, but never daring to touch without the excuse.

Behind came the 'Red Pimpernel', Hani's close friend Ronnie Kassrils; Joe Slovo, Hani's mentor and predecessor as Umkhonto we Sizwe chief of staff and Communist Party general secretary; and the rest of the ANC executive. As they emerged from the tents several of the women were openly crying. Kenneth Kaunda, looking much the same as ever despite his lost presidency, was dabbing his eyes with a large white handkerchief, the rest of the men were just looking sad.

But when they got up onto the platform they immediately led the crowd into a thunderous toyi-toyi, silver-haired Slovo making prodigious leaps that graphically gave the lie to the latest rumours that his cancer has brought him to the point of death. Winnie Mandela arrived shortly afterwards. She gave a ferocious clenched-fist salute to the platform, but only a scattering of fists replied, and she was led off to the back of the dignitaries. Nelson joined them, and the dancing and the speechifying went on into the evening, the sloganeering getting more militant as the leaders drifted away and the night lengthened.

Outside the stadium small groups stood huddled from the cold around fires in the veld, like soldiers on the eve of ancient battle. When the dawn broke over Johannesburg's golden-white mine dumps, more than two-thirds of the crowd had melted away. But those remaining included marauding youths and battle was soon joined with security forces guarding an adjoining industrial showground and a nearby motorway.

'The police are misbehaving outside,' the ANC Secretary-General, Cyril Ramaphosa, told the crowd. Outside two derelict mine buildings were burning. White troops had thrown up a razor-wire barrier on a pedestrian bridge. A fat youth jumped to his feet and then staggered wildly, for all the world a black Billy Bunter playing the fool in a schoolyard, before collapsing with a gunshot wound.

In the corner of the stadium grounds two ambulances were picking up the wounded. A man stood over a prostrate, bare-chested youth, holding up a saline drip. But the drama was ignored by the crowd as the familiar red, bullet-proof Mercedes of Mandela led the funeral cortege back into the amphitheatre.

A military band struck up 'Abide with Me' as the coffin was lifted onto a dais. Fighting raged on outside. Seven companies of MK guerrillas marched past the coffin, the portly figure of their commander, Joe Modise, taking the salute. It was a piquant moment: Modise sentenced Hani to death in the 1960s for mutiny after the young guerrilla protested at the incompetence of the command.

At 12.56 pm it was time to go. Past the mayhem they went, around the commercial capital to the cemetery outside his hometown of Boksburg where another huge crowd waited. An MK commander stepped forward to hand three white doves to the widow and their three daughters who were fighting back tears by the graveside. They released them on a nod, as a uniformed guerrilla pulled a pistol and fired a volley of shots. They were echoed by sympathetic gunfire crackling between the tombstones.

One of the birds fluttered, hesitated and then dived into the pit next to Hani. If anyone needed reminding, the dove of peace was dead.

V677
Pretoria Central Prison
Private Bag 45
Pretoria

9/2/65

My beloved loveliness,

An interesting & very useful side-effect of the Ritalin is that I seem to think more clearly now. It's hard to express briefly what I mean: essentially it's a matter of maintaining proportion between the different elements in a piece of thought. In retrospect I can see how I've exaggerated or minimised the importance of different parts of chains of thought – sometimes from day to day. For several days now I've had a sort of calm & balance against which I can judge the 'erraticity' of previous thought.

You have such a galaxy of wonderful characteristics, darling beetle. I sit & reflect on just one – say, your unselfishness to me – & I can't plumb its depths or comprehend its extent. Sweet Ann, I am a hugely fortunate fellow to have such a splendid woman to love me …

Your John

V677
Pretoria Central Prison
Private Bag 45
Pretoria

11/2/65

My dearest one …

The story of the little Prince & the fox is so wonderful, my lovekin … As I told you today, buz, & as I said in a letter a couple of days ago the possibility that you may not have me is incomparably the worst feature of what faces me. Should this happen, my love, my love, we must remember the end of the same story: 'It has done me good,' said the fox, 'because of the colour of the wheat fields.' And remember, beetle, a relationship must be assessed in terms of intensity & profundity, not only duration.

   Just think of how extraordinarily privileged we are to have had & to have a relationship such that there is nothing of importance which:
a. can't be said between us,
b. needs to be said between us.

Your very loving husband,
John

Presumption of guilt

Before he became president in May 2009, Zuma and his supporters made much of the 'presumption of innocence' as he struggled to stay out of prison in connection with the corrupt arms deal that disfigured the ANC's first years in office. The party used the concept to justify what it represented as a duty to stand by their president. An accused 'must be presumed innocent until found otherwise in a court of law', said the ANC. It accused his detractors of taking the approach 'that Jacob Zuma is guilty, and it is up to him to prove his innocence.'

The principle of a presumption of innocence is, of course, one of the fundamental tenets of the legal system, originating in English common law. But, as the US Supreme Court has pointed out, it is not considered evidence of a defendant's innocence. It is merely an assumption made by the law for the sake of due process. It is limited to the law.

There is, for instance, no need for concern that Hitler is being cheated of his innocence, because he never had the benefit of trial. Nevertheless, if Hitler were to be found cowering in some jungle hideout, he would enjoy – so far as the courts are concerned – an assumption of innocence until brought to trial. There would be no need to restore him to the Chancellery pending his trial.

So it is with Zuma. But that does not amount to the assertion that he is innocent. The distinction is an important one. And it is difficult to imagine circumstances in which it has more importance than Zuma's.

There may be an assumption of innocence where the courts are concerned, but it can coexist with a presumption of guilt on the part of the rest of society.

In the same way it can be assumed that Zuma's secrecy about

his life – in particular those 15 'missing' years – justifies an assumption, if not a presumption of guilt. It is incumbent on him, as a man who is already under suspicion of criminality, to answer some of the obvious questions raised by the account I have given of what is known about his activities in exile.

Questions like his membership off the Communist Party. Was he a lifelong member? And, more telling, why did he hide the detail?

What knowledge did he have about the deaths of such as the popular Thami Zulu; Ben Langa, the brother of the chief justice; and Cyril, alias Fear. To borrow a term from the courts, he was 'at all material times' in a position to know, which in turn attracts an assumption that he did know.

He was after all the deputy director of the Mbokodo and, as such, privy to its secrets. He may protest that his specific responsibility was intelligence – as opposed to 'security' – but we have it from the Commission that the responsibilities of these two branches of the Mbokodo merged. At the very least, why did he not take action to secure the release of Thami Zulu and investigate the Langa killing with more purpose than the brief conversation with Joel Martins in Lusaka?

What transparency can he bring to bear on the fate of those who died in ANC detention? Will the President of South Africa tell the electorate about the 'executions'? Was a presumption of innocence extended to them in anticipation of their trial? Were they given trials at all? The forgotten people, like Derrick Lobelo alias Vusi Mayekiso, who one might safely hazard was no super-spy, but more likely just a man who let his smoking habit get the better of him.

From the above it appears that Zuma would have been well positioned to be informed and – being informed – carries a responsibility for the camps scandal and the scandal surrounding the mysterious death of Thami Zulu and the tragedy of Benjamin Langa.

'Perhaps one day information will come to light which will show that he [Thami Zulu] was the Third Man acting on behalf of the enemy,' one of the many inquiries into these much-troubled times remarked. The reference is of course a flippant evocation of the most famous spy story of the 20th century.

Perhaps a more telling reference would have been to the Sherlock Holmes classic, *The Hound of the Baskervilles*, and the dog that failed to bark in the night.

14/2/65

Darlingest Ann,

… Every time I read something good (& especially if I read it with some one), I can feel my insight grow a little, or perhaps even by an appreciable jump. This is the wonder of books; through them the individual can attain a maturity & a penetration (by entering into the considered thought & viewpoints of others) which would otherwise be quite literally impossible, except perhaps if one had the services of a large number of excellent tutors.

This is a key to the understanding of Man's progress. And yet there are intelligent men (fortunately few) who boast of how little they read! They so obviously fail to comprehend that greater understanding of the World & of Man is accumulated & transmitted to the individual in this way, & that he who does not read but relies on casual discussion & his own experiences is confining himself to scraps while a banquet is available.

Your very loving husband,
John

V677
Pretoria Central Prison
Private Bag 45
Pretoria

15/2/65

Ann love,

… My phrases & letters must be repetitive, my darling lovekin, but please try to consider each one as unique & freshly minted, full of force & sorrow. As I write each letter I pour my love into it, hoping that it will reach you with as much significance as it leaves me.

Your loving husband,
John

20/2/65

My sweet darling buzz,

… I still seem to find it virtually impossible to express my feelings at visits. Several times I've decided to make a real effort, but it just isn't easy, love. May my letters carry the warmth, the depth & the extent of my feelings to you, my dearest beetle.

Very enjoyable music this evening. Two songs by Ella Fitzgerald & one by Eartha Kitt – in the lyrics of the latter ('Always True to You Darling in My Fashion') there's a reference to 'Harris'!

… Your very sweet Valentine arrived a couple of days ago. Do know, darling one, that you are so forcibly for me too 'The only pebble on the beach.'

All his very best love from your buffle,
John

My darling

Now that thugs are coming ... it is more difficult to keep up a
fighting spirit. What makes thugs different is that we ... fight
together. We can be together, support each other in some ways.
Most of all in our sureness of our love and support for each other
but in the f ... itself we each have our own little ... and I need you
so much. You are so successful in you. I try very hard. You will
hardly recognise me. Certainly not the peaceful person any more.
I have taken over ...

　　Some special love in this corner and special kisses.

Your own ever loving
Ann

1/3/65

… Seeing the ring on your finger pleased me greatly. It was an excellent choice, & I'm so glad you really liked it. It was clever of you to open it with me – you are such a darling girl – I will fall in love with you over & over if I hadn't done so so completely.

4/3/65

My dearest love,

... In general she gave the impression that she & David will do what they can – & of this I have no doubt – but that chances are now *slim*. As we have said to each other, buz, any prediction or assessment is quite impossible, but we must accept that the prospects for clemency are not at all good. This being so, my love, while not crossing bridges I do think that we must continue to harden our shells, & continue to behave with all the fortitude we can muster in adversity. It's jolly fortunate, isn't it, that I've been *up* for the past 4 or 5 days. And at the time of writing this shows no sign of ceasing, though of course it must do so eventually.

Your very loving buffle

Sweetheart

A short message of love – mountains and mountains of it. Its length will end on how long I have to wait before seeing you, and then I will post it on my ... through town. My own special buffle, I love you very much. Thinking of you, I am ... conscious of just an overwhelming feeling of love. To think of what you have been through is unbearable.

I have just seen Dr van Wyk go in, so am not sure what is going to happen. Maybe I shall be able to come back this afternoon, as he will be with you for some time.

Darling John, you are being so wonderful now that the going is getting really tough. I know how dreadful it must be for you to be so completely tied as to action and decision.

Perhaps somehow or other your wonderful qualities have rubbed off onto me for I find ... to do hitherto dreamed of things ... suppose somebody or other – now I remember what I have in mind was St Paul saying what the ... of love is. If you still have your bible ... that bit. Maybe I am wrong, but I can't ... Up here, sitting on the bench. I'll take a look when I get home and see if that is what I meant.

This letter has no number as I really don't know where I had got to.

From your loving Ann

V677
Pretoria Central Prison
Private Bag 45
Pretoria

8/3/65

My darling,

… Then, on the actual 'feeling intellectually down': it seems to
me that though various people are being approached with the
possibility of making representations it could well be considered
that the sum of the points they make is not sufficiently weighty to
justify clemency. Ann love, it's in a way a matter of tipping a scale
– we have to get sufficient weight in the pan. It's always possible
that in over-eagerness one can be rather a bull in a china shop,
but then on the other hand (& remembering that one is aiming
at tilting a balance) one ought not to be overdelicate in making
those points which one considers to have weight. One should be
respectful & polite, of course, but one is still entitled to use the full
strength of points …

Very lovingly,
Your John

V677
Pretoria Central Prison
Private Bag 45
Pretoria

10/3/65

My sweet dear Ann,

Today I snapped at you at your visit – I'm terribly sorry that I hurt you. It is so good that I *know* you don't feel the least Whit less loving towards me. Try imagining that I'm holding your hand, love – you know how much I'd like to.

Your very loving husband,
John

Pretoria Central Prison
Private Bag 45
Pretoria

12/3/65

Dearest love,

… Two letters from you arrived here today. The first included the postcard from Meg.

The other letter (started on the 5th & finished on Monday 8th) was the one in which you spoke of your fears of what you will do if the worst happens & you don't have me. One thing which does comfort me slightly is that over last weekend I think you *were* down, & that you felt somewhat better after seeing Ruth on Monday. I hope I'm right in this, & that I haven't confused the times & days.

But apart from this *small* consolation there is so little I can say, my lovekin. If it happens – we'll simply have to accept it. And by far the worst for me is the thought of how it'll hurt you – all else is shadowy in comparison. I know you are afraid, my darling Ann, but what can I do to disguise the reality of the monstrous possibility? I'm very glad that you have brought up your feelings fairly explicitly, Ann love – it's right for you to tell me. But oh, my lovekin, how hard it is to know this & to be entirely unable to move my little finger to help you.

If it had been possible you'd have gone up in my estimation over the past couple of weeks.

What a delightful girl you are. I love you so much, sweet dear Ann.

Your buffle – John

V677
Pretoria Central Prison
Private Bag 45
Pretoria

14/3/65

Dearest,

I've just written a brief letter to Mom & Dad – it's difficult really to think of subject matter. Do try to keep contact with them, buz – they do value it. Mom especially particularly likes hearing from you, & of David …

Your very loving husband,
John

17/3/65

My beloved Ann,

I don't think I've used this particular salutation in a letter to you recently, if indeed ever before. This is perhaps odd, for you *very definitely* are my beloved one, & have been for the past superbly happy 10 years. The fact that the past is unchangeable – though of course very bad in a way – also means that the fine things are immutably fixed. And you & I know with such entire certainty how fine a thing our marriage has been. You know, lovekin, that in spite of what has happened to us over the past eight months this period has in a way displayed the true temper of our love with especial clarity.

Two factors have been at my core virtually from the day of our first meeting (which we could count as the church braaivleis, or perhaps more properly as the swimming bath at the beginning of September). The one is an intense consciousness of how superb a person you are. You are, quite objectively considered, a *very* fine person. This isn't just my opinion, buz – it's the unanimous opinion of the *very best* people we know, & we know some very fine people. I could very easily eulogise, & in later letters probably will, but in this letter I'll content myself with the conservative statements made above.

The other fact is the strength & quality of your love for me. It stirs & delights me every time you tell me of your love for me; but the innermost me has 100% locked-in knowledge of this love. My dearest, as regards *necessity* you needn't ever mention that you love me – I *know* it – full stop.

It's about 4 pm, & a short while ago I saw Ad (I'll come back to that in a moment). You are in Jo'burg now, plugging away, doing whatever you can, probably with David Soggot at this present moment. And tomorrow I'll see your dear face again – wonderful, lovekin.

Talking of Ad: what a *huge* comfort it is to me that you & our David are with her. I quite literally can't think of any person in the world who could possibly be her equal, let alone superior for the job of 'elder sister'. This is *immensely* relieving for me, my darling one. I've never believed that 'blood is thicker than water' (taking 'blood' to be relations & 'water' to be other links) and the affinities between you and Ad are another support for my view.

My lovekin, do be quite sure that I know you & our friends have left no stone unturned in your efforts to try to help me. Irrespective of outcome you will know that everything humanly possible was tried. And if it ever does occur to you that in one way or another rather different decisions should perhaps have been taken – as we've said before the wisdom of hindsight isn't available as one makes decisions. You've done your best, & I'm very proud of you, dearest Ann. Your magnificent quality has shone so steadily – I'm intensely warmed by my pride in you.

You have held yourself so magnificently upright, Ann love. There seems so little hope now, but we must summon all our fortitude, we must do our best.

The last chance was an appeal for clemency to the state president. The lawyers submitted it on 22 March. The submission read: 'The consequences of his act were appalling, but however gross may have been Harris's miscalculations, he was prompted to this act only by the highest motives of his idealism. In his own mind the idea of violence, the idea of injury to persons was repugnant; he neither intended to nor could he gain personally from this deed. In the history of South Africa many others have committed acts of violence for the realisation of their dearly-held beliefs in the liberty of men.'

Thursday, 18 March

Sweetheart John

I worry so much about how my own … is feeling. I know that you are not well at the moment. That is quite clear. By the time you get this letter we may well have the final decision.

In the meantime I find it very important to be hopeful. To keep on fighting.

At the moment I am on the way to Johannesburg. We are in Potgieter Street, just near you. I hope you are asleep.

Darling John, I love you a great deal. I think about you, under the surface all the time. We are so much one that really without you, I am only half a person. I have no doubts about anything all along the … I could not possibly have done too much. I only fear that I have done too little. But I know that you know I love you, and that all my actions have been dictated primarily by that …

Ann

Ann Harris prepared her own plea for mercy. She and John's father delivered it personally to Vorster in Cape Town on 24 March. 'I appeal for clemency for a man who made a tragic and foolish mistake that resulted in the death of an old lady – and not for a man who intentionally committed murder.'

24/3/65

About your working part-time or full-time, darling love, please don't try to carry all the financial burdens at the expense of your having to slave away, & at the expense of your seeing relatively little of Davey. The latter point is so important, buz – I do want him to know that *you* are his mother, & that *you* love him unstintingly & comprehensively. Of course I hope that you'll do whatever you can for Mom & Dad – but the welfare of you two – Ann & Davey – must be the top priority.

'What does one say?'

Wentzel went to say goodbye to Harris on the day before the execution. 'He was dressed in the khaki corduroy, which prisoners wear. His face was yellow from long days in prison,' recounts Wentzel. 'What does one say on such an occasion?' he asks rhetorically. 'I told John that I was distressed at our friendship being cut short and that history would judge him. He cried a bit as we spoke. He told me that Father McGinis who was visiting him had told him that the peace of the Lord would descend upon him. He said that he did not accept that it was the peace of the Lord, but that he felt at peace and able to face the execution.'

'There is a reality and an unreality together on such an occasion,' says Wentzel. 'The reality is the knowledge of the certainty of John's execution and the unreality [is] one's disbelief in this certainty, one's revolt at the concept of setting out to kill a young man with such organised ritual. This would seem civilised conduct debased and abused with all the trappings of form and legality … instead of bringing civilised order to violence and disorder the law itself is the killer.'

Thursdays were the hanging days in apartheid South Africa and on Thursday, 1 April 1965, he walked to the gallows singing, 'We shall overcome'. The apartheid state used to hang up to seven people at a time. But Harris died on his own.

He would have been hanged with a new rope; if he had been black it would have been an old, previously used rope.

Father McGinis, who was present at the execution, described how 'Harris had shaken hands with everyone inside the execution chamber and told them he bore no ill will. He had been anxious to be in control of his senses to the very end. He sang "We shall overcome" as they hanged him.' The hangman was quoted as saying, 'He was still singing as he dropped.'

His last words, according to Gordon Winter, were 'Some day …'

Death notice

On 1 April 1965, John Harris, a member of the African Resistance Movement (ARM), was executed for placing a bomb at Johannesburg's main railway station, resulting in one death and several injuries. Harris was the first and only white person in the mandate period to be hanged for a political offence. His widow told the Commission: '5.30 am was the time set for the execution. We were all awake, thinking of John … Not long afterwards the phone rang. The voice said: "Your John is dead."' She recognised the voice as one of the Special Branch men.

My Darling John,

I have written it so often. This is the last time I shall do it …
But before I write of the sense of loss I feel and which I know I
shall feel still more in the days ahead, I want to write, as I have
promised, of our last two days together.

They were such happy days, when we were both filled with a
feeling of happiness, safety and peace, which Father M [McGinis]
diagnoses as Divine Grace (your words) – the phenomenon is
certainly there, although I don't agree with the diagnosis. But we
had more. We had a feeling of exaltation … I feel it now, as I write
of those two nearly perfect days. Perhaps … it was caused by the
sense of oneness which we felt. We *were* one, in the most real sense.
As you said, physical reality, physical presence is ephemeral, easily
lost, but the oneness we felt has nothing to do with time or space.
I was with you in your cell up to the last minute. You were with
me here. You are still here with me now, safely inside, absolutely
invulnerable.

We have become one over a long period. I have marked you
indelibly, you have marked me. You and I as we stood together on
those two days were products of each other, with the same thought
patterns, ideals and ideas … And so you will live on in me, for as
long as I live. You said that. And of course you will live on in Davey
in a different way. And because you are living through me, I must
lead a full life; I have promised you that. Before I said goodbye I
said, 'I will try to lead a life worthy of your wife.' You said, 'I hope
I have led a life worthy of your husband.' And then you went away.
But it was only on the lowest level that we separated.

We were so conscious of our oneness on those last two days.
Ruth was trying to get permission for us to see each other in the
office without a mesh between us, but it was refused. We didn't
feel disappointed. By the time the last afternoon came, we were so
much at one that little things like that seemed far away beneath us.

So safe. You said that your great fear had been for me, either that I would crack when I heard the news, or that I would, with great effort, put on a brave front. I had been afraid too. I wrote to you a while ago that I was on a stormy sea. So far I have managed to keep afloat, but there had been one enormous wave looming ahead, and I had feared that I would go under. I had even written to you that I didn't know if I wanted to go on living without you ...

You knew that even now you are a hero to many Africans. We have heard, and you have heard it. And now I know that you died like a hero. You were happy to the end. You walked to the gallows singing 'We shall overcome'. Before you died you felt no bitterness, only forgiveness ...

On Monday ... you said to me, surely it is much better to die this way than anonymously in a motor accident. I couldn't answer you then. I was too overwhelmed by the news. But I thought about it on Monday night. That evening I had found, while watering the garden, a little puffadder under the flowers. Death is just around the corner at any moment ... That is what I said to you on Tuesday morning, that you had been given a wonderful way of dying – not anonymously, but as a hero. It was an honour to be hanged by Vorster, just as it is an honour to be banned by him.

Your death had so much meaning in it. First of all you acted for all the people who say, 'It should be done, but I am not the one who can do it.' At your funeral we read: 'Seek not to know for whom the bell tolls; it tolls for thee.' I thought of what someone had said to me: that as far as motive went, any one of us could have been in your position. You were dying for us all. But it was wider than that. You were expiating the sins the white people have committed against the black, those who realise their guilt and those who don't. There is much more expiating still to be done, but you have given your life towards the final settlement ...

Before we said goodbye, we talked about how much at one we would be in the next few hours. You told me what you were going to do. You said you would finish *Beau Geste*, which you had just got from the prison library, and eat your peaches. Then you were going to write letters. You would probably stay up late to do that. You said you would think of me driving home. I told you that I would be buying some flowers for you on the way. You said, 'For tomorrow?' And I said, 'Yes.' Then you asked what I was going to buy, and I said, 'Roses. Little roses.' And you asked me, 'Why little?' And I said, 'Because it seems right.' ...

Those last few minutes were in a way an agony, but an agony that had the perfection of a Greek tragedy, so that they were at the same time a happiness. I don't know what you thought as you walked down the corridor, but I know I was smiling when I came outside, and I said to Ad, 'We had a very happy afternoon together.'

You asked me what I would do on Thursday. You wondered whether I would be awake with you. You wanted me to decide. I said I would be with you, and you said that was what you wanted too. Then I said that on Thursday I would write down all that we thought and said and felt. And you said, 'Yes, write it soon, because it will fade.'

Now it is written. The happiness has faded, but I am still your Ann, as I promised. It is very hard without you, but I shall be strong as you were strong. Everyone who saw you felt your strength and felt strong with you. And you did send a last message. You asked Father M to tell me that you had died singing, 'We shall overcome'.

You said, my darling John, that it was such a support to you to know that I had been with you 'every inch of the way'. Your parents stood by you because they loved you because of the 'biological accident' of parenthood. I chose to stand by you. More than that, I chose to go with you. Our oneness made me with you 'every inch of the way', as only you and I really know.

And we have David, whom you barely knew at all. We didn't talk about him very much. He came to see you, and banged the wire, enjoying the noise, and then he crawled along the bench for you. When he was outside waiting in the car with Ad, a warder came and patted him on the head and said, 'Is this the Harris baby? Poor little chap!' And Ad said, 'He'll be proud of his father.'

We talked about our little boy and you said there was no need for you to tell me what you wanted done. You knew that because of our oneness, the way we loved one another, my decisions would be our decisions. Then you said, 'Watch him for corpulence. The Harrises have a tendency to corpulence. And watch him for melancholia.'

Sometimes when you cried you said: 'These are tears of happiness.' Once you said it was like the time when David was born. You said: 'I remember I cried. It was because you were all right and he was all right and everything was all right.'

Life after death

Ann Harris left South Africa in 1966 after a letter from the government saying she would not be allowed to continue to teach. She went to London with 18-month-old David on the Union Castle Line and after a few months was given a job teaching in Uganda by the Ministry of Overseas Development. It was a two-year appointment, and, despite the traumatic memories, a fulfilling one. She was offered a further extension but decided, as she puts it, that David 'should become an English boy'.

Back in London she worked in a small private secondary school for girls and shared a flat with John's sister, Jane. And David started primary school near to the Hain family in Putney. (Ad Hain, referred to in the letters, was the mother of the anti-apartheid campaigner and later UK minister, Peter Hain.) Taking a cue from John's urging that she should marry after his execution, Ann decided she would not 'make a career' out of being the husband of John Harris.

She was introduced to a scientist, Martin Wolfe, by a mutual friend. They were married in August 1970 and went to live in Cambridge where Martin worked at the Plant Breeding Institute. He resigned when it was privatised by Margaret Thatcher in 1987. David Wolfe, the babe in arms when his father battled for life in Pretoria's Central Prison, is today a leading civil rights lawyer in London. Ann and Martin now live in a 13th-century farmhouse near Diss in Suffolk.

In 2009, for the first time, I met her face to face. My youngest daughter came with me. She is a lovely girl and we had an enjoyable, teasing journey on the train in the summer's sun. A taxi was waiting and after a few wrong turnings we arrived at the farmhouse. It was, as I had anticipated, a happy home.

But there was one thing I had not expected. Unforgivably, I must have forgotten that she had told me she had Parkinson's disease like me. I knew from the moment she greeted me that I was going to have trouble understanding her. An inexplicable feeling, which I suppressed at the time, welled up which was somewhere between rage and frustration. Later, on reflection, an image of my father came to me.

I loved my father. I don't know where I had been, but I hadn't seen them for some time. My mother called out: 'St John's outside tending to his sweet peas.' Dad's pride in his sweet peas was a subject of family fun.

Sure enough there he was in front of the trellis where my eldest daughter, still in her nappies, used to 'garden' with him in muddy companionship.

He was on his knees, but must have heard my mother call. He got up and strode across the lawn to meet me, his hand outstretched in happy greeting, but, oh God, the words wouldn't come. I looked into his eyes and the utter bleakness I saw there haunts me still. He had had two strokes and the second had wiped out his communications centre.

Trophy

With the liberation of black South Africa in 1994 some recognition was finally given to John Harris for his courage when a service was held in his memory at Hero's Acre outside Pretoria.

There were, naturally, questions about the whereabouts of his ashes. The family assumed they had been scattered in the prison grounds. But it transpired they had been kept in an urn on a policeman's mantelpiece, presumably as a memento. Or trophy.

'Naming names'

They said John Harris was a 'softie'. But he seems to have been more of a courageous and gentle man, six feet tall and solidly built with receding hair and an irrepressible grin on his face.

Born the son of a car salesman, he was a bright young boy with a recorded IQ of 153. At the age of 14 he became a regular performer on the radio programme, *Quiz Kids*. He also had a passion for cars and airplanes. He was something of a romantic.

Asked to choose a nom de guerre he almost inevitably chose 'Robin', evoking Robin Hood and the English myth of restitution. Friends remember him as 'intellectually self-confident', which means he could be a bit pigheaded and impatient. He never seemed to sit still, striding backwards and forwards when he was thinking, tossing an orange or tennis ball from one hand to the other. He wore a built-up shoe, to compensate for the vestiges of a mild bout of polio in 1956.

The bombing of Johannesburg station has a particular place in the story of resistance to apartheid, largely because Harris was the only white to be executed for a political offence during the apartheid era. He was, to whites, the 'mad bomber'.

He was a teacher, married to an attractive young woman, Ann, who was also a teacher. The young couple had tried to make it at Oxford University – John studying modern greats – but were forced to give up the venture and return to South Africa when they ran out of money.

John Harris was a sitting target for South Africa's 'dirty tricks' department; it was like spear-hunting fish in a goldfish bowl. As chairman of SANROC (the South African Non-Racial Olympic Committee), Harris was a target for hatred among whites – the man responsible for depriving them of their precious sport. He was an active chairman; in February 1963 he had flown to Lausanne to deliver a passionate (and ultimately successful) plea to the International Olympic Committee (IOC) to exclude his country from the Tokyo Olympics, which were due to be held the following year.

On his return to South Africa the security forces were almost forced by white opinion to take action against him. So they seized his passport. But one could sense that this was not enough for the likes of 'Lang Hendrik' van den Bergh – 'the Tall Assassin', as one of his subordinates in the Security Branch was to dub him.

In February 1964 the Branch had Harris banned under the Suppression of Communism Act. The effect of a banning order was mainly to limit an individual's movements; surely the analogy of hunting in a goldfish bowl has never been as apposite.

Isolated from public activities, he became a member of the African Resistance Movement (ARM), made up mostly of radical young activists, student leaders and university lecturers. They did have recourse to violence, but until this point had attacked inanimate targets such as power pylons and railway lines. It is worth saying at this stage that Harris was not only not a communist, but was anti-communist, like so many liberals.

Writing in his unpublished memoirs, a friend of Harris, the lawyer, Ernie Wentzel, explains that 'the ARM members believed in a chain reaction theory of political change. They had the idea that the political temperature was just below the boil. One had only to trigger off a dramatic incident such as a bomb explosion and this would tend to trigger off action by groups as yet unorganised. This would gather momentum until the momentum of opposition could not be resisted.'

ARM's 'momentum' was not gaining much ground at the time that the station bomb went off. All of the members of ARM had either been detained or had fled the country with the exception of Harris and an accomplice, John Lloyd, a journalist. Harris was determined to show the authorities and the population that ARM was still active.

It was on a Friday, 24 July 1964, that Harris tried to trigger the chain reaction, phoning in a warning of a bomb in a suitcase on Johannesburg station. He called the railway police first and then two local newspapers, the *Rand Daily Mail* and *Die Transvaaler*.

An account of what happened after the explosion was given by the government agent, Gordon Winter, in his book on his years working for South Africa's notorious intelligence agency, the Bureau of State Security (BOSS).

The suitcase exploded as planned, at 4.33 pm on the Friday afternoon. Twenty-four people were hurt, one of them – an old lady – dying of her injuries.

'Less than seven hours after the bomb blast, Harris was arrested by Security Police officers and immediately interrogated by Captain JJ Viktor, a friend of mine who knew I was a spy,' recounts Winter. 'Viktor later boasted to me how he had persuaded John Harris to make a full confession within five minutes. This is roughly what he told me.

'"One of the latest tricks in interrogation is to lull the suspect into a false sense of security. You start by being overfriendly with him and then suddenly scream like a maniac," said Viktor. "I've always believed the only way to make a man talk is to give him a bloody good hiding. But there's something to be said for these new-fangled psychological methods. I tried my own variation and it worked."

'Viktor said he first sat Harris down on a chair in the middle of the room. Then he told him, "Look, John, you are a member of the South African Liberal Party, so I know you are not the kind of man to go around blowing people up with bombs; so I'm not going to waste time trying to interrogate you about the station blast ..."

'Instead they would have a chat about sport. "When I asked him to name his favourite sport, Harris said he preferred playing cricket and tennis. I told him that I was mad about rugby, but that I always made a hash of my dropkick, Harris said he was a keen student of rugby but didn't actually play the game, as it was too rough for him ..."

'Viktor then picked up a newspaper, crumpled it into a ball and walked back to the far wall with it. He ran forward three, or four steps and dropkicked the ball of paper at a table in the corner.

'"Harris told me he knew at once why my kicks went wide and said I swung my foot out as I kicked, which took the ball off course. I thanked him for his advice, picked up the ball of newspaper and carried it back to the wall. I ran forward again and delivered a massive kick, not at the ball, but right on John Harris's jaw. Harris hurtled backwards and somersaulted over the back of the chair. As he lurched to his knees he swayed dizzily, cupped his chin in both hands and blood spurted from his mouth as he coughed."

'Viktor kicked him again on the chin and then once in the stomach. "I'll talk, I'll talk, but for Christ's sake don't kick me again, you've broken my jaw," Harris managed to mumble. He had suffered two fractures to the jaw.'

Wentzel went to see Harris shortly after his (Wentzel's) release. He described the scene afterwards. 'The interview room is like a milk bar with high stools and a counter for the visitors. Then there is a barrier of glass and perforated board for hearing. John was a sickening sight. His face was heavily swollen where his jaw had been broken ... He was the most dejected person I had ever seen. His spirit, smashed down by violence, flickered now and then, but he was frightened and felt he had no means to deal with his future.' Wentzel says that Harris begged repeatedly: 'Don't let them hang me.'

Harris would not talk about the assault at first, because a colonel whom he trusted 'had promised him that if he made a confession and forgot all about the assault he would not be given the death penalty,' says Wentzel. 'I told him very firmly that he could not have any such trust and he told us about the assault.'

Describing the assault as 'especially savage', Wentzel said that in addition to his broken jaw, Harris's testicles were severely damaged, sufficient to show severe bruising seven or eight weeks later.

The judge in the case against Harris was Mr Justice Joseph Ludorf, a conservative man and, judging from his performance, a fervent anti-communist. He also had a drinking problem.

Ludorf seemed to see the assault as a pivotal facet of the case, although, ostensibly, he knew nothing about it, no evidence of it having been led. Nevertheless he dealt with the issue in his judgement as follows: 'In his confession to the magistrate on September 11 the accused said the news [of those killed and injured by the station bomb blast] ... put him into a state of confusion and that as a result he revealed to the police the hiding place of the [bomb-making] materials as he did not want anything like this to occur again. This is clearly in conflict with the evidence of himself and his wife as to his reaction on hearing the news. But this conflict we see as not simply a lie by the accused. It goes much further!

'The accused's jaw was broken after his detention. The police evidence was that this happened as a result of a rearrest after an attempted escape by him at the Security Branch headquarters known as The Greys. Phillips [senior Defence counsel] very correctly did not seek to have this issue tried. He informed the court that the Defence disputed this evidence, but because [the question as to] just how he had got his jaw broken was irrelevant to the case before the court, he proposed to lead no evidence and not even to cross-examine the officer who gave the disputed evidence.

'When Moodie, on behalf of the State, commenced leading evidence as to the voluntary manner in which the confession was made, I asked Phillips whether he objected to the admission of the confession and he said that he did not have any objection at all. Under cross-examination, when faced with the conflict between his evidence and his confession, the accused deserted the attitude of his counsel and said that the confession was not voluntarily made. And at the end of his evidence, when questioned by me, he said that he made the confession for fear of being beaten again by the police.'

Ludorf's reasoning is a little difficult to follow. But it seems he was trying to say – with his pejorative explanation mark – that Harris was a liar, because he had persevered in trying to tell the court that he had been savagely beaten by the police.

Harris pleaded insanity at his trial. The Defence team said he was bipolar and went to impressive lengths to prove it. But clearly he was not mad. None of his friends or relatives believe he was mad. In fact they can tell one the name of the friend who was bipolar and whose symptoms he tried to imitate. So the trial all boiled down to 'intention'. If he could be shown to have had the intention of killing, he would hang. Recklessness was sufficient to 'prove' intention. For the purposes of the law, he had in effect intentionally killed Ethyl Rhys, the 77-year-old grandmother who was the sole fatality in the explosion.

Harris's account of his motive in planting the bomb is consistent and not easily dismissed. The security police had started a crackdown on the African Resistance Movement earlier in the month with what became known as 'The Fourth of July Raids'. Harris, suddenly finding himself in a leadership position of the domestic anti-apartheid movement, which was fast collapsing, decided on one last spectacular act – a warning of the consequences to white South Africa if they did not reform.

The testimony on which Harris's life turned in the trial came from his accomplice, a 23-year-old journalist working for *The Post* newspaper, John Lloyd.

Lloyd described a dinner he had at Harris's house a week before the bomb. At this dinner, he says, Harris told him that he had decided against a tentative plan they had to set fire to post office boxes in Pretoria – by posting incendiary devices – in favour of a bomb at a railway station or an underground parking garage.

'I had strong objections to these two, as targets, because of the possible loss of life involved, and we had some considerable argument on this point,' said Lloyd in his testimony. 'His contention was that any possible risk of life involved in striking at such targets would be justified as a long-term political move. He foresaw it as being a strategic move, which would foreshorten any political struggle of violence in this country and in that way save many lives.' Harris, in the judge's words, 'stoutly denied this allegation by Lloyd'.

Ludorf came down on Lloyd's side. 'Although he [Lloyd] may have been induced by a motive of self-preservation to blacken the conduct of the accused and to whiten his own, he must have been, we think, also motivated by saying as little as possible against his friends,' he said.

So, in the end and despite the cautionary principle that the evidence of an accomplice should be treated with 'suspicion', Ludorf backed Lloyd. His reasons for doing so can only be described as unfathomable.

'In truth, the prevailing winds were set for a hanging and I doubt if there was any way of saving John,' said Wentzel afterwards. 'John felt this and in his broken state he needed some hope, some idea of working constructively at his case. This is what his defence gave him and gradually his strength was restored,' said Wentzel.

'John never seemed to falter in his good spirits, his interest in what was going on both inside and outside prison,' said Wentzel of Harris's wait for the hangman.

Although Harris confessed to the station bomb, he did not betray any of his colleagues. He even declined an attempt by Judge Ludorf to get him to name names in court and, by Winter's uncontested account, he refused an offer by Van den Bergh shortly before his execution to release him if he would spy on his colleagues.

The toll

In his unpublished memoirs, Ernie Wentzel offers the thought that capital punishment is 'undiscriminating like John's bomb. Not only was John struck down but all around him others were destroyed, or injured.'

One who was destroyed was John Harris's mother, who committed suicide after her son's execution. There were also repercussions for John Lloyd, the crucial witness against Harris.

Lloyd got his immunity and was released after the trial, immigrating to Britain. In the UK things went well at first. He went into politics. He rose through the ranks of the Labour Party in Exeter, serving on the city council. In the 1992 general election he recorded one of the largest swings in Britain, albeit as an unsuccessful parliamentary candidate. Then he was elected chairman of the Exeter anti-apartheid movement and someone tipped off *The Guardian* about his background.

'It [the trial] was 30 years ago; it was an extremely distressing period and it is something that has marked my life ever since,' Lloyd said when I interviewed him in 1995. 'If I had been a free agent I wouldn't have done it [turned on Harris]. I was in detention under interrogation and I saw events partly through the eyes of my interrogators.'

Lloyd, it seems, came close to recanting. Harris's solicitor, the late Ruth Hayman, in an extraordinary personal initiative that could have resulted in her disbarment, flew to London and saw Lloyd, making a personal appeal to him to withdraw his evidence. At one stage a statement had been prepared for Lloyd to sign and an appointment agreed for him to do so, with just two days to go to Harris's execution. He did not show up for the appointment.

'Judas took his own life, but Adrian and Lloyd continue with theirs,' said Wentzel in a withering judgement on John Lloyd and Adrian Leftwich, the latter of whom turned state witness in a separate ARM sabotage trial in Cape Town.

'Lloyd – as far as I know – was quite a fiery radical in the ARM. At the Harris trial he had some opportunity to say a word that might have helped Harris, but refused to do so and in fact emphasised Harris's guilt,' continued Wentzel.

'Even when in London, snug and safe, he was asked to say something that might save John Harris. He not only refused, but even threatened to report the request to the South African security police.

'There is depth of depravity in this action. The weakness of Lloyd is human weakness, but this was a decision taken by an evil man who was prepared to place himself and his above John, or Ann, or their child.'

But there are aspects of Lloyd's story that raise questions as to where the true depravity lies.

Lloyd was arrested on 23 July – the day before Harris's arrest. The bomb exploded at 4.33 pm on the next day, the Friday. Lloyd completed his confession in the early hours of Saturday morning.

A striking aspect of his confession is that it does not mention the actual blast. There is no indication that a bomb explosion had taken place … more than eight hours after it had gone off.

Which is peculiar. The police made a point – when detaining various suspects in the bombing – of exaggerating the fatalities, claiming there were as many as 15 dead. The intention was obviously to frighten them into confession. So why did they make an exception of Lloyd?

Brigadier van den Bergh arrived at The Greys, at 7.10 pm on the Friday evening – more than two hours after the bomb had exploded. Why did he not tell Lloyd the bomb had gone off?

At 11 pm he had Harris arrested and brought in – later going on the record as saying that he had done so after Harris's name popped into his head 'from nowhere'.

A courageous lawyer

Some time ago the civil rights lawyer, David Soggot, went to visit a friend in hospital, emerging to find that Johannesburg's busy thieves had been at it again; they had stolen his car.

As is so often the case, the loss of the car was not as serious as the loss of his briefcase and the papers it contained. So he was much relieved, back at chambers, when a parcel arrived – delivered, the commissioner said, by a well-dressed young man who had declined to give his name. Inside was the missing briefcase with all the papers intact.

The tribute paid so silently by the anonymous thief was appropriate to the life of the Johannesburg silk who died in the city of his birth in May 2010, aged 78. Born of Jewish and Lithuanian descent and graduating from the University of the Witwatersrand, David's peers were the leaders of the South African Bar and he ranked with the greatest of them – Kentridge, Chaskalson, Mahomed and Bizos, among others. To witness the warm smile on Nelson Mandela's face on seeing him was to appreciate his standing among the great and the good.

In his days as junior counsel he represented John Harris. In Harris's farewell letters to his wife from death row, David's name keeps popping up, always in admiration for the 'terrier' who carried Harris's hopes of beating the hangman. That he did not win reflects on the country's security chiefs at the time, John Vorster and General Hendrik van den Berg, who are believed to have rigged the case against Harris.

Essentially a defence lawyer, the names of the clients David represented and the judicial hearings in which he was involved echo through the pages of recent South African history: Biko, (Winnie) Mandela, Delmas, Broederstroom, Mayekiso, Goldstone, the Eikenhof Three ...

David found much of his legal practice in what was then South West Africa (Namibia) where he established a particularly close association with SWAPO (the South West African People's Organisation.) He made his reputation in the protectorate through another case rigged by the Special Branch – popularly known as the case of the 'Kaiser Street Matahari' in which the security police were caught planting an agent as a typist on his Defence team. The trial, which involved two death sentences, was vitiated by the Appeal Court in Bloemfontein, by a bench led by then Chief Justice Rumpff. When the news got back to Windhoek there was literally dancing in the streets of Katutura township.

David also had pride at having appeared in the kingdom of Swaziland, in a case in which he represented an Opposition MP thrown out of Parliament. When David won the case the king suspended the Constitution and declared him a prohibited immigrant – a status he enjoyed until the day of his death.

Among his friends he was known as 'the frugal hedonist', having a passion for good music, good conversation and good food – the latter of his own cooking. Recently he took up painting under the tutelage of one of his daughters, Thea, who is a professional artist.

Where others are remembered in the glory of their office, memories of David are to be discovered in his humour and his quiet courage.

Humour stands on its own, but courage is not an easy attribute to justify, particularly when it came from an intensely private man. It was in the late stages of his life – after the stroke that so cruelly took most of the advocate's speech – that I saw and heard that quality, of courage, in a question he quietly asked me: 'Do you think I should wait around?' He did, for seven years, and the lives of his friends were richer in consequence.

On the weekend he died, as he was wheeled into the operating theatre, he looked around and said: 'It looks like Pretoria Central [maximum security prison]'. They were his last words.

A final twist in the hangman's tale

It is a bizarre story, that of the 1964 station bombing, replete with unanswered questions ranging from the basic conundrum that faced Judge Ludorf – whether Harris intentionally killed Mrs Rhys – to such as the possible involvement of an Israeli 'terrorist' organisation. And, above all, there are the questions raised by Gordon Winter.

Many strange people have been attracted to South Africa's shores over the years. Among the strangest was Winter, the journalist and self-confessed spy. Born in Derbyshire in 1931, he immigrated to South Africa and worked as an undercover agent for South Africa's elite Intelligence agency, Boss. He was, for a while Van den Bergh's 'blue-eyed boy'. He was deported from South Africa in 1966 – the deportation being used to give him 'cover' with the British press. He had a falling out with Boss and went into retirement to write a well-known book on his experiences, *Inside Boss*.

In this book, Winter claims that the bomb that killed the Mrs Rhys was not only allowed to go off by the railway police without any attempt to clear the concourse, but that the decision to do so was taken by Brigadier van den Bergh and endorsed by the then Minister of Justice, John Vorster.

The two government officials knew each other well, both men having been interned in Koffiefontein internment camp, as neo-Nazis and enthusiastic supporters of Hitler. Winter says they had a 'hot line' – a red telephone – for urgent communications with each other. Winter, who claims that the story of the phone call was confided to him by Van den Bergh himself, says the exchange was brief, the security force chief telling Vorster the bomb was in position and Vorster replying 'let it happen'. The implication was, of course, that they had discussed the bomb previously and were prepared to let it go off in a public place for the propaganda effect.

The effect was sensational. One blast had destroyed the Liberal Party as well as an underground revolutionary organisation at what was no doubt to them the negligible price of the life of a 77-year-old woman. Which leaves one speculating as to whether depravity had yet taken sufficient hold on the police – as it certainly did in later years – for them to have done what they accused Harris of doing; murdering 'innocent' people for political gain.

A naïve man, Harris may have inadvertently tipped off the police, if not about the bomb, then about the imminence of a 'spectacular' protest event.

Recently declassified police documents show that Harris had been under close scrutiny since at least 12 February 1964, which was when he was banned. One intelligence report in particular quotes him as saying, at a meeting of the Liberal Party: 'I'm no fortune-teller, but something will happen in the future, I don't know when, the present government will disappear and also white supremacy … we will govern the country with respect for all races.'

Was this a reference to the bomb? Certainly the declaration – reminiscent of Ernie Wentzel's analogy to a 'chain reaction' in describing the African Resistance Movement – is likely to have set off alarm bells at Compol (security police headquarters in

Pretoria) if they had not previously been rung.

Vorster and Van den Bergh seem to have been covering up something in connection with Harris's arrest. The two men made much of the general's 'intuition' in deciding that Harris was the bomber.

Ironically (in view of Harris's recent leadership of SANROC), Vorster was attending the Johannesburg screening of a film marking the 75th anniversary of the South Africa Rugby Union when the bomb went off on the other side of the country's commercial capital.

Vorster recalled later, in a biography: 'When I got to the station I found Hendrik van den Bergh and his senior officers there. We looked at the mess and I discussed the affair with them before I telephoned Dr Verwoerd. He was terribly shocked when he heard the news, but I gave him the assurance we would have the man by midnight. He asked me how I could say this and I replied: "Doctor, I live with my men and if they tell me that they will have the culprit by midnight, then I believe them." I well remember how we stood on the station platform and that is really where I got respect for those police officers of mine. They started discussing possibilities, the pros and cons of this one's involvement and that one's involvement. They asked each other, could it be this man or that woman. Then Hendrik van den Bergh said, "Let's forget everybody and concentrate on John Harris." And John Harris it was. By eleven o'clock that evening I could telephone Dr Verwoerd to tell him that we had our man … and that my officers had been right in saying we would have him by midnight.'

The veracity of Winter's account of a plot involving Vorster and Van den Bergh is encouraged by the fact that two other tales he tells in connection with the Park Station bombing are born out by ancillary evidence. The fact that he had his jaw broken is confirmed by Judge Ludorf, among others.

In his book, Gordon Winter also tells how Van Den Bergh played mind games in his efforts to 'break' Harris. At one stage, according to Winter, he organised a bogus 'escape'.

A young warder was roped in, who got word to Harris that an escape could be organised for £6 000, £1 000 as a 'deposit'. On the night of the escape the warder brought in civilian clothes and a tin of black shoe polish. The plan, according to Winter, was for Harris to scale a wall and get away in a waiting car.

But when the appointed hour came, his cell door swung open to reveal, not the young warder, but the lanky figure (he stood two metres tall and weighed 180 lbs) of Van den Bergh himself. 'Come on John, give me that thing you have in your pocket [the toy gun],' the security police commander said to Harris. Winter says that the whole thing had been organised by Van den Bergh from the beginning and adds that the brigadier made an offer to Harris the same night – about two weeks before the execution – to let him escape if he would agree to work for South African intelligence. Harris refused.

Significantly Ann Harris confirms the plot. She says she had to borrow the money from her lawyer (the indefatigable Ruth Hayman again) and her parents. She did not believe the offer was genuine. But what else could she do? It was her husband's life. The money was never recovered.

And then there is the puzzling Ann Swersky, nee Kerson, a close friend of Harris dating back to their university days. She now lives in Israel. Swersky is known to have helped Harris hide the bomb, in an underground cellar at her home, and was apparently the person who came up with the suggestion that a warning be telephoned in to police and the newspapers. The telephone strategy is, of course, well known nowadays because of its use by the IRA. But it seems to have been a fairly novel idea in 1964, although it was used in the Middle East conflict – notoriously in the 1964 bombing of British military HQ in Jerusalem's King David Hotel. Ninety-one people died in the blast, after a 25-minute warning.

In his testimony to court, Harris said he had told Swersky that he was involved in sabotage. 'I did not plan to, but it just came out, because she was a very nice girl,' he told the court. Swersky is believed to have been detained by the security police after the station bomb as a possible accomplice, but little more is known about her role in the bombing. Asked, during cross-examination, whether she had encouraged him with the bomb plot, Harris replied: 'Did she encourage me? She did not.' As it now transpires, she did more than 'encourage' him; she seems to have actively helped him construct the bomb.

I managed to trace Swersky to Israel, where she is chairperson of the national debating society. On the telephone she sounded charming, but was totally unhelpful. I traced her through Google. It was a fascinating, if brief, journey – on the Internet, I mean.

The first 'hit' I got was reference to her and her husband attending the funeral of Shmuel Katz, a South African immigrant to Israel. Katz, it transpired, was not any old immigrant. He was one of the seven-strong command of the Irgun, the 'terrorist organisation' responsible for blowing up the King David Hotel. Others in the command included prime ministers Menachem Begin and Binyamin Netanyahu.

From there Google took me to a book, *The Road to Democracy in South Africa: 1960–1970* (published by the South African Democracy Education Trust). It notes that Ann Swersky was vice-chairperson of a Zionist youth organisation 'whose sympathies allegedly lay with the former underground terrorist group, the Irgun'.

Fascists and the yarmulke

One of the more incongruous sights of the apartheid era was that of the then prime minister, John Vorster, in 1976, a yarmulke on his head doing obeisance at Yad Vashem, Israel's memorial to the Holocaust dead.

The incongruity lay in the historical footnote that Vorster had been locked up in Koffiefontein during World War ll, as a general in the fascist oganisation, the Ossewa Brandwag, which openly supported Hitler and the Nazis.

The apparent paradox is sometimes held up as an example of Jewish hypocrisy – a so-called 'unholy alliance' of 'strange bedfellows'. But understanding is there to be discovered.

Joe Slovo, Albie Sachs, Ronnie Kasrils, Anton Harber … the names of Jewish resisters against apartheid echo down the corridors of South African history. Of course it was not only politics that saw the disproportionate Jewish representation. And – if politics – not necessarily on the 'correct' side. Percy Yutar, the Jew who almost pursued Mandela to the executioner's chamber, was one striking example. But certainly the statistics of allegiance were disproportionate. Jews flooded into the country in pursuit of the Transvaal's gold and Kimberley's diamonds. Most of them came from Eastern Europe – Lithuania, Latvia, Estonia … By 1933, 70 000 Jews made up five per cent of the white population. By the time the National Party came to power in 1948 the figure had risen to 118 000.

The historian, Howard Sachar, observes: 'Jews were more visible than any other white element in their opposition to apartheid. Throughout the 1950s and the early 1960s Jews figured prominently at every level of the struggle – among reformist liberals and Communists, the courts (whether as defendants or as counsel for the Defence), in the lists of "banning" (political quarantine), and among those who fled the country to evade arrest. Thus, while Jews represented less than 3 per cent of South Africa's 4.2 million whites by 1960, they constituted 60 per cent of the nation's white political defendants.'

But, despite the 'disproportionate' contribution made by the Jews to the anti-apartheid cause, the priority of the community as a whole lay elsewhere, in Zionism.

South African Jews were intensely Zionist and were supported in that by Afrikanerdom. The Afrikaner leader, Jan Smuts, as a member of the British War Cabinet, was one of the authors of the Balfour Declaration and in 1948 he was one of the first leaders to recognise the state of Israel.

The dynamic lying behind this apparent confusion can perhaps be best understood through the life and times of the founder and leader of the Irgun.

Vladimir Ze'ev ('Wolf') Yevgenyevich Zhabotinsky, better known as Ze'ev Jabotinsky, was born in Russia in 1880, training as a journalist in early life. In the face of Russian pogroms at the turn of the century, he formed self-defence units to protect Jewish communities, bringing them together under the name of the Jewish Self Defence Organisation, a forerunner to the Jewish Self Defence League and Anti-Defamation League.

During World War I, Jabotinsky joined the British army and was decorated for bravery as well as being awarded the MBE. After his discharge from the British army he threw himself into Jewish self-defence work again.

In 1920 he was jailed for 15 years by the British authorities for the illegal possession of weapons, although he was released in the ensuing uproar. The British banned him from Palestine in 1930. He was informed of the ban while in South Africa.

His presence in South Africa at this time was not surprising. Jabotinsky found South Africa a fruitful place for fund-raising in the Zionist cause and it is recorded that he made three visits to what was then the Union of South Africa in the 1930s.

He had much in common with white South Africans, including racial ideology. In the early 1930s, Ben-Gurion, later Israel's first prime minister, called him 'Vladimir Hitler'. He believed in an extreme form of nationalism that had it that differing race groups suffered a different psychological profile. He regarded Arab culture as the 'complete antithesis to European civilisation, which distinguishes itself by intellectual curiosity, free investigation, dynamism and a minimum of interference of religion in everyday life.'

Jabotinsky's life – in particular its confusion of allegiances – helps an understanding of the apparent contradictions of Israeli-South African relations, which drew closer during the last two decades of the apartheid years. In 1976 – while the two countries were secretly collaborating on sharing nuclear military technology – the South African government yearbook explained their affinities: 'They are both situated in a predominantly hostile world inhabited by dark people.'

Sunday, 16 May 2010

Dear Ann Swersky,

It's me again – David Beresford in Johannesburg. I have not received an answer to my last letter to you, so I suppose you have no intention of replying. What I will do, therefore, is to summarise the facts I have put together with regard to your possible involvement in the 1964 bombing of Johannesburg's Park Station to give you a chance to reply to them.

There is a line of thought among anti-apartheid activists here which has it that John Harris had an accomplice who 'helped' him in the planting of the bomb. If this is true then there is a strong likelihood that you were that person.

You were very close to Harris. He said so at his trial, describing how he had confided all the details of the operation to you. As the judge, Mr Justice Ludorf, put it, you were held 'in the highest regard' by Harris. 'In giving evidence he (Harris) disclosed that he was highly flattered by the fact that this woman was prepared to participate in and encourage him in his activities,' said the judge.

It is a matter of record that you even bought some of the equipment to make the device. The judge said: 'Mrs Swersky bought two plastic four-gallon containers, one of which was used in the explosion …'

He also entrusted the explosives to you. You allowed him to hide the equipment for the operation in the cellar at your house, at Number 33 Oxford Road. Harris literally trusted you with his life.

You were also – by Harris's testimony – the person who suggested to him that telephone warnings should be given to local newspapers and the police. This was in imitation of what was done in Israel by the Irgun, most notably in the bombing of British headquarters at the King David Hotel.

(Incidentally, I believe that you and your husband, Barry, were close to Shmuel Katz, another South Africa immigrant to Israel who became a member of the Irgun's seven-strong command.)

I do not know how you left South Africa, but your husband, Barry, appeared as a state witness in your place. The two of you now live in Israel.

Ann, I am baffled as to why you are refusing to help me with the John Harris story. It is nearly half a century since the events that led to his death and South Africa is a very different place from those days.

Yours sincerely,
David Beresford

In the attic

The TRC never investigated the station bombing. Which is a pity, because it is clear that much more of the story could be told by musty old files in the government's archives. 'Why dig it all up again, why not let sleeping dogs lie, shouldn't these things be forgotten?' some readers may protest.

In answer one can call on a silent witness to the events of 1964: John Harris's baby son, David.

When he was 14 years old and his father long dead, he asked his mother if he could read the letters and newspaper cuttings he knew she kept in a trunk. He spent three days in the loft, reading them all.

'We didn't ever discuss it in great detail,' she recalled. 'You just read them and that was that.'

And that was that.

Was it?

Short-sighted seagulls

- *Careful, it'll sting you.*
- *I don't think so. Not when it's dead.*
- *It'll sting you. And then you'll be on television and you'll have to marry me. And a Portuguese man-o'-war will have claimed another victim.*
- *Mmmm.*
- *I'm feeling sad.*
- *Have you been to Bloubergstrand?*
- *A long time ago. When I was at varsity. Why do you ask? Here, draw a heart in the sand with our names. That's too small. It's got to be a huge heart, so all the gulls can see. They're short-sighted, you know.*
- *They're not!*
- *Yes. If you look carefully you'll see a reflection in their eyes. That's their contact lenses.*

– Idiot … I've got a stone at home from Bloubergstrand. Did I ever tell you about my first lover?

– No. I don't want to know you had a first lover.

– I was still at school. He was my Spanish teacher. We couldn't be seen together, because I would have been expelled from school if they'd found out and he would have been fired. So he had to hide me in his house. But I loved exercise. There was a strawberry patch next to the house, out the back. So he bought two badminton rackets and we used to go out the back and jump around the strawberry patch and hit the ball at each other.

– Shuttlecock.

– What?

– It's called a shuttlecock, not a ball.

– Smuttlecock, wattlecock. Whatever it was called, it was fun. But I wanted to do more with him. So one day we went to Bloubergstrand. We thought no one would see us there. And we walked along the beach. It was nice, walking with him. Just holding his hand. And I wanted to keep it, to keep the moment. So I picked up a stone and took it home and thought I'd keep the memory in it; the memory of the sand and of the sea and of Table Mountain over there and Robben Island over there and next to me my lover and in my hand the stone.

– Where is it?

– I don't know. At home. I used to keep it on the mantelpiece, but it's in a drawer somewhere now.

– And the lover?

– He went back to Argentina. He sent me a photograph of a painting he had done several years later. It was of me on the beach with a badminton racket.

– And did you send him the stone?

– No. I never told him about the stone. It was a secret, between me and the stone. It sat on the mantelpiece and every now and then I would look at it and think about the secret between us. But after a while it settled back to being just a stone. Sitting on the mantelpiece. So I put it in a drawer.

— *Stupid stone.*

— *Yes. It had a shorter memory than me.*

— *I used to collect stones. I had one from Tara, the Hill of Kings in Ireland. I told myself that Finn McCool had stepped on it - the legendary Irish warrior-king. And one from Isandlwana. From the hill itself, overlooking the battle site. I told myself it had seen the Zulu impis sweeping around the corner – 'thick as grass and humming like bees', the English scouts said. Before they wiped out the British army, I mean.*

— *So what did you do with the stones?*

— *Lost them. The one from Natal is probably in London, lying by the side of a road, and people walk past it without knowing that it saw the Battle of Isandlwana. It suffers terrible frustration, wanting to tell the passers-by about how they – the British – got beaten, about the battle and the terror and the heroism and the blood. But not being able to do so.*

— *Poor stone.*

— *I would like to have a stone that witnessed the story of David and Absalom. Maybe a stone that momentarily tripped one of the runners. Do you know the story of Absalom and David?*

— *From the Bible?*

— *Yes.*

— *Go on.*

— *Didn't you go to Sunday school?*

— *I did. Go on!*

— *Well, you know that Absalom led a rebellion against his father, King David?*

— *Mmm …*

— *Absalom was killed and the commander of King David's forces had to send word back to the king to say his son was dead. So he sent a soldier as a messenger, running to Jerusalem to tell David the news. And then a second soldier begged the commander to let him carry the news as well. The commander said, I suppose in irritation, 'Go, then!' The second runner overtook the first runner – you see, it's*

all about being first with the news: 'scoops'. Anyway, the second
messenger raced into the royal palace where he went onto his knees
in front of David and said they had won a great victory. David
said: 'And what of my son, Absalom?' The messenger, not wanting
to be the conveyor of bad news, lied and said he had seen a great
commotion, but he did not know what it had been about. Then a
message came from the guards at the gate that a second messenger
was approaching. He arrived and David said: 'How is Absalom?'
And the messenger replied: 'May the Lord deal with all the king's
enemies as he has dealt with the young man, Absalom.' The king
then went up to the watch tower above the city gates and in his grief
he cried across the stony desert: O my son Absalom, my son, my son
Absalom! Would God I had died for thee, O Absalom, my son, my
son!
- *That's beautiful.*
- *It's South Africa.*
- *The Bible?*
- *Yes. South Africa's an Old Testament tale. People, struggling to do*
  good, to do the right thing and failing. Because they're human beings.
  And as human beings they're always being corrupted by power and
  greed. Because that is what happens to human beings.
- *Maybe.*
- *I mean look at King David. He did the most terrible things. He*
  sent Uriah to be killed at the front – he murdered Uriah – so that
  he could fuck Uriah's wife. I mean, that's terrible. How many
  commandments is that broken? But he still saw himself as the leader
  of the chosen people. And so did his god. And his god continued to
  love him.
- *There wasn't much love after Sharpeville.*
- *No, you're right. The whites didn't cry after Sharpeville, or not*
  many of them. Nor after Soweto, nor after Langa, nor after Alex,
  nor after the Trojan Horse incident.
- *Did David cry for Uriah?*
- *No. He married his wife. Uriah's wife, Bathsheba. God sent a*

message to David, saying: 'That's a naughty thing to do.' But that is
what I am saying about apartheid. It was such an intensely human
story, all of it. It was mankind's fault, not the fault of the whites,
or the Boere. When mankind looks at Soweto and Sharpeville,
they're looking at themselves. It's a reflection of humanity, of them,
of people everywhere. It's the English concentration camps during
the Boer War and the death camps in Nazi Germany. It's the My
Lai massacre, it's Chatila, it's El Salvador, where they sewed up
a man's head in the belly of his pregnant mistress, it's Chile, where
they rammed cattle prods up women's vaginas. But they don't see it
like that. It was almost as if the world needed South Africa, as a sort
of ... I don't know ... a symbol of evil. So that they could say 'that's
evil' and therefore they must have been 'good', because they're not
there, they're not South Africa, they're not evil.

— *The 'puddle of brains' at the Bisho massacre?*
— *Yes, I was the messenger who arrived second.*
— *I'm getting cold. I must go.*
— *Already?*
— *You've finished the book, so you've finished with me.*
— *I suppose so. But you were so real.*
— *No, just your day-dreaming. Don't you remember your mother used*
to say what a day-dreamer you were? Anyway, I must go.
— *And leave me here. Alone?*
— *We are all alone.*
— *But ... but can't you explain? John Harris, the torture of the Dikani*
women, Tsafendas, the old crone laughing at me, at the church of
Ntarama ...
— *You want answers. There are no answers. We're anarchists. Authority,*
order, certainty are the enemy. Chaos is the creator. Hamlet, Lear,
Mozart, Van Gogh, Shaka, Verwoerd, they are just fragments of
existence, as we are as we stand here now. We try to make sense of
it, to impose our patterns on the tumbling dice. We fight for what we
must and we encompass what we can and call these little shells of
existence our world. But they have no meaning. Life has no meaning.

That is the glory of it. The man cried out on the cross: 'Eloi, Eloi, lama sabachthani?' – 'My God, my God, why have you forsaken me?' Even he was betrayed by the assumptions of life. That was what the war in heaven was about. Lucifer rebelled against the chaos of God. We think we want certainty, reassurance, but the Great Dice Player knows we are creators of our own past, the gods of our own destiny. We gaze into microscopes in search of the building blocks of life, but the certainties of the atom give way to the proton, the proton to the photon, the photon to the quark ... We gaze into the telescopes in search of the walls of the universe. But planetary system gives way to galaxies and galaxies to universes and universes to multi universes. And so it goes. There is knowledge out there, but no answers. There is only one aspect that offers any comfort and that is that there are patterns of irregularity in the chaos. And it is in them, if anywhere, that God exists.

Acknowledgements

My thanks go to: Georgina Hamilton, for her hugely generous support. David Pallister, my old colleague, without whose support, sympathy and penetrating advice this book would surely not have been finished. Piers Pigou, researcher "extraordinaire" whose ability to summon documents out of thin air at times seemed miraculous. Anton Harber and the generosity of the Taco Kuiper Fund for Investigative Journalism. Jonty Driver, Maeder and Leslie Osler for opening the door to John Harris's story. Gill Bond and Chris Austin, who picked me up and put me back on track. Hugh Lewin. Marianne, my big brother, Garth, and "my dearest coz", Rob and Hilary who are always there. My old friend William Barker, who may not remember it, but whose remarks got the whole thing going. David Wolfe and his mother, Ann (the son and widow of John Harris), and Martin Wolfe. Michel Pickover. Henrietta Dax of Clarkes Bookshop. Bram Vermeulen, Tim Dutton and Sappho Dias who have done so much to restore chivalry to the English. The staff of the Cullen Library and of the South African History Association (SAHA) and *The Guardian* newspaper who gave me that vital commodity – empty space in its many forms.